SEXUAL STATES

NEXT WAVE

NEW DIRECTIONS IN WOMEN'S STUDIES

A series edited by Inderpal Grewal, Caren Kaplan,

and Robyn Wiegman

SEXUAL STATES

Governance and the Struggle over the Antisodomy Law in India

JYOTI PURI

DUKE UNIVERSITY PRESS
Durham and London 2016

Printed in the United States of
America on acid-free paper ∞
Designed by Amy Ruth Buchanan
Typeset in Quadraat by Copperline

Library of Congress Cataloging-in-Publication Data
Puri, Jyoti, author.
Sexual states : governance and the struggle over the
antisodomy law in India/ Jyoti Puri.
pages cm — (Next wave)
Includes bibliographical references and index.
ISBN 978-0-8223-6026-1 (hardcover : alk. paper)
ISBN 978-0-8223-6043-8 (pbk. : alk. paper)
ISBN 978-0-8223-7474-9 (e-book)
1. Sodomy—Law and legislation—India.
2. Homosexuality—Law and legislation—India.
3. Criminal justice, Administration of—India. I. Title.
II. Series: Next wave.
KNS4216.P87 2016
345.54'02536—dc23
2015022772

Cover art: Paperwork piled up at the District
Commissioner's Office in New Delhi. Photo © Simon
Jacobs. Silhouette © mtmmarek/123rf.com.

CONTENTS

ACKNOWLEDGMENTS

As I get ready to send this book out into the world, it brings a moment of pause, an opportunity to reflect on the journeys the book represents. One journey began when I first came across a brief blurb in 2002 that an organization called Naz Foundation had launched a public interest litigation against the antisodomy law in India. On the road, I came into contact with new communities, traveled to new sites and ventured into new arenas of fieldwork, which collectively inform the critiques of states and governance that are the focus of this book. Yet, even as this book draws to a close, the other journey, to decriminalize homosexuality, remains unfinished. The appeals to the Supreme Court are underway and it is unclear how and when the court will weigh in on the 2013 ruling upholding the antisodomy law. More heartening, though, the broader struggle for sexual and gender justice, of which the legal campaign against the antisodomy law was just one aspect, continues more energetically than ever before.

In many ways, this book could not have existed without the input of the people who are part of this broader struggle, especially those who proceed with the understanding that undoing the social injustices of sexual orientation are contingent on undoing the harms of caste and class inequalities, religious discrimination, nationalisms, racialisms, gender hierarchies, and intolerances of gender expression. Indeed, this book takes inspiration from them. It is always a pleasure to be in conversation with Arvind Narrain—something to learn, something to share. Gautam Bhan has consistently supported this project; Alok Gupta's sharp and critical bent has been refreshing. In Delhi I was fortunate to have the insights of Ponni Arasu, Pramada Menon, and Jaya Sharma, who also generously shared loads of material with me. I learned from Saleem Kidwai and benefited from my discussions with Anjali Gopalan. Thanks also to Nivedita Menon for making time for lively conversations during the trips to Delhi.

Travels to Mumbai led me to Chayanika Shah, Vivek Diwan, Geeta Kumana, and Vikram Doctor, who without hesitation gave me access to material from his personal archive. Meeting with Ashok Row Kavi is always informative. My thanks to Anand Grover at Lawyer's Collective for being liberal with his time despite his many commitments. I am especially glad that the research process took me to Flavia Agnes's office, for she is someone whose work I much respect. On the way, Meena Gopal and Nandini Manjrekar have become interlocutors. A few more people to single out: in Delhi, Shaleen Rakesh, who was the former Naz Foundation legal representative and my first point of contact, and Aditya Bondyopadhyay, in Bangalore, Elarvathi Manohar, in Chennai, L. Ramakrishnan and Sunil Menon, and in Kolkata, Pawan Dhall. Not least, a collective thanks to the many individuals and representatives of organizations, both the supporters as well as the detractors of the campaign to decriminalize homosexuality, whose input directly or indirectly contributed to this book.

A Fulbright Senior Research Award allowed me to conduct a chunk of the research for this project. It remains an important U.S. taxpayer initiative at a time when funding for social science research projects, especially ones that are qualitative and based elsewhere, is being whittled down. My gratitude to the Fulbright staff in Washington and in Delhi. Simmons College, where I work, provided additional support along the way, including monies from the President's Fund for Excellence, the Faculty Fund for Research, and a course release from the Dean's Office, and Milo Kluk, Caroline Narby, and Heather Mooney helped me with the nitty-gritty aspects of the manuscript. My appreciation also to my supportive colleagues in my department and at Simmons.

The process of publishing represents another milestone. I was most fortunate to have two perceptive, exacting reviewers who nonetheless managed to be constructive in their responses. I am most grateful to both of them for helping me write a better book. Ken Wissoker was supportive of this project; I relied repeatedly on his brilliance in translating the reviewer responses and helping me hear them. It has been a pleasure working with Ken and the rest of the team at Duke, and especially Elizabeth Ault and Jessica Ryan. Amy Morgenstern's editorial skill aided in transforming the beginning and ending of the book in ways that were edifying, and Judith Hoover has given the book its finishing touches.

In between all of the research, the writing, and the quest to publish are the audiences with whom you can, if lucky, have fruitful conversations. Thanks especially to the colleagues and students at Brandeis University, Brown University, Connecticut College, Harvard University, Lund University (Sweden), Northeastern University, St. Lawrence University (thank you, Danielle Egan), Rutgers University, Tufts University, University of Chicago, University of Heidelberg, University of Massachusetts, Amherst, and Yale University.

More particularly, during the making of a book you look to people whose opinions you trust. I relied on S. Charusheela's keen intellect and friendship; I benefited much from conversations with her and her feedback on chapters of this book. I was equally fortunate to have the discerning eyes of Ania Loomba, Srimati Basu, and Geeta Patel on portions of the manuscript; Ania's clear-sighted comments, Srimati's acuity, and Geeta's incisiveness helped the manuscript in so many ways. I turned time and time again to Srimati and wish to express my gratitude to her. I would like to especially thank Anjali Arondekar for her astute readings and thorough assessments and Inderpal Grewal for her invaluable insights and encouragement during the crafting of this book. With colleagues such as Héctor Carrillo, Lawrence Cohen, Danielle Egan, Kathy Ferguson, Chaitanya Lakkimsetti, and Salvador Vidal-Ortiz and friends Angana Chatterjee, Harleen Singh, and Avinash Singh I had rich and rewarding conversations. I thank these friends especially for their warmth and affection. Kazi K. Ashraf's infinite intellectual curiosity allowed him to comment on portions of the manuscript, despite the distance between our disciplines. My engagements with him sustain me and remain a bright spot.

Then there are those who support you in ways that are indirect, helping you live beyond the intellectual in ways that enrich it. Many thanks to Fernanda Ghi, Guillermo Merlo, and Ana and Joel Massacote for fostering the joy of movement and music in my life.

Finally, the people whose impact on your life is immeasurable. Deepak, Manisha, Taranee, and Anchita provide a home in Delhi, and Nargis and Manohar Mhatre take care of me in Mumbai. Sangeeta K.

Malhotra, Vanita Seth, and Rajshree Kampani continue to be sisters to me. My family in the United States—Monica, Anil, Manu, Poonam, Gautam, Jennifer, and the not quite tykes anymore, Kabir, Resham, Arjun, Sia, and Vikram—have my gratitude for their love, nurturance, and gaiety. My parents, Manorama and Rajinder Puri, light up my life with their infinite affections and tenderness. Most of all, my gratitude to Rohin Mhatre, the creative nonconformist, who stands by me each day with a seemingly endless capacity for love and caring. Thank you a thousand times.

PART ONE

INTRODUCTION

CHAPTER 1

GOVERNING SEXUALITY, CONSTITUTING STATES

Bharatiya Bar Girls Union (Indian Bar Girls Union), Nityananda Hall, Mumbai, field observations:

In a large hall in Mumbai on an overcast July afternoon in 2005, some one hundred women have gathered to react to an imminent statewide ban on dance bars. The bar dancers are young, mostly in their midtwenties, dressed neatly in *salwaar* suits, trousers, and saris. Several dance bar owners are also present, not far from where I sit, but it's the women's voices that reverberate throughout the hall as each steps to the microphone. One woman wonders how bar dancers could be robbed of their jobs because of what they wear while performing, since the women in Hindi films (aka Bollywood) and discos dress so much more revealingly. Why, then, doesn't the government take notice of the film actresses? What about the women who perform in discos? Another woman counters state officials' accusations that dancing in bars is "easy money," lamenting the hardships of the work, the need to take loans from taxi drivers at times, among other indignities. Other bar dancers are intent on distinguishing themselves from sex workers. Many of them wonder about the government's claim to be "helping them" by closing the bars.[1]

With less than a month to go before some seventy-five thousand bar dancers lose their jobs due to a hastily passed state law, women's concerns, anxieties, and anger are palpable at the union meeting. Mere months before, a prominent elected official unexpectedly proposed such a ban on dance bars—where fully clothed groups of women danced to popular Hindi film songs for a male clientele—initially applying only to the state capital, Mumbai, but then encompassing the entire western Indian state of Maharashtra. It is puzzling, the women note, that state officials singled out dance bars over brothels, Bollywood, and bars and discos at posh hotels. Even though the bars had been a staple of the provincial state's nightlife for over two decades, subject to regulation, and a significant source of revenue, officials were now stridently condemning these bars for "corrupting rural youth" and "damaging the (state's) culture."[2]

Urging attention to these inconsistencies, the bar dancers at the meeting ask why dance bars, why now, in order to understand (and overturn) the regional state's edict. But interpreting the Maharashtra state's capricious actions is not easy, not least because of the confoundingly arbitrary discourses justifying the ban. The initial allegations of cultural depravity soon give way to criticisms that dancers are making "easy money," then projections that they are helpless victims of sex trafficking who need to be rescued, views hotly contested by the women themselves. Indeed state pronouncements oscillating between blaming and saving women and officials' empty promises of public assistance for the thousands who would be rendered unemployed lead to additional furious speculations at the meeting about the state's intents and irrationalities.

Some eight hundred miles north, in the nation's capital, New Delhi, another struggle for sexual justice is pivoting toward the state in ways that, too, are surfacing inconsistencies in discourses and practices of governance. Under way since 2001, these efforts are aimed at decriminalizing homosexuality by overturning the nationwide antisodomy law, Section 377, first introduced by the British colonial state in 1860 and retained in the postcolonial penal code. Unlike the bar dancers reacting to the proposed shutdown, this struggle was initiated by Naz Foundation (India) Trust, an organization established to fight HIV/AIDS, as part of a strategy to seek rights and protections for same-sex sexualities, beginning with a writ petition filed in the Delhi High Court against Section 377. As the legal process unfolds, these petitioners are foregrounding incongruities in how Section 377 is applied—for example, the law is being used to harass and extort from vulnerable same-sex sexual subjects—

and the irrationalities of administration, whereby the government is opposing decriminalization but the state-run National AIDS Control Organization is favoring it.

Coming to grips with these messy discourses, inconstant practices, and competing laws and policies through the edicts against dance bars or homosexuality underscores that states are fragmented and deeply subjective. Further, if subjectivity is redefined to mean not just inconsistency and bias but also the passionate, the affective, and especially the sexual, then it animates a more critical view of the states' injunctions on dance bars and same-sex sexual practices.[3] Recognizing states as subjective expands the focus on the state's impact on sexuality to asking how these instances of regulating sexuality serve states. Insofar as states are neither autochthonous entities nor mere material realities, a position I take, awareness shifts to how these preoccupations with managing sexual practices, forms of sexual labor, and such are discursively producing "the state" and serving to achieve state-effect (after, Timothy Mitchell).[4] In other words, these instances suggest that governing sexuality helps sustain the illusion that states are a normal feature of social life, unified and rational entities, intrinsically distinct from society, and indispensable to maintaining social order.

Most pressing, the issue of dance bars, which I discuss but briefly, and the criminalization of homosexuality that is the focus of this book underscore the expanding significance of sexuality to states. Unfolding as they are in the thick of liberalization's aftermath in India, these sites compellingly signal how regulating sexuality through a variety of mechanisms assumes importance, especially at a time when states are understood to be in decline. That is, states are seen to be diminishing due to the erosion of public services, the relentless drive to privatize, the ubiquity of market-based logics that are exacerbated by transnational flows of capital, and the pressures of transnational political structures, such as the World Bank and the World Trade Organization. While the sexual struggles emphasized in this book have kept Indian state institutions, practices, and discourses in the analytical foreground to an extent, widespread perceptions elsewhere of the scaling back of the state due to the effects of neoliberalism have intensified attention to sexuality in other sites of governance: personal relationships, consumerism, the media, and more. Useful as these studies are, the cases energizing this book show that regional and national states may be retreating from some aspects of social life, but the mandate to govern sexuality perpetuates the state as central, even crucial. The charades of the Maharashtra government's edict and the criminalization of homosexuality are cautionary accounts of how states continue to thrive by leaning heavily on sexuality's arguable potential to engender widespread social chaos.

With the concept of *sexual states*, this book advances the argument that governing sexuality helps account for the idea and inevitability of states, especially when they are in flux. It shows that regulating sexuality in its various dimensions, such as behavior, marriage, sexual health and disease, fertility, sexual labor, media representations, and the sex industry, are crucial mechanisms through which states are generated and the expansions and modifications in governance are justified. And it hones the understanding that the institutions and agencies, spaces, routinized practices, and discourses composing states are thoroughly imbued by considerations of sexuality. Efforts to decriminalize homosexuality and other sites of contestation flanking the book—closing dance bars, discourses of sexual violence, and policies against migration from Bangladesh—are crucial in demystifying states, foregrounding as they are the iterative, multivalent forms of governance giving heft to the illusion of states. Sustained attention to these instances offers insights into states' impacts on vulnerable groups while also revealing how these and other constituencies become implicated in upholding them.

Useful as the issues of dance bars and other cases explored at the end of the book are, it is the protracted struggle to decriminalize homosexuality in the contemporary Indian context that provides insights into sexuality's constitutive effects on states. When Naz Foundation sought the modification of Section 377 of the Indian Penal Code, the antisodomy law that declares "carnal intercourse against the order of nature," so that it no longer pertained to adult, consensual, same-sex activity, it was not the first attempt at decriminalizing homosexuality. That honor belonged to the AIDS Bhedbhav Virodhi Andolan's (AIDS Anti-Discrimination Movement, ABVA) attempt to repeal Section 377 dating back to 1994. But Naz Foundation's legal initiative is distinctive and worthy of sustained attention because it inspired a national-level campaign, beginning gradually, with the first cross-country coalition of activists and organizations aimed at securing rights for sexual and gender minorities.

Unlike the bar dancers' turn to the Maharashtra government as a result of its edict or the resort to national and Delhi-based state institutions during a watershed in sexual violence against women, Naz Foundation's turn to the state was premeditated. Seeking to use the antisodomy law as a threshold for long overdue rights and equal citizenship for same-sexualities, it attempted to engage a variety of state sites at the national, regional, and local levels, including the courts, government, and the Delhi Police. Parsing "the state," the Naz Foundation intervention gestured right from the start toward provisional and contextual understandings. As the campaign escalated, it yielded fresh insights, such as that the breadth of statecraft can get smaller as well as larger, from the local dynamics of policing to regionally specific patterns of governance, national-level agencies, and transnational discourses, and that what counts as the state is ever contingent.[5]

Presenting a rich, complicated, and performative arena animated by numerous constituencies, the Naz Foundation–led engagements of sexuality and state are best apprehended through fieldwork. One aspect of my research was focused on the Naz Foundation–led legal challenge, the gradual emergence of a nationwide political campaign, and the positions of supporters and detractors; the other was aimed at unraveling "the state" by pursuing the antisodomy law through a variety of state institutions, agencies, and practices. Spanning five major metropolitan sites—Bangaluru, Chennai, Kolkota, Mumbai, and New Delhi—my fieldwork also included Naz Foundation; its legal representative, Lawyers' Collective HIV/AIDS Unit; a range of sexuality rights, children's rights, and nonfunded groups; and HIV/AIDS organizations with a stake in this conflict. These forays unearthed concerns about the nature and impact of the antisodomy law and, more pressing, cautions about locating the state at the center of this activism.

Contesting the State: Sexuality, Law, and Reform

Naz Foundation's recourse to the state shadows histories of sexual regulation and reform in India. Pointing to this arc, Patricia Uberoi notes that questions of sexuality have been at the heart of the social reform agenda, its debates and contestations, in the colonial and postcolonial periods.[6] Others too have emphasized a tight link between sexuality and legislative social reform starting in the nineteenth century.[7] For the most part, though, such deliberations over the "woman question," or, for that matter, over marriage, pro-natalism, or population control, have been pegged to nation and nationalisms, while institutional analyses of state and sexuality are harder to find.[8] Further, state is frequently collapsed into nation, as seen repeatedly in treatments of sexual violence and trauma during the Partition of India and Pakistan in 1947.[9] In contrast, revised readings of this inaugural moment of the Indian state by Veena Das and Christine Keating's retelling of the framing of the Indian Constitution emphasize the weaving together of the social and sexual contracts, thereby helping reinsert questions of state and sexuality at the heart of Indian postcolonial history.[10]

State institutions are the hub of contestations over sexuality in contemporary India more acutely than ever before. Such contestations—related not just to homosexuality but also to HIV/AIDS, sex work, sex trafficking, sexual violence, population control, and media representations, among others—play out intensively in the Indian context, making it an especially useful lens to apprehend what is relevant in other settings as well.[11] Anxieties about obscenity in media representations or art, for example, have been defined in terms of the need to protect the moral and social fabric of the Indian nation but are actually channeled through local police stations and the courts.[12] Citizens and representatives of political and religious groups routinely register complaints; reportedly thousands of such complaints are pending, and although few prosecutions occur, state institutions remain the focal points of redress.[13]

More than any other institution, law and the attempts to enforce, reform, and redefine it in ways that match the aspirations of ordinary people, what Nandini Sundar calls law struggles, has come to define the interface between state and sexuality.[14] Not surprisingly, then, ABVA's abortive attempt at repealing Section 377 and Naz Foundation's subsequent intervention worked squarely within this paradigm. The antisodomy law had been increasingly commanding center stage due to the heightened contestations around same-sex sexualities amid the impending HIV/AIDS crisis. Marked by greater governmental scrutiny of same-sex practices and identities, deemed as high risk, this period also witnessed increased countermobilizations to protect people from the intrusions of governance. Increasingly Section 377 was identified as the symbol of institutionalized homophobia and an instrument of legal and extralegal persecution. Additionally, insofar as it criminalizes same-sex sexual practices and, by implication, gay, lesbian, and queer subjects, it was also seen as the barrier to securing necessary rights and protections for them.

Conceived as a legal strategy to be waged procedurally in the Delhi High Court, the Naz Foundation intervention was from the beginning circumscribed by its pivot to the state. Aimed at persuading the court to decriminalize homosexuality, the writ highlighted the antisodomy law's ill effects on same-sex sexualities and, most important, the violation of constitutional rights. In so doing it surfaced questions about the potentials but also the limitations of its bent, arguments, and strategies. For one thing, the writ sought to expose the inconsistencies and biases of state policies, whereby some state institutions acknowledge and serve same-sex sexualities even as the law criminalizes them. Yet its principal arguments were couched in a grammar of reasonableness: that decriminalization would ensure better public health and effective regulation, thus raising the greater concern for me about the extent to which decriminalization might actually lead to strengthening governance.

Curious about this and the complex relationship between state and sexuality that was emerging as a result of Naz Foundation's challenge to the antisodomy law, I spoke with a number of activists and lawyers who were part of the legal process. More and more intrigued about how the state was being imagined through the writ petition and how officials were representing notions of state, governance, and sexuality, I visited a number of state institutions and agencies in the first phase of my fieldwork. Looking to gain insight into the positions of the respondents (Delhi Police, Union Government of India, and others) named in the Naz Foundation writ and also the bureaucratic procedures and mechanisms through which such positions are crafted brought me up close to the state and the intricacies of governing Section 377.

SEXUALIZING THE STATE: CONCEPTUAL FRAMINGS

Alongside surfacing the inconsistencies and incongruities of state agencies and institutions, this ethnographic view also confirmed the need to dismantle the overarching idea of "the state." It dovetailed with poststructuralist understandings of the state as culturally and historically produced and reliant on active fashioning through ideas and practices, giving it the illusion of being monolithic, coherent, rational, permanent, and irrefutably "there."[15] Seeing the visits to police stations, gathering of police crime records, and other occasions through this critical lens in fact laid bare the state as fragmented, messy, contingent, and inconsistent. For instance, it raised questions taken up in chapter 3 about how to contend with a law that was intended to criminalize same-sex sexual behavior regardless of consent but that in fact has been used primarily to prosecute sexual assault on children. This approach also emphasized the need to interrogate how administering this code (among others) was continually breathing life into the state.

It became clear that the discursive illusion of the state could be confronted only through an investigation into the nitty-gritties of governance, their pedestrian, iterative qualities.[16] Following Foucault's emphasis on studying the micro practices of power affirmed the insight that engaging the state critically means attending to its constitutive elements, that is, the discourses and micro practices of governance, reports, documents, interactions, procedures, and more. Intent on uncovering this banal and therefore influential thick web, I became especially interested in the minutiae of Section 377, its case law and enforcement as also the ideological production of crime data, meanings ascribed in the government's legal responses, exchanges during the hearings in the Delhi High Court, and so on.

More crucially, my fieldwork raised questions about the role of sexuality in ways that could not be satisfied by seeing these discursive practices only as biased and inconsistent. For instance, my search for data, which is where chapter 2 begins, revealed that the difficulty of accessing statistics on Section 377 in contrast to the glut of tables on (hetero)sexual crime on women is not adequately explained by erratic institutional practices. Indeed, moments throughout the fieldwork reinforced the insight that the domain of sexuality blurs putative distinctions between the public and the private, or the political and affective aspects of the state.[17] Law, the seemingly dispassionate arm of the state, it turns out is colored, for instance, by justices' affects, passions, and anxieties that became evident during the Supreme Court hearings discussed in chapter 6.[18] Trailing the broader spectrum of institutional practices and discourses, though, suggests going beyond the scope of law to unearthing sexuality's far-reaching significance to governance and, in effect, the state.

Thus, although the Naz Foundation–led efforts to decriminalize homosexuality were invoking conventional understandings of the state, the struggle inadvertently triggered an analytic of the sexual state. First, it brought home the long-standing insight in feminist and sexuality studies that states are deeply subjective, preoccupied with regulating sexuality especially among vulnerable constituencies. Reaching for the nuanced analyses in this body of work paved the way for seeing that in fact sexuality impacts states just as much as states seek to define sexual normality, discipline bodies, and control populations.[19] Coming to grips with these complexities required shifting meanings of sexuality away from notions of individual or collective identity toward its structural connotations, as a domain at the level of relations, institutions, and more.[20] As such, the task expanded to tracking how applying the antisodomy law serves the state and, more broadly, seeing the state from the angle of sexuality.

Second, the view from the ground exposed sexuality's role in helping produce state-effect. The government's first legal response to the Naz Foundation writ was telling in this regard. Analyzed in chapter 5, this reply showcases how sexuality's seeming threat to society is used to produce and affirm the role of the state. Another pivotal moment at the National Crime Records Bureau (see chapter 2), which I visited to get a sense of the scope and circumstances in which crime under Section 377 is recorded, was equally illustrative. An "inside" view of this state agency revealed bit by bit not only sexuality's impact on its various aspects but also how these sexualized processes, spaces, functions, and interpersonal interactions cumulate into an idea of the state and the mandate to govern.

Third, a comprehensive view of the antisodomy law showed that concerns with sexuality implicitly and explicitly propel governance, often in incremental ways—as in the pattern of expanding judicial interpretations of the crime that Section 377 ought to cover. Equally important, the upshot was that not just juridical but also biopolitical and neoliberal rationalities are implicated in applying the antisodomy provision. This, contrary to the fact that sexuality is often left out of theories of biopolitics, with which I take issue in chapter 2, and that the state is typically overlooked in notions of neoliberalism, a point I reconsider in chapter 6.[21] In other words, issuing from this critical appraisal of the sexual state is the conceptual challenge of contending with multiple rationalities of governance rather than taking a teleological view of it (whereby neoliberal forms are seen as supplanting juridical and biopolitical modes).

Coming to grips with the sexual state in these ways highlighted the fourth aspect: that ordinary people also participate in animating it. Commonplace criticisms and ridicule of the state abound, yet it is difficult to sidestep the state in the search for justice, particularly for marginalized groups.[22] Vulnerable to the effects of state power, they are also likely to become implicated in fetishizing the state.[23] Setting into motion the legal process lasting for over a decade, the campaign to decriminalize homosexuality and the entire constellation of actors, constituents, opinions, and criticisms it prompted spun around projections of the state. Thus Naz Foundation's interpellation of the state as antagonist and protagonist mattered, as did more far-reaching critiques of the state offered by the coalition Voices against Section 377 (considered in chapter 6). Understanding the inciting of the state in these complex ways brings to light that in dispute between the Delhi High Court's decision decriminalizing homosexuality and the Supreme Court's subsequent overruling of it was the role and reach of the state.

Generating an ethnographically grounded appraisal of the sexual state yielded additional insights around which this book is constructed, beginning with the point that Section 377 is not, nor could it be, the principal law through which same-sex sexualities are governed. Even though the antisodomy law was intended to curb same-sex sexual activity (and other behavior seen as transgressive), a review of legal history indicates that it has for the most part not been used to prosecute adult consensual activity. Rather sexuality's significance to the state links a whole nexus of laws, policies, and discourses—among them the anti–sex trafficking act and lower order laws, including vagrancy and public nuisance, that are easier to enforce and therefore likely to have greater impact than the antisodomy law on same-sex sexualities, especially those vulnerable due to their gender expression and social class.

Pressed further still, it is debatable that sexuality's effects are limited to any one expression, pointing instead to an approach that goes beyond troubling states' heteronormative underpinnings.[24] Taking an integrated view of sexuality's disparate iterations has the distinct advantage of providing thoroughgoing critiques of the state, especially in contexts where the dualities of heterosexuality and homosexuality have not been foundational.[25] The examples of the dance bars, agitations against (hetero)sexual violence, and attempts to stall immigration from Bangladesh, alongside the struggle to decriminalize homosexuality, fruitfully expose contiguities between sexuality's various iterations and highlight its effects on states even when not easily perceptible, as in the case of emigrants from Bangladesh.

Gesturing to neither a single law nor a specific aspect of sexuality, the analysis also throws into question the premise that Section 377 imperils only, or mainly, homosexual subjects. The campaign against the law presumed that Indian legal history tracks closely with Foucauldian genealogies of the homosexual, who is seen as brought into history through institutions such as law only to be persecuted. But if, as noted earlier and explored fully in chapter 3, such a pattern is not borne out by case law, then it throws into doubt the presumed subject of this statute. More gravely, the ethnography examined in chapter 4 points toward the ways the law's enforcement is likely to target hijras and, significantly, religious minorities, especially Muslims, regardless of their sexual practices. Accounting for how some religious minority groups are racialized and pejoratively queered, the discussion provides a broadened understanding of the range of subjects impacted by the antisodomy statute. As such, a close analysis of this law, coupled with the other cases I consider, illustrates the need to bring "least powerful" constituencies—on the basis of marginalized social class and caste, sexual orientation, gender expression, and religion—and the numerous points of regulation into the same field of analysis, without of course collapsing relevant differences.

In sum, a critique of the sexual state advances radical appraisals of state, sexuality, and governance. This theoretical turn keeps states in the analytical foreground and demystifies them by drawing attention to the subjective and especially sexualized governance practices, laws, policies, and discourses that help realize them. Analyzing how states are constituted partly by the mandate to contain sexuality's putative threat to the social order, this stance looks at the ways sexuality easily affects every aspect of the assemblage abbreviated as "the state." Highlighting the banal as well as multiple iterations of governance actually giving substance to states, it encourages awareness of how race, gender and expression, and social caste and class are implicated in the exertions of power. Not least, this approach underscores that it is not only the nitty-gritties of governing that help produce state-effect but also the quests for sexual reform that (are obligated to) pivot around the state.

To illustrate the relevance of this approach beyond the efforts to decriminalize homosexuality, I return to the ban on dance bars for the rest of this introduction. Marking the differences presented by the dance bars—heterosexuality, sexual labor, and the politics of the regional state—from the decriminalization of homosexuality, I show the urgency of grappling with states' reliance on sexuality and striving further toward critical assessments of discourses and practices of rule.

Dance Bars and Remaking the Postliberal Regional State

Dance bars took center stage in public discourse once the regional state's deputy chief minister and home minister, R. R. Patil, suggested a prohibition on women's performances in these settings. When the state governor refused to sign an ordinance initially proposed by Patil to shut down dance bars, a bill (Bill No. 60 of 2005) was swiftly introduced into the Maharashtra State Legislature on July 8, 2005.[26] The bill, entailing an amendment to Section 33 of the Bombay Police Act of 1951, which regulates entertainment such as dance performances in restaurants, bars, and so-called permit rooms, was unanimously passed within two weeks:

> AND WHEREAS it is brought to the notice of the State Government that the eating houses, permit rooms or beer bars to whom licenses to hold a dance performance, have been granted are permitting the performance of dances in an indecent, obscene or vulgar manner;
>
> AND WHEREAS it is also brought to the notice of the Government that such performances of dances are giving rise to the exploitation of women;
>
> AND WHEREAS the Government has received several complaints regarding the manner of holding such dance performances;
>
> AND WHEREAS the Government considers that such performance of dances in eating houses, permit rooms or beer bars are derogatory to the dignity of women and are likely to deprave, corrupt or injure the public morality or morals.[27]

The inconsistencies of state discourses on dance bars encapsulated in the bill were conspicuous right from the start. This, not just because the bill exempted establishments with ratings of three stars or more or performances in Hindi- and Marathi-language films but also because of how the ills of dance bars were framed. Hinging on questions of women's bodies and sexualities, the discursive legitimation for closing down dance bars had as much to do with the vulgarity of the performances and the "easy money" women could net by dancing and manipulating men's weaknesses as with women's sexual exploitation and trafficking of women and girls. State logics alternated between the violation of the dignity of women and the threat that the women posed to public morality.

For those who opposed the state's edict, not least the bar dancers and feminist scholars and researchers mobilized by the implications of the ban, its rampant contradictions were fodder for contention. Since little was widely known about dance bars beyond the handful of popular representations and an account based on a sample too small to carry heft, two studies conducted by feminist researchers, "Background and Working Conditions of Women Working in Dance Bars in Mumbai" and "After the Ban: Women Working in Dance Bars of Mumbai," became crucial in countering the underlying schisms.[28] Contrary to state officials' claims, the first study showed that women were not trafficked into the profession, were between twenty-one and twenty-five years on average, and lived precariously on incomes of less than Rs. 15,000 (approximately $330) a month, entirely dependent on a share of the tips from customers.

Noting that bar dancers were largely from culturally and economically marginalized communities, this study and other emerging accounts troubled the uneven and unjust effects of state policy as well as its underlying motivations. From these counterhistories it became clear that as many as 42 percent of the women in the study were from caste-based and marginalized Muslim communities, where unmarried women supported families through some form of sexual labor.[29] Further, the injunction against dance bars stood to exacerbate, as it subsequently did, the vulnerabilities of women from migrant communities who had been forced to migrate from within the state and elsewhere due to the impact of uneven development.[30] Identifying the state's preoccupations with the dance bars as trails of earlier colonial histories aimed at reforming *nautch* (singing and dancing) girls as well as elitist attempts to rid Maharashtra of its regional sexualized entertainment forms, such as *lavani*, feminist critics rightly indicted the casteist, moralistic, hypocritical tendencies of the state.[31]

After the law was passed and the dance bars were closed on midnight of August 14, 2005, challenges to the biases and subjective hues of the Maharashtra state had little choice but to seek recourse from another state institution, namely law. A number of writs from the bar owners association, bar dancers union, feminist coalitions, and a variety of social and activist groups contested the ban in the High Court of Bombay primarily on the grounds that it violated constitutional rights—including the right to practice a profession, occupation, or trade; the right to life and livelihood; and the right to freedom of expression—while discriminating against this form of labor. In a prompt decision, *Indian Hotel & Restaurants Association v. The State of Maharashtra and Others*, the high court declared the state decree to be unconstitutional, while safeguarding the bar owners' and dancers' fundamental right to practice a profession, occupation, or trade and making much of the state's irrationalities in passing the law: that the injunction was arbitrary since it exempted other elite establishments and that if the dance bars were morally suspect, how could the state allow women to work as wait staff.[32] Rejecting the Maharashtra government's subsequent appeal, the Supreme Court upheld the high court's ruling and arguments and delivered a searing critique of the state's illogic, paving the way for reopening the dance bars in 2013.[33]

Despite the apex court's pronouncement, the state government remained defiant under Patil's leadership, seeking measures that would preserve the ban on dance bars.[34] Proposing in fact to extend the embargo to exempt elite establishments, the state government waded deeper into the mires of sexual regulation, reenergizing questions about dance bars' importance to the state.[35] Taking on this question, I build on feminist appraisals the regional state, while critically reading the state through the histories of dance bars and attempts to regulate them.

REGIONAL ITINERARIES OF THE SEXUAL STATE

The rise and fall of dance bars chronicles the remaking of the Maharashtra state over the past two decades. Emerging in the 1980s, dance bars flourished outward from Mumbai to its suburbs and satellite cities and then on to other cities and towns under a morass of regulations as well as extralegal arrangements that were the offshoots of the developmental state characterizing postindependence India.[36] Managed through an elaborate system of licensing and a density of state laws governing restaurants, serving liquor, and dance and entertainment that were gradually put into place over the years, the dance bars were lucrative sources of state revenue from taxes and fees, as well as extralegal payoffs for staying open past the official closing time, placating police, or contributing to various political parties.[37]

The apex and turning point of this economy of exchanges occurred in the mid-1990s under the right-wing coalition government of the Shiv Sena and Bharatiya Janata Party (BJP), just as the regional state was being impacted by liberalization. Introduced in 1991, liberalization measures ushered in the deregulation of markets and licensing control, foreign capital investment, and privatization, as well as increasing political decentralization that granted greater autonomy to states and oriented them directly toward transnational capital and global governance.[38] As Sarah Joseph notes, these changes represented the incorporation of market rationalities in the structures of the state and mechanisms of governance.[39] Subsequent efforts to revive Mumbai as a global financial and service center, for example, attest to how the regional state was and is being reconfigured, simultaneously repressing and abetting market rationalities and further blurring the boundaries with corporate capital and the interests of elite consumers.[40]

The Maharashtra government's increasingly fraught relationship with the dance bars by the late 1990s reveals the regional state's attempts to transition from a regulatory system embedded in licensing and payoffs to one that is more liberal and rational. Flavia Agnes explains that the strains initially involved a punitive excise tax hike of 300 percent and police raids in 1998 under the right-wing coalition government, which led to a bar owners' lobby and unprecedented public attention to a rally of some thirty thousand bar dancers.[41] Particularly noteworthy is that in 2001 the subsequent government, led by the Nationalist Congress Party, to which Patil belongs, introduced for the first time measures specific to dance bars that would have lessened corruption, but for disagreements with the bar owners later adjudicated by the courts.[42] Then, only a year before the dance bars were closed, the government issued a fresh set of rules in July 2004, levying restrictions on the kinds of clothes bar dancers could wear, establishing a barrier between the dancers and customers, and stipulating a maximum of eight dancers on stage at a time, among others.

These escalating public conflicts and protracted efforts to manage and eventually shut down the dance bars were undoubtedly part of a larger project, as critics have noted, to "cleanse" the city of lives and lifestyles incompatible with state-sponsored neoliberal visions.[43] But they were also signs of a state in crisis. In a postliberal era when the state is no longer the focal point or, as Joseph argues, is no longer seen as the guardian of public interests, dance bars provided an opportunity for the regional state to remake itself.[44] Rather than a calculus of retraction or expansion, the state's dogged attention to dance bars over the years and across the political spectrum reveals a crisis of relevance and legitimacy.[45] Speaking to these representational aspects, Akhil Gupta and K. Sivaramakrishnan observe that liberalization entailed shifts in arrangements between the state and economy and a change in "the way relations between state and other institutions and social groups are recast and re-imagined," thus raising the question of what was peculiarly significant about dance bars for the regional state.[46]

SEXUAL PERILS AND STATE-EFFECTS

Setting dance bars apart from other forms of sexual labor is the widely held view that they do not simply provide sexual entertainment to men but drive them to irrational sexual behavior and fiscal excess through the seductions of love and romance. Indeed over the years dance bars were gradually associated with the false promises of love and romance that would lead men to irresponsible and excessive behavior. Reinforced in the first extensive journalistic portrayal of dance bars, Suketu Mehta's book *Maximum City*, this is how dance bars came to be understood and reproduced once they were under the harsh light of mainstream media. Spelling out these discourses of excess and extraction, Mehta chronicles what he sees as a typical scenario:

> It goes this way: A gangwar boy might start becoming a regular at a bar. He might see a girl whom he fancies. He might imagine himself protecting her from villains, or he pictures the girl nursing his wounds after a gunfight or an encounter. So he goes up to the girl on the way out and asks to see her after the bar closes. She smiles and asks him to come back tomorrow. He goes back the next evening and sits there and now watches only her among the dancers. She remembers him from the previous day, smiles once or twice at him, and he asks the waiter to garland her with thousand or five thousand rupees. She dances a little faster for him, in his direction. He stays until the bar closes and then asks her again for her number. She asks him to come the next night; she will be waiting for him. And so he comes again and again to the bar, throwing a little more money over her head

each time, until one night, when he is least expecting it, she quickly thrusts a piece of paper into his hand. On it is written the magic telephone number and her name.[47]

Mehta's narrative sees emotional intimacies between dancers and patrons at the crux of transactions of cash, gifts, and sex, while showing how extraction and excess are inherent to dance bars.

These populist accounts further diverged into bar dancers as sexual predators and men as prey. It is for this reason that although portrayals of women as hapless victims of the trade entered state and mainstream criticisms of dance bars, they were consistently offset by apocryphal accounts of women earning staggering amounts of money from merely (!) dancing in bars. Mehta's chapter on bar dancers singles out one such woman with the pseudonym Monalisa, as if to suggest that exceptional cases such as hers illustrate the danger inherent in the trade. Similarly, soon after the ban went into effect, a Mumbai bar dancer, Tarannum Khan, was arrested on charges of illegal betting, gambling, and links to the underworld. She captured attention for having amassed vast wealth from dancing at the bars and reportedly being literally showered with 90 lakhs in one night by a male patron later indicted on charges of massive corruption. Raids by income tax authorities on the homes of several bar dancers and media reports of untold extralegal wealth further fueled the discourses of extraction and excessive accumulation. As one commentator observes, these images effectively displaced media representations of despair and desperation that emerged after the ban was enforced.[48]

In contrast, male patrons of dance bars were seen as gullible, easily seduced into fiscal irresponsibility, and needing to be saved from the dancers and themselves. A frequent point of concern was that men often squandered their entire monthly income on the bar dancers, thereby harming their "respectable" wives and mothers. If this discourse was implicitly about men from the working classes with dependents and limited income, another point of anxiety derived from the intersections of masculinity and surplus wealth, often associated with the underworld. The stories about men bestowing lakhs of rupees on the object of their desire, as Mehta describes, were stories about the overindulgences of money and masculinity. Indeed one of the five amendments proposed by the state prior to the embargo on the bars was that clients *could not* shower money on the dancers. What tied together the two discourses on masculinity was the fervent belief that dance bars make men behave irrationally, both sexually and fiscally. Despite the fact that the discourse of male irrational sexual behavior was not widespread, it dominated in the context of dance bars.

The notoriety of dance bars was and continues to be especially conducive to reassembling the illusion of a regional state with increasingly blurred boundaries and uncertain relevance. Introducing one regulatory mechanism after another, especially since the late 1990s, helped reassert the state's indispensability in managing sexuality's irrational, excessive, and ever-present potential to disrupt the social order. The imperative to "save" besotted men and the women who posed a danger to men as well as themselves aided in reproducing the state as the centerpiece of governance despite liberalization, or perhaps more necessary because of it. Positioned at the crosshairs of transnational capital and global governance, the regional state was produced as both modern and moral by dovetailing with U.S. State Department–led antitrafficking rhetorics and globalizing discourses of women's rights to justify the imminent dangers of dance bars.[49]

These sexualized edicts, policies, and discourses, then, are fruitfully understood as traces of the sexual state, which is reproduced amid changing regional, national, and transnational contexts and reflected in the struggle against the antisodomy law. Despite the differences between the two sites of contestation, not least issues of (hetero)sexual labor and (homo)sexual identity, accounting perhaps for their noticeable lack of engagement with each other, and the significantly different outcomes in the Supreme Court, a careful exploration of the injunction against dance bars illustrates that states continue to remain the hub of sexual regulation, governing through a nexus of laws, policies, and discourses rather than simply the injunction against dance bars or the antisodomy law. Consider therefore the sexualized regulatory mechanisms that both preceded and outlasted the closing of the dance bars: state officials' defiance of the apex court's ruling to reopen dance bars, the refusal to issue fresh licenses, proposals to make licensing fees prohibitively high and issue more stringent rules to discourage dance bars. Despite the rulings in favor of the dance bars by the Bombay High Court and the Supreme Court, the regional government remains committed to obstructing the reopening of dance bars and in so doing continually reproducing the state and justifying discourses and practices of governance.

The Roadmap

This book is about the intimacies of state and sexuality that play out widely in the Indian context, typically through law, sometimes at the behest of the state institutions and at other times through the pursuit of redress. Focusing on the struggle to decriminalize homosexuality, the book is organized into three sections. Supplementing this introduction, chapter 2 begins with a pursuit for statistics related to the antisodomy law in order to gain some insight into the extent to which this law is enforced. Bringing an up-close view of the National Crime Records Bureau, my fieldwork yields crucial insights about sexuality's impact on such agencies composing the state by holding up to scrutiny its spaces, iterative practices, and routinized procedures for crunching and reporting data on crime. The discussion revolves around the difficulty that heterosexual violence against women is emphasized and rendered into a social problem, whereas the numbers for Section 377 are deliberately omitted. Rather than heteronormativity, I account for this difference by way of the agency's concern with ensuring the biopolitical welfare of the population. Taking issue with the neglect of sexuality in theories of the biopolitical while emphasizing the connections between biopolitics and sexuality leads to the insight that seemingly objective measures such as statistics as well as state definitions of social problems are deeply subjective sexualized practices. It also makes clear that Section 377 is not the primary law but one among a thicket of decrees, policies, discourses, and iterative practices through which same-sex sexualities are governed and states affirmed.

Part II further disassembles the idea of the monolithic, rational state by exploring the subjective histories of law and law enforcement. Showing that case law and police crime reports (known as FIRs, First Information Reports) for the antisodomy law are primarily related to child sexual assault, chapter 3 reveals the irrationalities of a law used quite differently from its original intent. This approach leads to a fuller understanding of how law's practices and discourses regulate sexual crime and subjects in ways that reaffirm its indispensability and, by extension, the state in preserving sociosexual order. Reading case law from the angle of sexual violence on children, the analysis reveals a steady expansion in the range of sexual practices and discourses that fall within the ambit of governance. As such, I argue, case law or police crime reports do not support a Foucauldian understanding of "the homosexual" as the beleaguered subject of the antisodomy law, and I note the pitfalls of such readings. Arguing for the need to disentangle the homosexual from these records of child sexual violence, I also caution that Foucauldian readings of law and homosexuality risk strengthening the state—by assuming it as the primary site of injustice and then as the arbiter of justice.

Continuing the focus on juridical aspects of the state, chapter 4 turns to the antisodomy law's significance to law enforcement. Fieldwork conducted among the Delhi Police helps highlights the subjective, sexualized aspects of law enforcement in three ways. First, pivoting around discussions with police constables and more senior members of the force, the chapter shows that the generic homosexual is not the primary target of law enforcement. Rather the crucial insight is that policing in Delhi is likely to imperil racialized religious minorities, particularly Muslims, whom the police associate with sexual crimes. Making the case that Muslims are being racialized within the national context and specifically within police discussions, the chapter explains the inconsistencies of policing and the endemic forms of prejudice that so quickly rise to the forefront in relation to enforcing the antisodomy law. Second, indicating the ways police also target hijras, the analysis speaks to the flexible uses of Section 377 that permit governance well beyond the law's scope. Third, revealing dissent among the Delhi Police, this discussion notes that while there may be some leeway in the policing of the generic homosexual, the regulation of racialized religious minorities and gender nonconforming persons is more intractable.

Following the groundwork laid in the two previous sections, part III shifts course to documenting the legal campaign to decriminalize homosexuality that ends abortively with the 2013 Supreme Court decision. Framed against the previously established insights that the antisodomy code is not the only law governing same-sex sexualities and its potential impact is not limited to same-sexualities, chapter 5 begins with a discussion of how the Naz Foundation writ was constrained by a pivot to the state and a necessarily reductive understanding of the antisodomy law. Drawing on fieldwork at Naz Foundation as well as interviews with sexuality rights activists and visits to organizations across five major metropolitans, I account for early criticisms of the writ and its evolution into a national-level campaign focused around the antisodomy law and the generic gay subject. Also building on fieldwork conducted among state agencies, especially the Ministry of Home Affairs, I underscore the subjectivities of the government's legal response opposing decriminalization, exposing its appeal to the perils and excesses of sexuality in order to preserve the integrity of state institutions and justify state intervention. Leading to the writ's initial dismissal by the Delhi High Court in 2004 on a mere technicality, the chapter concludes by chronicling Naz Foundation's plea to the Supreme Court and the subsequent directive instructing the High Court to decide the case on its merits, thereby rendering Section 377 as the flashpoint for a national legal and political campaign for justice.

Delving into the second phase of the struggle against the antisodomy law (2006–13), chapter 6 juxtaposes the 2009 Delhi High Court ruling decriminalizing homosexuality and the subsequent 2013 Supreme Court decision recriminalizing it. The chapter begins with the decisive impact of Voices against Section 377, a coalition of Delhi-based groups, on the historic Delhi High Court ruling. Reading this decision alongside the apex court's overruling, I make the case that the two judgments represent diverging views of the relationship between state and sexuality in postliberalized India. Thus, the argument goes, the lower court seeks to reduce the reach of the state, except that it does so by deploying an individualized, assimilationist, and neoliberal rights regime. Turning to the Supreme Court 2013 pronouncement, the analysis comes to grips with the ways it too is shaped by the imperatives of postliberalization. The chapter shows that, in contrast to the lower court's vision, the apex court seeks to reaffirm the state and prolong governance through legislative intrusions into the realm of sexuality.

The postscript, "Afterlives," offers a summary and discussion of the implications of the arguments developed in the previous chapters. It also extends the implications of the concept of sexual states through an analysis of the agitations around sexual violence that swept India after December 2012 and its applicability to a site where the imperatives of sexuality are not so obviously marked, namely migration from Bangladesh into New Delhi, before ending with the concept's relevance outside of India.

CHAPTER 2

ENGENDERING SOCIAL PROBLEMS, EXPOSING SEXUALITY'S EFFECTS ON BIOPOLITICAL STATES

States' preoccupations with sexuality are everywhere in evidence. In the United States the military has lifted the ban against lesbian and gay soldiers, the Supreme Court has mandated the recognition of gay marriage at the federal level, the Food and Drug Administration has approved the over-the-counter sale of the "morning after" pill, and numerous regional states have introduced legislation against sex trafficking. In the United Kingdom, the Office of National Statistics has started to track lesbian, gay, and bisexual members of the population. In Russia lawmakers have passed legislation against "homosexual propaganda," and Nigeria has expanded and intensified the criminalization of homosexuality. Instances of sexualized forms of governance—legislation, policy shifts, decriminalization or intensified proscriptions—are numerous. Coming to grips with them illuminates how they help produce the state as an elemental, normal, if not natural, feature of social life and as ever more important to ensuring social stability.

The usefulness of tracing governance's recourse to sexuality became amply evident in what started off as an innocuous quest for statistics related to the antisodomy law, Section 377. Seeking insight into the Naz Foundation–led struggle, I wondered how numbers would inform the efforts to undo Section 377. Would they be low, thereby confirming the established wisdom that police routinely harass and extort but do not formally charge same-sex sexual subjects under Section 377, or would they be high, asking for a different account? While exploring policing and criminal prosecutions was important to understanding the context in which Section 377 came to be the lightning rod of state injustice, numbers promised rough and ready insight into the law's landscape.

Helpful police constables recommended that I visit the National Crime Records Bureau (NCRB), which serves as a clearinghouse for crime statistics. But gathering the data related to Section 377 turned out to be no straightforward task, and the process of gaining access to the information was also complicated. My first foray into NCRB might well have ended abortively, with a frustrating side note in field logs on impossible bureaucratic hoops and a footnote in this book explaining the absence of numbers. As it happened, the initial lack of available data, a series of encounters with state representatives, and paths from cubicles to larger and larger offices winding through a series of administrative sections gave me insight into the complexities of sexuality and governance practices at a seemingly dry, bureaucratic, number-crunching state agency.

The visits to NCRB highlighted inconsistencies in the processing of data, for while numbers for Section 377 are omitted, (hetero)sexual crime against women is processed into statistics and elevated to the status of a social problem. Further, these irregularities foregrounded the significance of the agency's iterative practices, such as tracking numbers for crime, processing statistics, and generating reports, thereby surfacing the banal and unremarkable and, as such, more impactful aspects of governance.[1] This dovetailed with the added insight, that considerations of sexuality affect biopolitical forms, measuring and indexing crime in order to govern and ensure the well-being of the population as a whole—a point that has been routinely neglected by a long line of scholars, including Giorgio Agamben, Henry Giroux, Michael Hardt and Antonio Negri, Achille Mbembe, Aihwa Ong, and more recently Akhil Gupta.[2] And not least, what became repeatedly apparent are the implicit and explicit ways sexuality impacts not just the functions of crunching numbers and producing reports but also NCRB's spaces, structures, and procedures for handling the interpersonal.

Providing a nitty-gritty glimpse of a typical bureaucracy, the quest for numbers lays the groundwork for coming to grips with sexuality's effects on state agencies such as the NCRB. Especially since the agency (or "the state") is not a monolithic thing or a presumptive reality but a cultural and material assemblage and effect, delving into the elements, functions, and procedures that make it work is a means of unearthing how sexual ideologies help sustain its idea and importance. And insofar as NCRB is not a constituent part of "the state" (for that would mean seeing the state as overarching and everlasting), NCRB's discursive practices and spaces are windows onto the idea and inevitability of the state itself.[3]

This chapter begins by dwelling on my first field visit to NCRB, for the interactions and observations look beyond the question of numbers or reports to the subtleties of sexuality's effects. As such, it sits squarely within a rich tradition of anthropological and sociological ethnographies of the state that use the minutiae of fieldwork to critical ends.[4] Dwelling on the deferrals and obstacles in dealing with this bureaucracy, this approach teases out their sexual inflections in ways that are relevant not only to NCRB but to research trips to government offices, state-run libraries, and archives, to name a few. As such, it presses against the tendency to see such field-based encounters as a backdrop to data gathering and not the data themselves. At the same time, heeding Gupta's cautions about fieldwork's unassailable claim—"I was there"—this chapter takes the position, following Jacqueline Stevens, that our experience of the state is embedded in its discourses.[5]

The second section revolves around the difficulty that numbers for crime under Section 377 are not easily accessible even as crime against women is more fully processed and reported. Analyzing the differences between numbers and statistics, I explore how, in contrast to crime related to the antisodomy law, crime against women is constructed as a social problem in ways that help reproduce state institutions such as NCRB and legitimize their purpose. While such disparities may be consigned to heteronormative ideologies, I argue instead for the need to look more deeply into the biopolitical practices and techniques of governance producing the disparities and neglect. Coming more fully to grips with them, the last section argues that crime related to Section 377 is being actively written out of measures aimed at assessing and ensuring the welfare of the population. The analysis also leads to the insight that the antisodomy law is not the only site through which same-sex sexualities are likely to be regulated, thereby clearing the way for a more complex understanding of how Section 377 is used and the implications thereof.

Banal Quests and Emerging Insights

New Delhi, scene one:

I arrive one July afternoon at the NCRB in New Delhi. Stating my business at the check-in window as a researcher who is looking for statistical data, I am sent up to the next floor to Kavita Paul's cabin [cubicle], joint assistant director in the Systems Development division.[6] Partially transparent partitions carve up the large room into individual work areas, with several desks in the center. Stacks of files, bound copies of reports are crammed everywhere in cabins, by the desks outside, against the wall.

Kavita Paul greets me graciously from behind her desk in her corner cabin. Our meeting is short, lasting but a few minutes. The information on Section 377 does not exist since the data are reported by offenses, not the penal code, she says. Paul offers me data on crimes against women instead; that is no problem, she says. Stacks of files, paper, records everywhere, but no information related to Section 377?

I persist, and Paul asks to see my authorization letter. Then, somewhat sympathetically, she says, "Come with me," and takes me to N. K. Agarwal, joint additional director in Systems Maintenance. His is also a cabin, but partitioned from floor to ceiling. He and his assistant confirm that this information can be derived from the system. After expressing doubt over my letter of approval since it doesn't say anything specifically about NCRB or Section 377, he waves me on to get permission from Mr. Nair in the Operations division.

On the ground floor, past the odor of the women's and men's bathrooms, past the double doors into a common space lined with cabins on the left and a couple of work rooms on the right, is Mr. Nair's cabin. Blue plastic lines all of the windows and the glass panels on the doors, which, coupled with florescent light, radiates a moon-like glow. Protecting the computers and the records, not ambiance, is the likely purpose. My first task is again to explain my interest in data on Section 377 and furnish my letter of approval. He says that I should state my interest in a letter so that my request can be approved by Deputy Director of Computer and Systems Satish Dubey. It seems wise to use institutional letterhead instead of the blank paper he offers, and the letter, Nair's assistant and my escort, Sanjay, and I are sent on to Mr. Dubey.

Dubey's is a small but full-fledged office on the second floor. He is amenable to my request, indeed affable and interested in my research. However, I have to get permission from the director, he says. He cannot be serious!

To encounter the NCRB is to encounter the material histories and imaginations of the state.[7] In 1986 several state agencies that kept track of crime data, including the Central Fingerprint Bureau and the data section of the Central Bureau of Investigation, were amalgamated to establish the NCRB, based on the 1979 National Police Commission recommendation to establish a "nodal agency" to standardize crime records and to create sharable databases across police stations.[8] Its charge is to provide police with information necessary for law enforcement by serving as a clearinghouse for crime statistics and to improve public service through the web, for example, by providing information on stolen vehicles and authenticating secondhand vehicles to be purchased. Located in R. K. Puram, a suburb of the capital city, NCRB is housed in a low-level, unassuming building. What is it about the state that makes one expect resplendent structures, especially where national crime statistics are managed? The signboard is unimpressive: basic black and white lettering on metal, typical of Indian postcolonial state institutions. Then again, cultural and historical discourses of the state constantly filter every encounter with its buildings, spaces, documents, agents, and discourses.

But a culturalist reading of the NCRB needs elaboration in light of C. J. Fuller and John Harriss's strong claim that scholarship on the modern Indian state shortchanges it as an idea or does not embrace it in the idiom of the state-idea (after Philip Abrams).[9] The same is true, they suggest, of ordinary people's understanding; *sarkar* (Hindi, encompassing state, government, and state officials) has etched itself as a material reality in the minds of ordinary Indians. To insist on a culturalist approach, then, is either to be at odds with scholarship and popular discourses on the state in India or to claim a more radical contribution on this point than is warranted. Fuller and Harriss are right to suggest that scholarly attention remains on analytical narratives of the trajectory, successes, and travails of the modern Indian state, but Partha Chatterjee's history of the postcolonial Indian state is as much a political as a cultural narrative of the changing idea of the state.[10] Similarly Sudipta Kaviraj's and Ashis

Nandy's analyses are each premised on the subjective imaginations of the state, and Gupta's analysis of the discourses of corruption in rural northern India points even more clearly to how people construct the state symbolically.[11]

As a state agency dedicated to processing and managing crime statistics, NCRB embodies notions of the neutral, rational state, compared to, say, impassioned perceptions of political corruption, making it that much harder to reconcile it with the subjective understanding of the state that I introduced in chapter 1. If anything, the NCRB seems to conform to the impersonal and rational characterizations that derive from Weber's combined view of the state as a compulsory organization, with a monopoly on the use of force and binding authority over a defined territory, and a bureaucracy, characterized by division of labor and jurisdictions, hierarchy of authority, abstract laws or administrative regulations, and general rules of functioning.[12] But such foundational assessments of rationally minded, bureaucratically driven states have been faulted, and by none more cogently than Ann Laura Stoler's concept of affective states: "Such a focus opens up another possible premise: that the role of the state is not only as Antonio Gramsci defined it, in the business of 'educating consent.' More basically, such consent is made possible, not through some abstract process of 'internalization,' but by shaping appropriate and reasoned affect, by directing affective judgments, by severing some affective bonds and establishing others, by adjudicating what constituted moral sentiments—in short, by educating the proper distribution of sentiments and desires."[13] Still, to rethink NCRB as subjective means extending Stoler's arguments by noting that the challenge lies not only in tracing states' use of affective strategies but also in recognizing that rational techniques are not asubjective. Said another way, rationality is not opposed to affect but is in fact another form of it, thereby raising the stakes to showing that irrationality can be constitutive of something so seemingly impersonal as number crunching and report making. Stoler's gesture toward affective states also needs to be extended by accounting more directly for sexuality, for despite her careful attention to it in terms of colonial governance, sexuality is visibly absent in these reflections on the state.

In contrast, Begoña Aretxaga's analysis provides a more thoroughgoing critique of the state as a site of libidinal passions and sexual fantasies. In the accounts of strip searches of Irish Republican Army women prisoners by prison guards in March 1992, Aretxaga sees chilling eruptions of state fantasy, a phantasmatic heterosexual mass rape of the prisoners conducted by male and female prison guards. In the process, Aretxaga notes astutely, "state power lost the neutral, rational mantle that legitimizes it to reveal a thoroughly sexualized, symptomatic body politic." But unlike the episodic and violent displays of state sexual fantasies and passions brilliantly analyzed by Aretxaga, my encounter with NCRB is humdrum, if not routine. Gathering numbers for police crimes recorded under Section 377 may not be a daily occurrence, but its site is qualitatively different; there is no event putting the state *in a state*, as Aretxaga describes the torrent of violent sexual fantasies unleashed by the state.[14]

NCRB is saturated with matters of sexuality in ways that are routine, unremarkable, and minute, perhaps harder to identify but more powerful as a result. Contrary to the notion of the impersonal state, especially in a number-crunching agency, gendered and sexual bodies are everywhere. Indeed the metaphorical similarities of states and bodies have been noted.[15] Bathrooms and bodily odors that are hard to escape in government buildings in India are constant reminders of the inextricability of stateliness, embodiment, and sexualities. What greater prompt of the sexual state than how sexual respectability must be routinely managed on site. As a normatively presenting woman researcher, in no case did I meet with a male state agent by myself behind a closed door. Glass partitions and open doorways sifted encounters and contained the threat of sexuality. In other cases, when office doors were shut to reflect status, give privacy, or maintain the efficiency of air-conditioning, at least one additional person was always present to maintain decorum—of sexual respectability and, of course, status.

THE DATA TRAIL: GRIDS OF SPACE AND STATUS

To obtain the necessary information, I traverse the ground and first floor of NCRB, the hierarchy of cabins and offices, as well as three divisions that manage information and the technology used to produce it. Should I have cut to the chase and gone directly to the director of NCRB? Perhaps. But the role of the representative at the receiving window is to direct me to the right official, precipitating appropriate rituals and procedures. Curiously neither N. K. Agarwal nor Mr. Nair anticipates that such a request would need the director's approval; rather they simply send me on to their superior in the chain of command. The state, after all, is an exercise in authenticity to be practiced routinely and minutely.

The lateral and vertical grids of NCRB enact the state structurally and functionally.[16] Henri Lefebvre's point that the primary role of the modern state is to prevent the collapse of a political, economic, and social edifice through a system of hierarchical places, functions, and institutions explains how tasks are distributed.[17] The management of crime records is organized into three units: Systems Development, Systems Maintenance, Systems Operations. At issue is not so much efficiency (or lack thereof) of work and its distribution (on which I cannot comment adequately) but the practices guiding the data trail through the three divisions, up and down the building, in and out of the cubicles and offices of joint assistant directors, joint additional directors, and eventually the director, even though the task finally comes to rest in the hands of a couple of relatively junior state employees.

Further, some functions are appropriate to cubicles, some belong in offices, and others occur in common workspaces that, as Foucault suggests, are governed by seeing and surveillance. Paul is in a cabin that allows mutual looking between her and her neighbor, while remaining partially shielded from the common work area immediately outside. Agarwal's cubicle is sturdier, fabricated partly out of glass and protected by a door. Nair's cabin also has a door, with a view of the common work area of the ground floor, the network of computers, assistants, and working bodies. He is partially shielded from and has partial visual access to the work area. As I observed from my vantage point in the common area on a number of occasions, glass doors to the row of cubicles can be covered with blinds. Cabins, offices, common work areas, glass, and gazing create homogeneous and fractured spaces and states.[18]

Visitors like me are an oddity at the agency. On the one hand, NCRB facilitates the work of other state agencies and institutions, for it is not intended to interact directly with the public. Any wonder, then, that the pursuit of data is confusing, a matter of negotiating opaque and uneven lateral and vertical grids? It feels like a game of snakes and ladders; at any moment of encounter, one might well hear the dreaded words, "It is not possible to give you these data," which once uttered would be difficult to take back. On the other hand, as a visitor I am instrumental to the procedures of governance and, in effect, stateliness. Paul asks to see my letter of authorization before we can proceed further, before she can inquire about the availability of Section 377 data not to be found in published reports. It is as much to verify my access to data as it is to relegitimize state authority. The letter of authorization does not convince Agarwal initially since it does not mention data on Section 377, but then he abruptly shrugs off his ambivalence and leads me to the next step.

At a subsequent moment, however, the paradox of governance practices assumes fuller proportions as I become further implicated in the process that sustains state authority at the behest of Nair, who asks me to put in writing my request for data on Section 377. A blank piece of paper will do, and it is furnished. The purpose? First, it is to freight state records with the power of the written word in ways insightfully captured by Emma Tarlo's concept of "paper truths."[19] Second, the authority invested in the position of the deputy director is performed in response to the written request, for he has something on which to imprint a seal of the state and his signature. Third, the purpose of putting down my request in writing is to leave a paper trail, especially if my request is granted and Nair's is the unit charged with providing me the data. It is his insurance, for, as Tarlo explains, paper truths leave trails of bureaucratic workings (that in some instances also make them vulnerable). But I offer letterhead from where I work in place of the blank paper, to counter state authority with the power of an institution of higher education in the United States and the priorities of research more generally. It works, but at the cost of becoming a willing, even enthusiastic instrument for securing the nexus of stateliness, U.S. imperialism, and Western institutions of higher education. One dances to the tune of the state, but hopefully while deliberately messing up the steps.

Statistical Technologies and Gendered Social Problems

Had I been willing to settle for data on crimes against women, my encounter with NCRB would have been limited to a few minutes with Paul and a pile of reports and documents. But my request for Section 377's numbers triggered a series of interactions, foregrounding the partialities of enumerative practices of governance and, in effect, NCRB. To begin with, these interactions indicate that the data on crime against women are abundant, which, as it turns out, has to do with the subjective differences between numbers and statistics. This is to say that while state agencies and units might enumerate all kinds of things, only some things are endowed with the gravity of statistics (thereby giving the notion of statistical significance different and expanded meanings).

NCRB performs its function as a clearinghouse for crime data by collating numbers from police stations around the country, which are then transformed into statistics and statistical representations, such as tables. Tables provide a snapshot of crime statistics in various categories, and, to make it more visual, maps of India demarcated into states and overlaid with each set of crime statistics have been added. The visual representations are processed into annual hard copy and electronic reports on crime statistics for major cognizable crimes and local and special laws. The reports are organized into various chapters based on vulnerable populations, such as "Crime against Women" and "Crime against Children," or types of crime—juvenile crime, violent crime—and so on.

In the chapter "Crime against Women," only those crimes that target women qua women are included and organized into categories related to sections of the penal code: rape; kidnapping and abduction for different purposes; homicide for dowry deaths or their attempts; torture, both mental and physical; molestation; sexual harassment; importation of girls (up to age twenty-one). A second overall classification covers crimes committed under (somewhat) gender-specific laws, including the Immoral Traffic (Prevention) Act (1956),[20] the Dowry Prohibition Act (1961), the Child Marriage Restraint (Amendment) Act (1979), the Indecent Representation of Women (Prohibition) Act (1986), and the Commission of Sati (Prevention) Act (1987). Tables, graphs, maps, and brief interpretations keep prose to a minimum so that statistics appear to speak sufficiently; for example, crimes classified by penal code, that is, cruelty by husbands and relatives, molestation, kidnapping and abduction, rape, and the like, account for 95.8 percent of the crimes, and those related to special or local law provisions 4.2 percent, according to NCRB's 2011 report.[21]

Statistics and statistical accounts on crimes against women are based on the assumption that aggregates, totals, and trends yield important information *as a whole*, despite the loss of specifics related to each case or the relevance of social class, ethnicity, religion, and region to crime.[22] Classifications such as crime against women and its various subcategories that are especially attentive to sexual crime (rape, kidnapping, molestation, child marriage, the Immoral Traffic [Prevention] Act, indecent representation of women) sustain the need for new rounds of numbers, fresh statistical analysis, and, in effect, practices of governance. It is also true that governmental statistics—and this is particularly true about crimes against women—can be variously interpreted and used to expand governance. Even though nongovernmental organizations (NGOs) and semiprivate institutions share the massive burden of counting and classifying the population in India, agencies such as NCRB still carry the appearance of legitimacy, if not the weight of authority. NCRB's statistics are regularly used by numerous constituencies—women's groups, NGOs, police, newspaper editorials, websites—to demand state accountability and to argue for more resources, better enforcement of law and crime prevention, more policewomen, improved systems of redress, and a more sensitive judicial process—all of this most visibly related to matters of sexual crime.[23]

The question, then, is when and how did attention to crime against women come to occupy such a central place in practices of governance? The answer lies generally in the colonial histories of crime and statistics and the specifics of defining women as social problems in the Indian context.

COLONIAL HISTORIES

Describing the explosion of statistics as a technique of governance between 1820 and 1840 in Western Europe, Ian Hacking suggests that this period of the "avalanche of printed numbers" led to an unprecedented growth of state bureaucracies and typologies of enumeration: census, surveys, maps, among others.[24] As Nikolas Rose argues, statistics was a means of rendering territories into pulsating objects of knowledge, which was nowhere more relevant than in the seemingly impenetrable colonies.[25] Placing the rising significance of numbers, statistical techniques, genres of officially sanctioned histories, reports, and the like also around 1840, Richard Saumarez Smith suggests that they were aimed at apprehending and administering colonial India, while also centralizing the role of the colonial state.[26] Thus the use of statistics in the colonies was, according to Arjun Appadurai, about the ability to domesticate the clutter of narrative prose "into the abstract, precise, complete, and cool idiom of number" and a way of constituting rather than reflecting reality.[27]

But the function of statistical techniques in colonial India was no mirror image of the metropole, as Appadurai and others are quick to underscore. Although in Western Europe statistics emerged as a "moral science," as Hacking details, that is, the study of immoral behavior and criminal behavior, Appadurai argues that in the colonies a focus on crime and deviance encompassed the *entire* population.[28] Numbers were used by states before they were used in the colonies, but it was their deployment as statistical measures, imbued with the appearance of scientific rigor and aimed at the governance of the population, that set them apart in colonial India. Focusing on the Criminal Tribes Act of 1871 that institutionalized notions of hereditary criminals, for example, Sanjay Nigam sees the legislation as a commentary on Indian society as well as on a subsection of the population whose deviance was traceable to Indian culture.[29] Appadurai further argues that statistics served justificatory and disciplinary functions in the colonies by marshaling support for arguments, debates, and rhetoric on committees and boards, enabling comparisons among groups, and providing narratives for otherwise incommensurable aspects of the social and human landscape. Most important, statistics became alibis for colonial interventions into cultural practices especially to do with girls and women, such as sati.[30]

A second point to be underscored is that the conjunctions of statistics and the "woman question" were framed by perceptions of social problems plaguing the colonies. But, as critical sociologists usefully explain, social problems are not objective conditions; rather they are subjective judgments about what constitutes harm or requires problem solving.[31] That is, numbers, statistics, and reports did not represent colonial India as much as they helped constitute it as a collation of social problems that required scientific modes of apprehension and degrees of intervention—to which the debates on women's illiteracy, sati, and child marriage as social problems requiring intervention and reform attest. Backed by the authority of science, objectivity, and universality, statistical technologies, methods of sampling, and probabilities were used to define and assess sociological priorities.[32] Scholars of colonial India, such as U. Kalpagam and Gyan Prakash, tend to imply rather than analyze the construction of social problems in the colonial context, but their work amply illustrates the processes through which administrators selectively defined, intervened in, and socially engineered parts of colonial society.[33] If statistics and the contested terrain of women's social life was one angle of the gendering of social problems in colonial India, then crime against women is its postcolonial avatar. The point, though, is not to offer a presentist reading of history or constrain present-day complexities into an increasingly distant past but to call attention to technologies of governance with institutional histories.

ENGENDERING SOCIAL PROBLEMS IN POSTCOLONIAL INDIA

I spoke with representatives of the Delhi Police to understand how Section 377 is perceived and enforced. Although the police commissioner dismissed me after but a few minutes, he sent me on to another senior police official, N. N. Khanna, who dealt with legal writs that named the Delhi Police as a respondent, including the one filed by Naz Foundation challenging the scope of Section 377.[34] Unaware of the Naz Foundation writ at the time, Khanna nonetheless sought to deflect my interest in Section 377, saying, "This is a peripheral aspect. Because of the total volume of crime, very little attention is paid to Section 377 by the police. . . . The social attitudes to women's issues and gay criminal activity cannot be compared. You should be studying Section 375 [rape law], not 377. There is more social impact of 375. If you want to make a contribution, you should study crime against women."[35] On several other occasions as well police and other state officials instructed or encouraged me to focus on crimes against women, especially sexual crimes. Some, including a senior-ranking policewoman, a joint commissioner of police who was in charge of the crime against women police cell, were puzzled: Why would I want to focus on Section 377?

Framing the apposition between sexual assault on women and the antisodomy law are the perceptions that sexual crime against women is an egregious social problem because of its scale and seriousness, and Section 377, covering crimes related to unnatural sex, does not warrant attention. As a result Khanna suggested that Section 376 ought to be of greater interest to me as a (woman) researcher, echoing Paul's offer of statistics related to crimes against women in place of Section 377 and the puzzlement of the policewoman heading the crime against women cell. Their apprehension about heterosexual violence against women is not unimportant; however, it is used to diminish attention to Section 377 and imply that rape may be a social problem but not an unnatural one. Pressed on this issue by Khanna, I could not help but respond, "Yes, you are right about violence against women. We do not even protect women from their husbands when there is marital rape." He, who was to become the next police commissioner of Delhi, simply ignored my interjection.

Rendering crime, especially sexual crime, against women as a social problem of national prominence derives from the collusions of modern forms of governance, which, as James Scott notes, are characteristically focused on making the social easily legible through statistical and other techniques and national and transnational women's activism.[36] Feminist agitation has been crucial to rendering violence against women a pressing social problem in India through what Malcolm Spector and John I. Kitsuse would describe as an interactional and interpretative process that involves claims making and responding activities.[37] The result is that dowry-related deaths, custodial rape, battering, homicide, and torture became issues of social concern and sites for state intervention and attention, as reflected in the NCRB reports, the creation of special police cells in cities like Delhi, and more recently the expanded definitions of and punishments for sexual assault.

Trailing colonial histories of the "woman question," transnational gendered discourses of human rights have placed the burden on postcolonial states like India for defining and addressing the problems of violence against women. As Inderpal Grewal writes, the formula "women's rights as human rights" re-creates "new forms of governmentality that reshape the relations between the West and non-West, and between populations and states."[38] The need to protect women and endow them with rights, Grewal suggests, was supported by international and national development agencies speaking the language of women in development.[39] Even as a large number of developmental organizations and state institutions started to keep statistical information on women, police in cities such as Delhi and the judiciary began receiving training in human rights and the problems of violence against women, lending added significance to tracking crime data.

But critical feminists have also distanced themselves from such institutional attention to sexual violence, for it has served above all to expand the scope of governance rather than bring relief to women. Focusing on the sexual violence agenda and the inescapability of feminist organizations having to comply with state regulations to become eligible for resources in the United States, Kristin Bumiller notes that even as the resources available for women decreased, the state's reach was expanded as sexual violence was defined as a social, medical, and legal problem.[40]

In India the Protection of Women from Domestic Violence Act (PWDVA) of 2006 was a hard-won victory after protracted negotiations with state institutions, but it was also a source of more intimate governance, for it extends the reach of governance through protection officers and a series of protective legal measures to stop violence, including offering monetary relief, restoration to the household, and custody of children.[41] Looking to state intervention to solve the problem of sexual violence ignores the ways the Armed Forces (Special Powers) Act, the Unlawful Activities (Prevention) Act, and other laws that are ostensibly aimed at securing parts of India in fact exhort state violence, especially toward women, as Navsharan Singh and Urvashi Butalia assert.[42]

The imperatives of historically, nationally, and transnationally engendered social problems address why crime against women is discursively produced, but the question of why the numbers for Section 377 are unavailable is still unclear. Crime against women is reported through a combination of offense and sections of the penal code, which only confuses why crime under Section 377 is not enumerated and interpreted. That the numbers are too few, have not been tabulated, or are not statistically significant may all be true, but wouldn't statistical analyses be the only way to determine that for sure? If their statistical insignificance had indeed been determined, why was it not registered with asterisks or other signs, which is standard procedure? The imperative, then, is to delve further into what the omission of Section 377 tells us about the complexities of unnatural sex and the exigencies of governance. Put differently, the point is to consider Simone Abram, Jonathan Murdoch, and Terry Marsden's caution: a fate worse than being captured by numbers is being neglected by them.[43]

Sexualizing Biopolitical Governance

An obvious difference between being registered and being erased by statistical measures has to do with their heteronormative underpinnings. Heteronormativity has been useful in coming to grips with statistical technologies of governance, exemplified by Michael P. Brown and Paul Boyle's study of how census surveys and reports in Britain and the United States continue to closet gays and lesbians.[44] Using the metaphor of the national closet, the authors call attention to the quotidian and complex interweavings of governance, sexuality, and the census that result in such erasures of sexual identities. The explanation, they suggest, lies not only in the issues of privacy, tyrannies of categories, and statistical rigor but also in societal and governmental heteronormativity.

But the degree to which heteronormativity explains the biases in NCRB's reports is debatable, for its history does not travel well to the Indian context. The idiom of the closet does not adequately resonate in a setting characterized as much by partially obscured histories of same-sex eroticism as by the hypervisibility of queer subjects (not least hijras, Kinnars, Aravanis) and practices that, as scholars of colonialism and sexuality have repeatedly found, were only partially erased in attempts to make the colonies comply with bourgeois ideals of sexual normalcy and propriety.[45] Heteronormativity is also incongruous with the language of Section 377, which emphasizes "unnatural carnal intercourse," or same-sex as well as cross-sex sexual practices outside the putative realm of nature and normality. This explains why a subset of the case law under Section 377 has to do with women petitioning for divorce on the grounds of unnatural sex imposed on them by their husbands.[46] Finally, by mapping the differences between crime against women and Section 377 in terms of presence and erasure, heteronormativity does not facilitate grappling with sexuality's effects on governance practices when they do not align neatly along axes of heterosexuality and homosexuality.

The gap between what is available and what is untabulated in the data trail at NCRB cuts to the crux of biopolitical governance and its imbrications with sexuality. Crime records are an essential part of biopolitical modalities that seek to interpret, predict, and intervene in social relationships and events. NCRB's defining purpose, assessing crime statistics, producing reports year after year, serves to regularize life and mortality, to manage violence with statistical techniques, analyses, and policies. Perhaps crime and violence cannot be completely erased, but they must be managed to ensure a relative equilibrium between crime and the economy (especially given their complex interconnections) for the collective well-being. Corporations, NGOs, and the media are among other constituencies that gather statistics and data about populations and groups, but what is distinctive about NCRB and other state institutions, following Foucault, is that biopolitical techniques are aimed at improving the life and quality of the population, controlling the random and the accidental through calculation and forecast, while justifying regulation in the interests of the population or its regularization.[47]

Foucault's thinking on biopolitics has spurred scholarship along two dimensions: the terrain of biology, medicine, and science through which matters of life, health, genetics, and disease are addressed, and the formation and fault lines of political community, wrought by defining states of exceptions.[48] The concept of the biopolitical can be extended in these disparate ways precisely because it engages the deeper questions of what counts as life, death, and the collective, and it opens up connections between the use of surveys and statistics and discourses of nation and territory, between genocide and census data, between the individual and the planet. Indeed the thread common in Foucault's discussions on the biopolitical and subsequent engagements by Agamben, Mbembe, and, more recently, Gupta, is the production and regulation of the collective, alternatively known as population and political community.

Missing from most engagements with biopolitics, of which Agamben's is the most often cited, are the domain of sexuality and the structures of racism. Few engage race at the intersection of life and politics, despite Foucault's attention to the ways race differentiates between "what must live and what must die."[49] Sexuality, Foucault argues, takes effect not just in terms of constituting subjects; it "exists at the point where body and population meet," a point that ironically is missed by Agamben, who questions Foucault's inability to connect the exercise of power at the level of the subject and the collective or the body politic.[50] Mbembe offers a thought-provoking revision of Foucault's reflections on the biopolitical with the concept of necropolitics, to argue that contemporary life is subjugated to the power of death.[51] Using historical and contemporary examples drawn from Nazi death camps, slave plantations, the occupation of Palestine, and the sustained violence and genocide in Africa, Mbembe, like Agamben, neglects a reading of power and sovereignty deepened by attention to the ways the domain of sexuality serves as a pathway of power; for example, HIV/AIDS is significantly absent as a crucible of the biopolitical and the necropolitical in Mbembe's analysis.

Sexuality is foundational as much at the level of the subject as it is to the forging and governance of political and social collectives, whether as population, national body, or community. Calibrating fertility rates or the ratio of births to deaths, tracking sexed and gendered bodies across the life span, estimating rates of sexual activity or the composition of households, in fact what might be summarized as reproductive and nonreproductive sexuality, is central to regulating the population and the rhetoric of collective interest. What possible interest does the state have in restricting and recording marriages—not just the lineages of property and prohibiting miscegenation but also regulating reproductive and nonreproductive sexuality? At the level of the social body, sexuality stages our anxieties about morality and beliefs about the natural dimorphism of humans, and the gendered essence of humans. Notwithstanding medical reproductive technologies and beliefs in divine intervention, sexuality is seen as the ontology of human existence. In this framework the appropriate and adequate management of sexuality ensures a healthy population and a state of equilibrium to prevent sexual repression, sexual chaos, too many children or too few, population explosion, hunger, disease, HIV/AIDS, and the list goes on.

Remaining attentive to sexuality's foundational relevance to biopolitical governance helps reframe the subjective differences produced by statistical discourses. While violence against women is elevated to a social problem and a matter of biopolitical governance, the omissions from Section 377 point toward the fault lines of biopolitical practices through which populations, or the collective that matters, are forged. In his reflections on statistical enumeration and biopolitical regulation, Gupta notes that even those who must be ignored (or sacrificed) must be known, codified, enumerated, and (this is the point that he stresses) separated from the rest of the population.[52] In contrast, tracking numbers for Section 377 and governance practices at NCRB indicates that biopolitical practices are riddled with sexual anxieties that affect who gets counted and who counts.

As a criminal code, Section 377 is typically deployed when there is a complaint about nonconsensual sex involving adults of the same sex, differently sexed adults, or assaults on children. While I develop this point at greater length in chapter 3, it is worth underscoring here that the vast majority of charges related to Section 377 have to do with sexual assaults on children. Until the 2012 Protection of Children from Sexual Offences Act introduced legislation for children, the antisodomy law was used to charge and prosecute sexual assault against boys and aggravated rape or sexual assault against girls. Much of the crime reported under Section 377 is not organized along heterosexual or homosexual axes, and until recently, because of narrowly defined rape laws, egregious male sexual assault against women was arraigned under it. Despite the substantial numbers of child sexual assault cases being charged under Section 377 and a section devoted to crime against children in NCRB reports, the data are not reported. The letter K under the heading "Crimes Committed against Children Which Are Punishable under the Penal Code" mentions "Unnatural Offenses, Section 377," but no other description or numbers are presented, suggestive of the kinds of sexual anxieties that are driving omissions in statistical reports and discourses.

The numbers for Section 377 are also going unreported under crimes by penal code, perhaps because sexual activity is mostly consensual and therefore not registering statistically or because police stations around the country are not funneling numbers related to Section 377 to NCRB due to lack of enforcement. But anecdotal and research reports indicate that legal and extralegal policing of same-sex sexual practices is widespread and socioeconomically marginal same-sex sexualities are especially at risk, thereby raising two possibilities. The first is that policing does not result primarily in formal charges filed under Section 377, which is quite likely, for that is no easy task. A medical examination to prove offense is the bar that must be met before charges against offending parties can be filed by police, which frequently opens the door to extralegal abuse. Thus, instead of charging homosexual men under the antisodomy law, police usually solicit either sexual favors or money.[53]

This foregrounds the second likelihood, that while same-sex sexual and gender minorities, especially those without the protection of social class, may be vulnerable to Section 377, it is not the only law through which police harassment and violence can occur. Indeed an ensemble of vagrancy laws, allegations of theft and disturbing the peace, and the Immoral Traffic Prevention Act (amended most recently in 2006) variously place same-sex sexualities at risk.[54] For example, Section 268 is the law against public nuisance that capaciously includes any act of commission and omission "which causes any common injury, danger or annoyance to the public or to the people in general who dwell or occupy property in the vicinity, or which must necessarily cause injury, obstruction, danger or annoyance to persons who may have occasion to use any public right," making it a more likely candidate to harass and charge same-sex sexualities or gender minorities. Priyadarshini Thangarajah and Ponni Arasu point out that despite the perils of Section 377, queer women are at greater risk from the laws on kidnapping, abduction, compelling a woman to marry, and wrongful concealment or confinement of an already kidnapped person.[55] Paradoxically, honing in on crime data for

Section 377 points away from Section 377 and toward a complex network of laws, policies, practices, and modalities of governance that regulate same-sex sexualities.

One way to develop a critique of the sexual state is to unravel the histories and practices of a regional state that seeks to regulate dance bars through a variety of mechanisms that have outlasted the judicial ruling to reopen them. Another way is to look at state agencies up close, through fieldwork, to reveal sexuality's effects on routine practices and mandates of these agencies and, by extension, the state. My search for statistics related to the antisodomy law paved the way for a series of interactions with and deferrals by state officials at NCRB that, in turn, exposed how bodies and sexual propriety are monitored through the ordering of workspaces. Across numerous field visits to many state buildings throughout the research process, it is difficult to identify a unit that is not attentive to the management of gendered bodies and the possibility of desire, and NCRB is no different in this respect. Indeed the lived, embodied aspects of state institutions and agencies are a crucial part of what defines and sustains them, even though as researchers we have not given them their analytical due.

Being attentive to sexuality also sheds light on why some issues defined as social problems, such as crimes against women, are measured, quantified, processed, and reported in ways that justify the rationale for NCRB and even the expansion of governance practices—harsher laws and punishments, for example. The reason same-sex issues are not similarly represented, however, is not predicated on heteronormativity, for that would be to deny the point that Section 377 is used to prosecute heterosexual violence against girls and women. Accounting for the discursive differences between violence against women and the antisodomy law through a focus on biopolitical governance draws attention to a broader view of sexual anxieties that do not align along the heterosexual and homosexual divide. Such a focus on biopolitical practices aimed at the welfare of the population suggests that the neglect of numbers for Section 377 in NCRB's tabulations and reports is deliberate and that the omissions gesture toward a complex web of juridical measures and provisions, of which Section 377 is only a part, governing same-sex sexual subjects.

Sexuality's significance to biopolitics extends beyond statistical discourses and deliberate silences on sexual crime, for it has everything to do with the biased ways populations are understood, measured, and calibrated and is implicit in matters of demography, assessments of health and disease, marriage and inheritance. The inconsistent attention to crime featured in this chapter is an entry point into the broader conjunctions of sexuality and biopolitics and an invitation to rethink theories of biopolitics (and necropolitics) that systematically neglect sexuality. Gupta's book *Red Tape* addresses the puzzle of why poverty is still widely persistent in India, despite numerous state-based initiatives. Using detailed ethnographic insights, Gupta juxtaposes the embodied aspects of governance and their biopolitical dimensions to explain how well-intentioned programs can nonetheless reproduce violence structurally, but without attending to the relevance of sexuality to the inconsistent, messy, and fragmented state. For a program such as the Integrated Child Development Services considered by Gupta, which is energized by population control and enlivened by state officials, staff workers, villagers, and the ethnographic researcher, sexuality remains an unresolved piece of the puzzle.

Coda

New Delhi, July 2005, final scene:

A little later I find myself in the spacious, second-floor office of Mr. Vishnu Dev, the ninth director of NCRB. Dressed in a beige safari suit, Dev, a man in his sixties, listens without much reaction, befitting a director with a background in the Indian Police Service.[56] The information is already available, he says, and calls in a Mr. Nath to confirm. Nath seems nervous, ill at ease at being called into the office unexpectedly and having to confirm the bad news, what Kavita Paul and Satish Dubey have already established, that information on Section 377 is not already in the records and tables.

The subsequent deliberations are nerve-wracking, hard to read across the massive desk that separates the director from the rest of us. Would he say yes? Would he approve the conversion of numbers into data, of figures into statistics? Dev wonders aloud whether the information even exists, for he believes that there are hardly any cases and Section 377 is hardly used. Even that is information that needs to be confirmed, I insist valiantly. Dev confirms that the information can be culled, and, then, in the tone of those used to granting or denying requests, in the tone of those who occupy large offices and sit behind enormous desks, says succinctly, "It's approved." I thank him and return approximately six times to gather the numbers.

PART TWO

SEXUAL LIVES OF JURIDICAL GOVERNANCE

CHAPTER 3

STATE SCRIPTS

Antisodomy Law and the Annals of Law and Law Enforcement

According to the National Crime Records Bureau, 2,243 First Information Reports (FIRs), or police crime logs, were registered under the antisodomy law statute over a ten-year period, 1996–2005, for twenty-five states.[1] The state of Madhya Pradesh had the most crime reports for Section 377 (401), followed by Rajasthan (337) and Haryana (312), while, at the other end of the spectrum, the states of Sikkim and Tripura reported only two such cases. The accuracy and consistency with which FIRs are channeled to the NCRB is unclear; for example, Madhya Pradesh reported eighty-four cases for Section 377 in 2003—the highest for any state in any year—but as few as four cases in the previous year.

These numbers are often compared with figures for Section 375, the law that criminalizes rape. Against the 2,243 cases for Section 377 over ten years, 18,359 cases of rape against girls and women were registered nationally in one year alone.[2] For metropolitan Delhi, which is home to some fourteen million, the reported figures for Section 375 are more than seven times higher than those for Section 377. As one senior police official noted, social taboos and fear of the police and criminal procedures mean that some number of rapes are never reported.[3] Even though crime committed under Section 377 is also likely to be underreported for similar reasons, the volume appears to be considerably less, confirming the view that rape represents a social problem but numbers for Section 377 do not warrant attention (see chapter 2).

Case law for Section 377 parallels the pattern from law enforcement; since 1860 only an estimated twenty-six to forty-six cases, depending on the cutoff date, went through the higher courts. Even when the tally increases to the ninety-nine cases that I was able to collate for this chapter, or in the case of the final Supreme Court verdict on the Naz Foundation writ, which covers 140 cases, it still does not compare to the voluminous case law for rape.[4] But statistics tell incomplete stories, and numbers gesture toward only the most preliminary comparisons. While charges under rape law require evidence of the lack of or inability to consent, consent is irrelevant to Section 377, and although rape is not seen as normal, neither is it seen as unnatural.[5] If rape laws are meant to protect, the antisodomy law is meant to punish. Whereas the rape law refers to violations involving "sexual intercourse," the antisodomy law uses the language of "carnal intercourse against the order of nature" to create a tautology between unnatural sexual practices and criminality.

In contrast to its pattern of sporadic (formal) enforcement, the antisodomy statute became the centerpiece of gay, lesbian, and queer activism in India in the years preceding the Delhi High Court verdict; originally known only in limited circles, it rapidly became the icon of homophobia in national liberal discourse. Marking the law's ascent into the public limelight, an open letter signed by the highly regarded novelist Vikram Seth and many other Indian luminaries argued that Section 377 jeopardizes human rights and fundamental freedoms as well as the spirit of a democratic and plural nation and should be revoked. In what he described as an exceptional gesture, the Nobel laureate Amartya Sen supported this appeal, arguing that the criminalization of gay behavior contradicts human civilizational progress; however, he begged the question of why a relatively little-used law warranted an extraordinary response on his part.[6]

Plaguing Section 377 are not the number of crimes recorded or the cases adjudicated, for numbers, after all, are unreliable and inadequate as measures of violence and injustice. Rather driving the struggle against Section 377 is its discursive history—that it inaugurates and institutionalizes the sodomite in Indian legal history, and by extension social history, and that it facilitates the persecution of homosexuals not least through law and law enforcement. As such, the 2001 Naz Foundation writ challenging Section 377 makes the case that the law's letter and spirit discriminate against homosexuals and serve as a barrier to equal and full citizenship for sexual and gender minorities.

These tensions between a sporadically used but abused law that is also an icon of injustice raise questions about juridical governance and histories: Does the law indeed import the sodomite as personage, in the Foucauldian sense, into the Indian context? If the law is not being enforced, why does it linger? What are the patterns of juridical governance across the law's more than 150-year history? Is it used at all, and, if so, does case law indicate the continued persecution of same-sex sexualities? Or does it yield a different picture, and would it hold across the annals of law enforcement, such as police crime logs?

In this chapter these questions segue into an analysis of case law and FIRs that articulates with the critique of the sexual state in the following ways. First, I expose the subjectivities of law, the institution that, in South Asian history, is seen as the emissary of the state or, more broadly by theorists such as Weber, as the source of its legitimacy and meaning with particular attention to sexuality.[7] Building on previously established insights, I trace the disjunctures and inconsistencies between the statute's history and its use to primarily prosecute sexual violence against children. Instead of treating it as a ready archive, I disarticulate and disaggregate the body of case law, marked as it is by the instabilities of meaning—stretching tautly across 150-year colonial and postcolonial histories—and the uncertainties of numbers: which cases have been left out and which ones qualify. Taking the caveat that legal materials are not merely descriptive but normative, and the caution that legal archives are often used to produce the very histories and subjects that they ostensibly corroborate, I read legal archives from the perspective of child sexual assault to highlight law's irrationalities and affects.[8]

Second, I track the increasing range of sexual practices and discourses that have fallen within Section 377's ambit over the years, thereby powering the reach of law and law enforcement and implicitly securing the state. Section 377 may not be frequently deployed to register or prosecute crime, but its documented history tracks closely with expanding judicial definitions and understandings of what constitutes unnatural sexual practices, which, without exception, are articulated in the context of sexual assault on children. Third, taking issue with Foucauldian genealogies of homosexual persecution institutionalized into law, I invite more complex renderings of colonial and postcolonial histories of homosexuality. Coming to grips with these histories in ways that do not presume a beleaguered homosexual subject at the outset draws attention to a broader and multiphonal set of discourses—unnatural, wrongful, perverse, depraved, and habitual—that animate how Section 377 is governed. Not least, I also bring to the forefront the nuances of gender, age, and social class that mediate sexualized practices of governance helping produce state-effect.

Taking the ambiguities of the legal-juridical framework (after Janaki Nair) as my point of departure, I begin by analyzing the discursive intent of Section 377 and locating it within a history of colonialism, penal codification, and criminality.[9] The chapter's emphasis then shifts to inconsistencies between the intent of the law and its archival life and the passions of its gradually expanding scope. I end by reflecting on the pitfalls of reading an ongoing history of homosexual persecution, or a Eurocentric Foucauldian genealogy, to drive the struggle against Section 377.

Formatting Discourse

Section 377 was part of the 511 criminal codes that composed the Indian Penal Code, introduced by the colonial state in 1860, and has been amended only a few times since then. It reads, "Whoever voluntarily has carnal intercourse against the order of nature with any man, woman or animal, shall be punished with imprisonment for life, or with imprisonment of either description for a term which may extend to ten years, and shall also be liable to fine. Explanation: Penetration is sufficient to constitute the carnal intercourse necessary to the offence described in this section." Section 377 was the revised version of Clause 361 that was part of the draft first submitted in 1837. Although Section 377 aimed for greater precision, Clause 361 makes clear that the intent is to penalize what is defined as unnatural lust regardless of consent: "Whoever, intending to gratify unnatural lust, touches, for that purpose, any person, or any animal, or is by his own consent touched by any person, for the purpose of gratifying unnatural lust, shall be punished with imprisonment of either description for a term which may extend to fourteen years, and must not be less than two years."[10] Section 377 replaces "unnatural lust" and the vagueness of "touching" with "carnal intercourse against the order of nature," which requires penetration, as Arvind Narrain points out. But it also retains an expansive scope compared to, say, the specificity of rape law, requiring continual judicial interpretation.[11]

Some versions of the Indian Penal Code provide further clarifications on the intent of Section 377: "General Comments: This section is intended to punish the offence of sodomy, buggery and bestiality. The offence consists in a carnal knowledge committed against the order of nature by a person with a man, or in the same unnatural manner with a woman, or by a man or woman in any manner with an animal." The general commentary serves to further emphasize the intent of Section 377 in ways that were earlier achieved by providing what were called "illustrations," aimed at facilitating legal interpretations of some of the codes due to the absence of an established body of case law to serve as precedent.[12] Also notable about the general comments is that they amplify what is implicit in Section 377: that the law applies equally to men and women.

Despite the relevance of consent, Section 377 was placed in chapter 16 of the penal code with other violent offenses relating to the body, such as rape, kidnapping, and assault. In terms of punishment, life imprisonment or ten years rigorous imprisonment (hard labor) and a fine are severe for consensual sex but represented an improvement over the death penalty for sodomy in England.[13] It is important to note, however, that in England sodomy was sporadically prosecuted through its common law tradition, and there existed no direct parallel to Section 377 in law or in the acts that subsequently legislated same-sexual sexual activity in nineteenth-century England, namely Blackstone's *Commentaries on the Laws of England* (1769), the Offences against the Person Act of 1828, the Criminal Law Amendment Act of 1885, and the Offences against the Person Act of 1861.[14] Section 377, then, was a specifically colonial invention that was shaped by extant meanings of sodomy in England and the exigencies of colonialism, crime, and social relations in a context at once far removed and linked by rule.[15]

COLONIALISM, CODIFICATION, AND CRIMINALIZED SUBJECTIVITY

Attempts to standardize law by codifying the Indian Penal Code of 1860 were fundamentally about discourses of desire and sexuality that encompassed the breadth of colonial rule in ways noted by critical scholars such as Anne McClintock, Ann Laura Stoler, and Robert Young. Law was a particularly charged site through which the excesses associated with the colonies could be produced only to be harnessed by impositions of European law, synonymous with reason and universality, for, as Piyel Haldar notes, the East was fabricated, fantasized, and even envied as the other side of law in colonial representations, while helping constitute Occidental legality.[16] These oscillations between the East and Europe, between lawlessness and the rule of law, between multiple confusing legal systems and a universal system helped rationalize the drive toward codification in the Indian colonial context.

Nair suggests that although the process of codifying law started after 1772, it became an urgent matter in the 1830s, leading to the formation of the First Law Commission in 1835, under the stewardship of T. B. Macaulay.[17] The draft, prepared mostly by Macaulay, was submitted to the government of India in 1837 but adopted only twenty-three years later. Influenced by Jeremy Bentham and the Utilitarians, Macaulay strongly espoused the need to standardize criminal law to ensure universal jurisprudence even though the definition of universality was severely mediated by race, gender, and nation in the colonial context. While the codification of law was highly contested and divisive, its legacy has been predominantly understood through the discourses of modernization and reform.

Through the decades support for codification oscillated between the need for law and the need to reform a legal morass; less disputed were the underlying premises of ushering Indian law into history and codification as progress. That the penal code stabilized the rule of law by systematizing, standardizing, and simplifying amid multiple, confusing, and complex legal structures is a position shared by Macaulay and his supporters well beyond the colonial period. Writing across the distant shores of historical space, Macaulay and the present-day legal historian M. P. Jain paint similar modernist narratives of rupture with the past. The state of law prior to the Indian Penal Code is repeatedly described as chaotic, confusing, and uncertain as a result of multiple colonial and precolonial structures of law that varied by region, religion, and jurisdiction. Thus in his "Introductory Report upon the Indian Penal Code" Macaulay describes an uncertain legal system in India that must be superseded by a uniform penal code:

> It appears to us that none of the systems of penal law established in British India has any claim to our attention, except what it may derive from its own intrinsic excellence. All those systems are foreign. All were introduced by conquerors differing in race, manners, language, and religion from the great mass of the people. The criminal law of

the Hindoos was long ago superseded, through the greater part of the territories now subject to the [East India] Company, by that of Mahomedans, and is certainly the last system of criminal law which an enlightened and humane Government would be disposed to revive. The Mahomedan criminal law has in its turn been superseded, to a great extent, by the British Regulations. Indeed, in the territories subject to the Presidency of Bombay, the criminal law of the Mahomedans, as well as that of the Hindoos, has been altogether discarded, except in one particular class of cases; and even in such cases, it is not imperative on the judge to pay attention to it. The British Regulations, having been made by three different legislatures, contain, as might be expected, very different provisions.[18]

If Macaulay fails to note the ironies of a legal morass, which was an administrative effect of colonial rule and the imposition of conquest, then it is also lost on Jain in his narrative on codification:

> The chaos with which the legal system was afflicted in India could be effectively dealt with only through the process of codification, *i.e.* reduction to a definite written form of law which had previously been unwritten or written only in such form as reported cases. Codification envisages reduction of different branches of law to a clear, compact and scientific form. Only through codification it was possible to achieve certainty for uncertainty, a written and stable law instead of a wilderness of judicial precedents which were bewildering to the litigant and confusing to the court. It was only through codification that homogeneity of law in the country could be achieved, and the law could be systematized, simplified and made somewhat clear and precise.[19]

The grammar of the excesses of law mixes with metaphors of wilderness to affirm codification as inevitable and an improvement.

Codification of law was also a reach for secularization, away from what Bernard S. Cohn has described as the theocratic understanding of the Indian state, whereby Hindu and Muslim became administrative categories of convenience to stabilize complex and hybrid legal and cultural practices.[20] Macaulay and Jain each note that although English law applied in some parts (presidency towns), other parts (*mofussil*) were governed by Hindu and Muslim law depending on the religious-cultural affiliations of the subjects.[21] This nominalization of Hindu and Muslim law was first undertaken by colonial agents and later partially undone by administrators such as Macaulay for whom secularization became the pretext for excluding local law. It was argued that even among presidency towns and the mofussil there was lack of uniformity due to judicial decisions and interpretations; non-Hindus and non-Muslims were governed by a different set of laws depending on where they resided; and the highest court often had to weigh in on which particular aspects of law applied in which areas. All of these elements were cited as arguments for a universal, secular, modern penal code.

But the colonial discourses of reform, modernization, and secularism were also feints for making systems of governance intelligible and subject to European orientations. David Skuy, who argues that the Indian Penal Code was not about the reform of the Indian primitive criminal justice system but was a British attempt to modernize its own criminal justice system, suggests one angle of critique. Characterizing the British criminal justice system as primitive, Skuy notes that by the time Macaulay started his work on the Draft Code of 1837, Britain's messy, bloody, and inchoate legal system had been under reform for half a century and that India received a penal code that reflected the needs of England.[22] Although Skuy's analysis ignores the particularities of the colonial context, it is useful in unsettling the persistent narratives of modernity and reform that shape not only colonial but also postcolonial discourses of law. Elizabeth Kolsky takes a different approach; she argues that codification was driven by the exigencies of the local, particularly the need for colonial authorities to harness lawlessness among European communities.[23] Both Skuy and Kolsky start by relating histories (after Kumkum Sangari) of the metropole and colony but point to different sites of significance. My point is not to reconcile these different analyses but to note their critiques of modernity while underscoring law as the means through which the East and excess are produced and (unevenly) harnessed.

Rather than a progression of history and modernity, Section 377 represents what Radhika Singha has called the despotism of law possible within an authoritarian context.[24] Lost in the colonial and postcolonial liberal narratives on codification as inescapable and inevitable is the underside of introducing criminal laws like Section 377 where they did not previously exist. Seen from the perspective of Section 377, the rupture between past and present, modernity and its predecessor is not celebratory but suspect. In his introductory notes on the Draft Code, Macaulay emphasizes the need to meld simplicity and precision in any law and declares law a travesty, an "evil," if it does not adequately convey meaning to the people who must abide by it. He seems to have missed entirely the irony of his own beliefs; one wonders what greater evil or travesty there is than the introduction of a law against unnatural lust where it did not previously exist. Indeed there is scant explanation in the written record about the introduction of Clause 361. Macaulay's "Introductory Report upon the Indian Penal Code," for example, makes references to this clause only to forestall public discussion on it: "Clauses 361 and 362 relate to an odious class of offences respecting which it is desirable that as little as possible should be said. . . . We are unwilling to insert, either in the text or in the notes, anything which could give rise to public discussion on this revolting subject; as we are decidedly of the opinion that the injury which could be done to the morals of the community by such discussion would more than compensate for any benefits which might be derived from legislative measures framed with the greatest precision."[25] Macaulay drew heavily on Bentham, but regrettably he appears to have been unaware of Bentham's polemic that homosexuality should *not* be treated as a crime.[26]

Section 377 introduced the criminalization of nonprocreative sexual practices in a way that did not have a precedent in precolonial India, and although the code does not overtly interpellate any specific persons or what have come to be identified as sexual orientations, the consensus is that it inaugurated the homosexual into legal history. Taking a Foucauldian stance, Narrain notes that while homosexual intercourse, contingent on subjects' caste and gender, could be punished for violating religious-legal texts, the "deviant" or "criminal" homosexual did not exist in precolonial India.[27] Similarly Alok Gupta argues that Section 377 is a law not merely about sexual practices but about homosexuality, for its target is not transgressive sexual acts but the transgressive person: the consenting homosexual.[28] Aniruddha Dutta crystallizes the analytics of the modern homosexual and the attendant homophobia: "Section 377, though externally imposed without consultation, becomes part of the process of re-mapping and re-figuration of extant categories of gender/sexual difference vis-à-vis a modern taxonomy of sexual acts and subjects and allows for the retroactive consolidation of tendencies phobic or resistant to such difference into a loose yet powerful assemblage of something like modern homophobia."[29] Thus Section 377 can be seen as intended for persons who have the appearance of being homosexual and therefore likely to commit aberrant sexual acts. Not surprisingly, as Anjali Arondekar elaborates in her critique on retrieving sexual subjectivities from the colonial legal archive, one of the very first cases under Section 377 had to do with the prosecution of a hijra for a crime without an eyewitness, a victim, or a chronology of events, but merely the appearance of homosexuality.[30] Thus Narrain speculates that Section 377 "contributed to the very emergence of the homosexual as a rights bearing subject who would one day question his/her very criminalization."[31] Section 377 may have served the imperatives of colonialism and governance of sexual subjectivities, but, as Upendra Baxi asserts, it is not enough to register the emergence of law as discourse, for it must be analyzed more thoroughly.

Law's Subjectivities and Expansions

As an imprecise collation of judgments, sentencing, and appeals mostly from the high courts and the Supreme Court, case law for Section 377 is a rough rather than ready archive. Some records are lengthy, others are brief, and the handful of studies on Section 377 identifies varying numbers of legal cases. For example, Suparna Bhaskaran bases her analysis on some twenty-seven cases, while Shamona Khanna identifies thirty cases and Gupta forty-six.[32] I was able to locate ninety-nine cases due to a combination of search methods, improved online search engines, and additional cases in the past few years, but even this is not an exhaustive list. The law reports are not always thorough, the search engine is not comprehensive, and there are human errors, for example where Section 377 is mistakenly recorded for Section 337. The list is also partial because it is drawn from the higher courts, as records from the lower courts are difficult to access. If only those high court cases that mention Section 377 are considered, even when the charges are not filed under this code, the cases multiply. Still, if one were to hold more closely to cases that are primarily charged under Section 377, the problem extends beyond identifying a numerically stable archive to reading an archive spanning 150 years and shifting conditions.

In her work on U.S. colonialism and law in Hawai'i, Sally Merry explains that case law always emerges through an "interpretive screen,"[33] which in the context of Section 377 has to do with the decriminalization of homosexuality. Notwithstanding the significance of legal precedence, case law on Section 377 has been collated and analyzed due to scholarly or activist interest, including this study, not least because law dictates the terms of its contestation. Inasmuch as Section 377 might be understood to criminalize homosexuality, any criticism or challenge thereof must show how the law constitutes the sodomite and unfairly and unreasonably discriminates against homosexuals.

Critiques of Section 377 range from the discriminatory spirit of the law to the records as proof of that discrimination. Bhaskaran's analysis of case law is undergirded by the AIDS Bhedbhav Virodhi Andolan writ, submitted in the Delhi High Court in 1994 to decriminalize homosexuality by repealing Section 377 (see chapter 5 for more on this writ), and Gupta's and Khanna's discussions of the legal archive occur in the context of the 2001 Naz Foundation writ, also aimed at decriminalizing sodomy. These analyses of case law are driven by the need to show inherent legal biases against the sodomite as a precursor of the homosexual. My point is not to take issue with these insights, for I build upon them. Rather I wish to underscore the point that the engagement with case law thus far has been primarily deployed as evidence of the legal bias against homosexual subjects and to hold it up as emblematic of contemporary homophobia, the origins of which lie within the colonial state.

UNYIELDING BODIES

But case law on Section 377 does not so easily yield. Rather than figuring the sodomite, it turns out to be a collection of sexual offenses that lie beyond the pale of the natural and normal, including consensual and nonconsensual sex between adult men, sexual assault on children and women by adult men, anal and oral sex coerced by men from their wives, and bestiality.[34] In fact the vast majority of Section 377 case law involves the sexual assault of boys and girls, typically young children, by adult men. This is not an innovative insight into case law by any means, for Bhaskaran skims this point in her analysis while Gupta notes that more than 60 percent of the forty-six cases in his study are about child sexual abuse, with a trend toward increased use of Section 377 in the 1990s to prosecute sexual assault on girls.[35]

Since the Indian Penal Code offers only narrow definitions of rape in Section 375 and makes no provision there for sexual assault on children,

Section 377 has until recently been the only way to prosecute sexual violence against male children and male adults, as well as aggravated sexual assault against girls and women.[36] The format of Section 375 offers a narrow understanding of sexual assault so that women and girls are consistently reproduced as heterosexual subjects whose bodies are violable, and men are produced as violators. "Forcible penis penetration of the vagina by a man who is not her husband" remains the operational understanding of rape, as a result of which a judge of the Delhi High Court did not hold responsible the father who repeatedly sexually assaulted his young daughter in the infamous *Jhaku* case on the grounds that the harm caused her did not fall under the criteria of Section 375.[37] In contrast, Section 377's imprecise but adaptable grammar of carnal intercourse against the order of nature allows for the prosecution of sexual violence on boys, otherwise excluded from Section 375, and also aggravated sexual assault that exceeds the scope of forcible penis penetration of the vagina. The irrelevance of consent under Section 377, or what is the crux of the problem for same-sex consenting adults, ends up facilitating prosecutions in cases of child sexual assault, as is amply evident in the legal case record.

Despite this the legal record for Section 377 has been analyzed from the angle of adult homosexuality. Gupta observes that, ironically, of the forty-six cases in his study only six are related to adult male-male anal intercourse, of which one case alone involves consensual sex.[38] Similarly, of the ninety-nine cases collated for this chapter, seventy-one of the victims are children: forty-four boys and twenty-seven girls.[39] These cases do not lend themselves to facile characterizations, even though the record starts dismally in 1884 with the higher court setting aside the conviction of Bapoji Bhatt by a sessions judge in the state of Mysore partly by expressing doubt about the nine-year-old boy's testimony in *Government v. Bapoji Bhatt*. Another case from the same year, *Queen-Empress v. Khairati*, has to do with a hijra whose appeal is granted since she was convicted of a "crime" without any substance or witness or harm to anyone, but not without the judge railing against her as a habitual sodomite.[40] Although not all appeals are upheld in the higher courts, most of the archive contains pleas to the rulings or sentences of lower courts in cases of child sexual assault.

When considered from the vantage point of child sexual assault, the most conspicuous pattern in the legal record has to do with the plausibility of the case, which is primarily based on whether a child can give testimony or the testimony of a young child can be credible, much like in *Bapoji Bhatt*. Years later, in the relatively brief record of *Sardar Ahmad v. Emperor* from 1914, the judge rejected the appeal that the uncorroborated testimony of the thirteen-year-old boy should not be the basis for conviction.[41] Even though there appear to be no other cases in the years between *Bapoji Bhatt* and *Sardar Ahmad*, the judge upheld the district magistrate's reliance on the child's "practically uncorroborated" testimony without much discussion and let the conviction stand. The very next case in the archive, *Ganpat v. Emperor*, decided in Lahore four years later, presents a stark contrast despite similarities in the basis of the appeals.[42] The petitioner appealed his conviction under Section 377 for assault on a fourteen-year-old boy, and this time the presiding judge set aside the conviction and acquit him on grounds of uncorroborated evidence by a young child. These contrary judicial conclusions are not without consequence, for *Ganpat* was cited as recently as 2010 to deny conviction for sexual assault on a young boy in *State of Himachal Pradesh v. Yash Paul*.[43] A more recent case, *Raju v. State of Haryana*, related to sexual assault on a nine-year-old girl, reveals the persistent ambivalence toward children's testimony in Indian law. The judge wrote:

> In a long chain of decisions, it has been observed that children are a most untrustworthy class of witnesses, for when of tender age, they live in a realm of make believe, they are prone to mistake dreams for reality. They are pliable as clay and repeat glibly as of their own knowledge what they had heard from others. However, there is no rule of law in India that evidence of child witness cannot under any circumstances be acted upon. . . . When the oral testimony of the child witness is found to be thoroughly honest and straight forward and implicitly reliable, even the solitary testimony of the child witness is sufficient to sustain the conviction of the accused.[44]

Of particular importance in cases involving children are judges' concerns about questionable motives and spurious allegations by victims. In the 1947 case *Mirro v. Emperor*, the judge set aside the conviction established by the assistant sessions judge, reasoning that the accounts of the boy, the blacksmith who tried to intervene, and other witnesses who gathered at the behest of the blacksmith did not add up plausibly.[45] In particular the judge referred to the petitioner's concern that the accusation was the result of "bad blood" between him and the community of

Chamars, to which the boy belonged. Dismissing any question of "communal feelings," the judge set aside the conviction on the "impression" (his word) that the accused was seen as an undesirable person and the accusation was the result of enmity.

Mirro is also important as a case in which plausibility was at least partly based on medical evidence. Continuing a line of reasoning present in the earliest case, *Khairati*, *Mirro* extends the role of medical evidence as the gap in the prosecution's story. In her discussion of *Khairati*, Arondekar writes that in a case tried under the antisodomy law, without a complainant or a specific crime, no location of the alleged crime, and no witness, medical evidence of a subtended anus and signs of syphilis was damning.[46] Arondekar emphasizes the heightened role of medical jurisprudence in colonial history involving offenses against the body, including under Section 377. What *Mirro* extends after *Khairati* is further amplified in *Ghanashyam Misra v. The State of Orissa* in 1957, where the petitioner, a schoolteacher, appealed his conviction for raping a ten-year-old girl student under Sections 376 (rape laws) and 377 in the Orissa High Court.[47] In considering the appeal, the presiding judge carefully weighed the various facts but also repeatedly emphasized the role of the medical examination. The petitioner's appeal was rejected and the sentence was actually increased based on the medical evidence of a tear in the girl's hymen, her blood-stained sari, the abrasion on the prepuce of the petitioner, the standards of medical jurisprudence that required a satisfactory explanation for the injury on the penis, and the medical opinion that penetration, though incomplete, likely occurred.

Across this archive medical jurisprudence is consistently refracted through the lens of legal guidelines and what is considered commonsensical reasoning. Thus the question of plausibility in these cases extends beyond the matter of child victims and witnesses to the integrity of the overall case, and judicial reasoning requires putting together the jigsaw puzzle of facts, legal arguments, and medical jurisprudence. Corroborating children's testimony with other children and adults to whom they report sexual assaults, the sequence of events in which the assault occurred and was reported to the police, and the circumstances under which the assault occurred are among the points of consideration in the archive. Put together with legal precedence and judicial interpretations of the letter and spirit of the law, the legal archive of Section 377 becomes subject to its own discourses and performance. On the one hand, judicial decisions in upholding or modifying convictions and sentences have all the appearance of legal and commonsensical reasoning. Their authority is derived from such appearances, affirmations about plausibility, recourse to legal precedence, and reiterations of the spirit and logic of the law. On the other hand, the archive and sometimes the individual cases are quite arbitrary. For example, close reading of the letter of the law in relation to legal precedence sometimes means upholding convictions, at other times overturning them. And, as noted earlier, reasoning used for similar circumstances sometimes leads to entirely different conclusions, for neither legal guidelines nor common sense are free from subjective and contrary sociolegal discourses.

LAW'S EXPANDING SCOPE

Also evident across the unwieldy archive is Section 377's expanding scope, not in reference to the homosexual as sodomite but consistently in cases to do with child sexual assault. In *Bapoji Bhatt* (1884), the judge accepted the appeal to conviction from a lower court because he considered the testimony of the nine-year-old to be doubtful but also because, in his reasoning, oral sex with a nine-year-old boy did not fall under the scope of Section 377. Arguing that "Section 377 is almost word for word the same as the form of indictment prescribed by English law for cases of Sodomy," he concluded that judges in England did not see a man's forcing his penis into the mouth of a child as constituting sodomy.[48] A similar appeal some decades later in *Khanu v. Emperor* (1925) that oral sex with a child does not constitute an offense under Section 377 was rejected. *Khanu* serves as a point of rupture in case law by arguing that oral sex involves sexual euphoria but is nonprocreative and therefore is against the order of nature. Further spinning out sociolegal discourses on sodomy, the court also weighed in on the question of why "modern states, now freed from the influence of superstition, still make the sin of Sodom punishable," only to conclude that it is to encourage legitimate marriage, to discount unmanly and less useful members of society, and to prevent the premature sexual indoctrination of the young.[49]

Khanu is cited frequently and used to expand the scope of sodomy to crimes of nature involving bestiality, buggery, and oral sex, leading to a conviction of three men for sexually assaulting a boy by forcible, if incomplete, penetration of the mouth with a penis in *Lohana Vasantlal Devchand and Others v. The State*.[50] As Narrain notes, *Lohana Vasantlal*

Devchand settles the matter of sodomy by including in its purview any unnatural sexual activity involving the sexual organs of either of the participants.[51] The judge wrote, "It could be said without hesitation that the orifice of mouth is not, according to nature, meant for sexual or carnal intercourse. Viewing [*sic*] from that aspect, it could be said that this act of putting a male-organ in the mouth of a victim for the purposes of satisfying sexual appetite, would be an act of carnal intercourse against the order of nature." The following year, in *State of Kerala v. Kundumkara Govindam and Another*, the Kerala High Court justice cited *Khanu* at length and ruled that forcible sex between the thighs of a fourteen-year-old girl was within the ambit of carnal intercourse against the order of nature and was therefore punishable under Section 377.[52]

Alongside the expanding statute's scope, case law was also proliferating discourses of sexual perversity, mostly through cases of sexual assault on boys. In *Fazal Rab Choudhary v. State of Bihar*, the Supreme Court interpreted Section 377 as synonymous with sexual perversity while weighing an appeal from Fazal Rab Choudhary, who had been sentenced to three years of rigorous imprisonment for what was described as an unnatural offense on a young boy.[53] In deliberating the merits of the appeal, the justices wrote, "The offence is one under Section 377, . . . which implies sexual perversity." The justices who furnished the historic judgment *Naz Foundation v. Government of NCT of Delhi and Others* in 2009 summarized the legal record of Section 377 as spanning "from the non-procreative to imitative to sexual perversity."[54]

Discourses of morality, excess, and the unnatural flourished throughout the legal record as judges considered cases and appeals related to sexual assault on children. Persisting in the discourse is the language of depravity, heinousness, and sexual perversity associated with unnatural behavior that cannot be directly traced to Macaulay's notion of the "heinous crime"; whereas Macaulay seems to refer to the heinousness of consensual sex among men, the heinousness in the legal record is primarily about the monstrosities of sexual assaults on children by adult men. In *Mirro*, involving sexual assault on a young boy, the judge characterized the accused as a terror and a morally depraved man. More recently, in the *State of Maharashtra v. Rahul alias Raosaheb Dashrath Bhongale*, the presiding judges repeatedly used the language of depravity to deny the appeal of the petitioner.[55] Characterizing the ferocity with which the accused sexually assaulted and murdered the young girl, this legal record is replete with phrases such as "depravity of the accused," "depravity of the mind," and "depravity of nature" to register shock and dismay at the vicious crime. Crime under Section 377 is often described as beastly and heinous, but perhaps no word is more frequently used in child sexual assault cases than *unnatural*, where it is both a synonym for sodomy and a means to characterize excess that cannot be contained within the realm of nature (or, really, culture). Thus *unnatural sex* is frequently used to signal coerced anal or oral sex but mostly for cases of excessively violent or brutal crimes committed on young children.

Case law spanning some 150 years can be broadly read as shifting from initial preoccupations with nonprocreative sex to interpreting and expanding the scope of unnatural sex by the early decades of the twentieth century. The homosexual as sodomite may well have been the reference point in early case law, which is why oral sex forced on a nine-year-old in *Bapoji Bhatt* would be seen as outside the scope of Section 377. But the relentlessness of cases of sexual assault on children forced judges to gradually enlarge the scope of Section 377 and include an increasing range of practices—oral sex, forcible sex between the thighs, and so on—within its ambit. Across the archive the reference point shifts away from the putative perversity of the homosexual as sodomite to the persistence of perversity, sexual depravity, and heinousness in relation to adult male sexual violence on children. Seen from the angle of child sexual assault, the legal archive of Section 377 is inconsistent with the ideological underpinnings of the code and is suggestive of law's irrationalities.

Before proceeding, I would like to juxtapose the legal record with police crime records, for they are the foundations upon which convictions are won and lost in the courts. The handful of analyses on the legal record of Section 377 does not take into account police crime records, perhaps because they are difficult to access. Providing more immediate insight into what sometimes ends up in the higher courts, police crime records serve a twofold purpose in this discussion: they provide a useful point of comparison with the trends of case law for Section 377, and they speak to another facet of Section 377's illogics. Therefore I turn to a sampling of sixty-six FIRs related to Section 377 for the period 1999–2005 obtained from three police districts of New Delhi, covering tens of police stations, to explore the uneven ways in which state institutions and procedures format sexuality, governance, and criminality.

Wrongful versus Unnatural Acts: Police Crime Records

First Information Reports are mandated under Section 154 of the Criminal Procedure Code, related to what are classified as cognizable offenses. Section 377 is a cognizable offense, which means that a case may be investigated and an arrest made without a warrant. Section 154 reads:

> Information in cognizable cases. (1) Every information relating to the commission of a cognizable offence, if given orally to an officer in charge of a police station, shall be reduced to writing by him or under his direction, and be read over to the informant; and every such information, whether given in writing or reduced to writing as aforesaid, shall be signed by the person giving it, and the substance thereof shall be entered in a book to be kept by such officer in such form as the State Government may prescribe in this behalf. (2) A copy of the information as recorded under sub-section (1) shall be given forthwith, free of cost, to the informant.[56]

FIRs are the written reports related to the commission of an offense that is supposed to be recorded in writing by the police, based on the testimony and attestation of the informant. As affidavits, they serve as another iteration of "paper truths" of the state.[57] Like many other state records, FIRs are standardized, aimed at registering the same information in each case while leaving room for each case's peculiarities. They format otherwise unmanageable details of crime reports into the following categories: police district and date of record; relevant sections of the penal code; the day, date, and time of the crime and the place, date, and time where the complaint was filed; details of the complainant or information, including name, father's or husband's name, date of birth, nationality, passport details, occupation, address, and telephone number; details of the accused; reasons for delay in filing a police report, if any; details of any stolen property; details in a case of murder; and the details of the crime, as well as the name of the person creating the record.

The sixty-six FIRs from New Delhi corroborate what is evident from the legal archive; the vast majority (fifty-nine) are crimes committed on children; forty-nine are about sexual assault on boys, while ten chronicle crimes against girls. The ages of the victims were not recorded in three of the cases, although the narratives suggest that two were boys and one was a girl. The FIRs also include four adult men as victims or complainants; their ages were eighteen, nineteen, twenty-five, and forty. The nineteen-year-old reported that a classmate committed the crime; the eighteen- and twenty-five-year-old were assaulted while trying to find employment. In what appears to be an unusual case, the forty-year-old reported being abducted by two men in a van, robbed, and sexually assaulted while he was walking to work one early morning. None of the four cases involving the adult men, nor any of the other sixty-six cases, bears obvious traces of consensual rather than coerced sex, even though the circumstances could be more complex than what is recorded.

These FIRs also provide additional insight into what becomes the legal record of Section 377 through the higher courts. The informants or complainants logged in the FIRs are either the victims of crimes or, typically, family members who intervene on behalf of their children. A twelve-year-old boy may be identified as the complainant, but at other times a father or mother may be recorded as such. Typically a mother or father is listed as the informant or complainant when the child is younger than ten. Women are more likely to register the FIR for their young daughters. Children are typically listed as students, and the adults are generally from the working classes, listed as laborers, owners of a small business such as a juice stand, or engaged in other low-skill occupations. Almost all the women are described as housewives. At least based on these sixty-six FIRs, it appears that the working poor and the lower middle classes are the ones reporting crime related to Section 377. Most of the accused are neighbors; in only one of the cases the identity of the accused was not known. The age of the accused is rarely noted, but there are ample references in Hindi to *ladka/ladke* (boy/boys) or *aadmi* (man). Since *ladka* might be used to describe a boy or a young man, it is hard to ascertain the age of an accused, whether he is also a minor possibly assaulting another minor or legally an adult committing a crime on a minor.

STATE SCRIPTS AND WRONGFUL ACTS

FIRs are not simply "factual" records of crimes or "paper truths" that are freighted with the power of the word in the modern state; rather they are better understood as *state scripts* that produce and mediate narratives on crime in three ways. First, they are forms, having a number of different fields where information is condensed and easy to read. In fact the FIRs gathered for this study include two versions, the earlier of which was phased out. The later version uses twelve fields of information related to the details of the informant or complainant and the crime, a narrative section, and another three fields at the end related to the police officer recording the FIR. The many more fields of data in the later version create a more detailed record, including age, occupation, and passport number of the informant or complainant, and is easier to read at a glance. The logic of governance appears to be dictated by the standardization of detail, which allows for more efficient gathering and tabulating of information. This is precisely the kind of information that is used by centers such as the National Crime Records Bureau to generate reports in increasing detail.

Second, FIRs are literally scripted. Since the FIRs are from Delhi police stations, all the fields are handwritten primarily in Hindi and partly in English, especially numbers, dates, and occasionally names. They are stored as paper copies and listed in hardbound ledgers, kept in the Records Room of local police stations. Third, there is relative consistency in the narratives, despite the particularities of cases, the different police districts from which they were obtained, and the five-year period from which they are drawn. It's not that the details of age, gender, and occupation of the informants or complainants do not matter, but that the formatting of the narratives gives the FIRs a kind of uniformity. While no case is the same as another, the representation of the crime and its circumstances repeat across the FIRs into what emerge as a few familiar scenarios. A FIR from the North West police district recorded in 2001 lists a twelve-year-old boy as the complainant and a male of unknown age as the accused. In the first-person account of the boy, he says that he was promised a new and bigger kite by the accused, who took him inside the house, locked the door of the room, clamped the boy's mouth with his hand, took off the boy's pants, and performed a wrongful act on him. The boy's mother knocked on the door, causing the accused to flee. Several other FIRs read similarly, as boys and girls are lured by a neighbor or an older boy or man from the neighborhood and then assaulted behind closed doors. In this case the accused was charged under Section 377 as well as Section 342 for wrongful confinement. Cases involving young girls are sometimes charged under Section 377 and Section 376 (for rape), but only under Section 377 when the girls are young. For example, a mother registered a FIR for sexual assault on her three-year-old daughter, reporting that she left her daughter in the care of a neighbor, the mother of the accused; when she returned she found her daughter crying and later learned from her that the accused had put his "*ungli* (finger, but possibly a child's word for penis)" in her "private parts" (written in Hindi) and caused her pain. Another scenario repeated in the FIRs is captured in the case of a thirteen-year-old boy who accused three perhaps older boys of taking him by a small temple in a park and sexually assaulting him; when he cried out, they ran away. He returned home and told his father, who took him for a medical examination after calling the police station and then to the police station to register the FIR.

The FIRs format discourses of sexuality and criminality, but in ways that are not consonant with the code. In contrast to the ideologies of unnatural sex, the sampling of police crime records is dominated by the discourse of *galat kaam* (Hindi), which roughly translates as *wrongful act*. The recorded accounts of the children, the adults reporting on their behalf, and the adult men who file complaints are thick with references to *wrongful act*; it is used to describe mostly coerced anal sex but also coerced oral sex and rape. One way to understand this discourse is as a euphemism for *sexual assault* in the case of children. But if euphemisms are necessary, especially in sexual crimes involving young children, *unnatural* serves just as well; indeed more linguistically formal references to *apprakrit maithun* (unnatural sexual intercourse) are found in the crime records, but only sparingly.

What seems to be at play here is a disjunction between the law and narratives of crimes under it. Unlike the discourse of unnatural sex and its association with that which violates or transgresses what is natural and therefore legitimate, a wrongful act is replete with injustice and injury. Rather than being generated at the threshold of nature or culture, the discourse of the wrongful act is specifically about the cultural universe of harm and the act of wronging another, especially compelling in terms of children. Whether it is generated by the person giving testimony—the children who report crime and testify to the police or the adults who file complaints on behalf of children—or the police constable who records it, the discourse clearly prevails in the context of child sexual violence and is incongruent with Section 377's origins and intents.

Contemplations on the Code, Case Law, and Criminal Records

The egregiousness of a law criminalizing sexual practices among adults regardless of consent is inarguable, but the antisodomy law's records point toward more complex histories of juridical governance. Underscoring Section 377's subjective and contradictory aspects yields a thicker understanding of how such juridical mechanisms bring within its fold a web of crime, sexual practices, and subjects—child sexual assault, sexual assault on women and men, adult male perpetrators, but also occasionally women seeking divorce and adult sexual and gender minorities—thus reaffirming the indispensability of law and, by extension, the state in preserving sociosexual order. Though Section 377's unwieldy archive has been read primarily from a Foucauldian viewpoint to show how law introduced and wrongly criminalized the homosexual, underscoring law's sexual ideologies offers a more thoroughgoing appraisal of governance and better serves efforts at undoing it.

Highlighting the dissonance between the provision and functions of the antisodomy law helps cast doubt on its usefulness. The intent of Section 377 may well have been to repress and prohibit sex between males and females, but in fact case law from the higher courts—and this is supported by the sample of police crime records—has been primarily used to prosecute sexual assault against children, especially boys but also girls. Complaints, supported by the medical examination required under the statute, are likely to be filed in cases of crimes against children, not in relation to the adult consensual sexual practices that may fall within the ambit of Section 377, throwing its effectiveness into further doubt. If the antisodomy law is not targeting same-sex sexual practices (or other practices that were originally implied) and is an inadequate substitute for prosecuting sexual offenses against children, then it is hard to justify.

Second, discourses of sexual perversity, depravity, and the scope of sex against the order of nature have been consistently articulated and elaborated through cases involving sexual assault on children, not in relation to the so-called sodomite or the homosexual. Gupta observes that the foremost contribution of cases such as *Lohana Vasantlal Devchand* has been to mark sexual perversity in Indian law and trigger a growing linkage between sodomy, perversity, and homosexuality without distilling a space for consensual same-sex sexual practices.[58] But to make this case is not only to homogenize a complex and unwieldy set of records but also to fill a lacuna in the case records that is worth utilizing differently. By underscoring that institutional discourses and expansions of the scope of sodomy law are generated through cases of sexual assault against children, it is possible to suggest that social concerns about unnatural sex, sexual perversity, and the like are consistently being expressed on account of adult male violence on girls and boys rather than targeting homosexuality.

Third, taking a subjective view of law encourages more nuanced representations of the homosexual, not least by sifting him from the child sexual predator. In fact even though the Section 377 archive has consistently been criticized for encoding biases against homosexuals, it would be more politically efficacious to argue that the archive is *not* about the persecution of adult consenting homosexuals. It is not that biases against the sodomite or the homosexual do not color legal archives, but reading them systematically into the case law unwittingly reaffirms the homosexual as child predator. That law and law enforcement do not sustain homosexual persecution, despite the law's intents, becomes a way of highlighting law's irrationalities, as well as extricating the homosexual from the child predator.

I am also suggesting that by presenting the legal archive of Section 377 as *primarily* about child sexual assault and not about the homosexual it is possible to rewrite precolonial as well as colonial and postcolonial histories as ambiguous ones. Most significant, the archive does not evidence a clear-cut sociolegal history of persecution against homosexuals in India. (To suggest otherwise is to produce a Foucauldian genealogy of the homosexual as sodomite where it does not unequivocally exist.) Such a position also risks giving greater strength to the state, by assuming it is the site of injustice toward same-sex sexualities and also the wellspring of justice, accounting for Naz Foundation's emphasis on seeking recourse from the judiciary. One would go a lot further in demonstrating the irrelevance of the antisodomy law by rewriting legal histories of homosexuality wherein the colonial context has limited impact and the postcolonial setting shows little indication of systematic persecution of same-sex sexualities as well as by raising questions about a penal code and legislative system that, until the passing of the Protection of Children from Sexual Offences Act (2012), did not have laws and provisions to deter and prosecute sexual assault on children. And, not least, building a more capacious case challenging discrimination and injustice against same-sex sexual subjects would necessarily implicate a whole nexus of laws, policies, and discourses in lieu of a narrow focus on Section 377.

A fourth and concluding point: the archive is hardly free from homophobic discourses. To say that there are few cases of adult homosexual consensual sex in the higher courts is not to say that troubling discourses are absent, for the issue is never just about numbers. In a recent analysis, Gupta discusses how specific cases—*Queen Empress v. Khairati* (1884), *Noshirwan Irani v. Emperor* (1934), and *D. P. Minwalla v. Emperor* (1935)—constitute (homosexual) personhood pejoratively.[59] Khairati was initially apprehended for being male bodied while dressing and singing in women's clothes, and then convicted by a lower court for having the characteristic signs of a "habitual catamite." In *Noshirwan Irani v. Emperor*, the judge railed against the "vice of a catamite" in the case of the eighteen-year-old Ratansi, with whom the appellant was trying to have sex; they were observed by a policeman and neighbor, who subsequently marched the two of them to the police station.[60] Even though the conviction was set aside—because of discrepancies in earlier and later testimonies, the likelihood that the neighbor and policeman had a grudge against the young Ratansi and did nothing to intervene on his behalf, and because no penetration could be proved—the language described the catamite as despicable and anal sex as a vice. In *D. P. Minwalla v. Emperor* one of the two accused of sodomy appealed his conviction under Section 377 for what appears to be consensual sex with a young man described as a lad.[61] The judge of the High Court of Sind pored over the evidence, arguments, and plausibility of the crime to uphold the conviction under Section 377, but revealingly chastised the accused for inviting "a lad to perform upon him an odious and unnatural abomination." These and similar cases proliferate the recursive and pejorative logic between sexual acts and (homosexual) personhood.

What stands out troublingly from the language of the cases involving consensual sex between men is the discourse of the "habitual sodomite." The language varies superficially as the "habitual sodomist," "the vice of a catamite," and "the vice" (of sex against the order of nature), but its underpinnings are about criminality and habitualness. Starting with the legal record of *Khairati*, the notion of the habitual sodomite finds sporadic though consistent expression in the archive of Section 377. The habitual sodomite is part of a larger matrix of discourses of habitual and hereditary offenders who are codified into the policies and practices of criminality by the late nineteenth century in colonial India. The ideology that some groups are predisposed to crime through habit or heritage was enacted into law first in the Habitual Criminals Act of 1869 and then the Criminal Tribes Act of 1871 and its subsequent iterations, casting entire communities as imminent criminals, subject to surveillance and control of mobility and coercive resettlement.[62]

Although Satadru Sen does not address crime related to Section 377, his reflections on the distinctions between habitual and hereditary offenders shed light on how to interpret the traces of the habitual sodomite. Sen argues that while the hereditary criminal was typically associated with the countryside and intergenerational transmission of crime, the habitual criminal was seen as his urban counterpart, hardened to crime but not predisposed to it. Additionally important, according to Sen, is that "the colonial discourse on hereditary criminals was based on a cultural, rather than the biological, model of hereditary. The biological model was always present, but was distinctly secondary."[63] If notions of the hereditary criminal are based on social heritage, then the habitual criminal is seen as someone who is accustomed to crime and likely to continually repeat it; for him, committing crime becomes a settled practice or condition, perhaps even an inward disposition.[64]

When judges use the grammar of the habitual sodomite or the vice of sodomy (the habit or defect of an immoral or depraved nature) in the case law of Section 377, they rehearse it as a crime that is continually repeated or becomes part of the inward or mental disposition, and therefore an inevitable practice. It seems to me that the most persistent and injurious discourse on homosexuality decried in the legal record is that it is a settled, habitual practice that will inevitably be repeated, the implications of which become especially palpable from the angle of a rights-bearing homosexual. Even though for the Delhi Police the arc from the habitual to the criminal is to some extent negotiable in the case of homosexuals, it is intractable in the case of other groups who are seen to be accustomed to unnatural sex and criminality.

CHAPTER 4

"HALF TRUTHS"

Racializations, Habitual Criminals, and the Police

Little is of greater concern in state regulation of sexuality than the policing of sexual and gender minorities.[1] In their report on lesbian women in India, Bina Fernandez and N. B. Gomathy indict police coercion and threats of public exposure as the principal form of state violence.[2] Police intimidation also makes gay men vulnerable, according to *GayBombay*, a community group in Mumbai, to extortion of money and sex.[3] A report by the well-regarded People's Union for Civil Liberties, Karnataka, "Human Rights Violations against the Transgender Community," documents the vulnerability of hijras to, among other institutions, everyday police harassment, abuse, and sexual violence, further intensifying the need to understand policing.[4]

As Foucault notes in "*Omnes et Singulatim*," the police as a collective institution is an institution of the state as well as an overall strategy of governance, which accounts for why activist and scholarly concerns have been directed at "police states" (for example, Arendt in *Origins of Totalitarianism*), with an eye to the institution as a site of violence—excessive, ongoing, exhibitionist, spectral, and routine.[5] Feminist social scientists and scholars of race, ethnicity, religion, and nationalism continue to grapple with police violence that targets ethnic and racial minorities, migrants and refugees, the urban poor, women sex workers, and tribal communities, among others, but what is frequently missing are systemic analyses of the institution and its histories.[6]

The police is among the most opaque state institutions in India, and though several studies have taken to task its colonial histories and postcolonial legacies, contemporary ethnographic accounts are still uncommon, leaving journalistic impressions to fill the void. Indeed the Delhi Police have a research cell that monitors aspects of the institution but disseminates its findings only internally. Turning to fieldwork, then, becomes a way of creating an archive of the state, a task made all the more imperative due to the impenetrability of the police. Delving into two discussion groups in Delhi, one with twenty-five constables at a Delhi Police station and another with some forty-five station heads, inspectors, and others from the middle rungs, this chapter brings representatives from a range of police stations in the Delhi area into the fold of research.[7] Supplementing this analysis are my numerous visits to police stations and conversations with constables that offer glimpses into the institutional discourses and practices governing sexuality, with the proviso that their perspectives are neither representative of police in India nor exhaustive portrayals of the Delhi Police.[8]

Complementing the discussion in chapter 3 on the legal archives of the antisodomy law, this chapter analyzes the subjective, sexualized aspects of law enforcement. In an added twist, I argue that policing related to Section 377 likely imperils those communities that are seen as inherently hypersexual and criminal, especially Muslims and hijras. Although gay men, men who have sex with men, and lesbians are not immune to the brute impact of legal and extralegal policing, the Delhi Police point toward the ways in which law is subjectively administered or, put differently, how the antisodomy code is routinely flexed to imperil entire groups regardless of their sexual practices.[9] Coming to grips with these passions and prejudices, this chapter substantiates the argument that Section 377 serves to enhance law enforcement's reach and justification, providing another view of how sexualized governance practices and discourses help secure institutions that constitute the state. In the process it expands the focus on gender as normative womanhood to include hijras and adds awareness of racialized religious-cultural minorities to this analytical mix.

However, invoking racialization in India's present to understand police narratives linking crime committed under Section 377 and religious-cultural minorities requires reconsidering existing analytical apparatuses. Although pejorative representations of Muslims by mostly Hindu police in Delhi would typically be explained as communalist biases—that they are the result of mutual sectarian prejudices and hostilities—the inference of reciprocity makes communalism analytically inadequate in a context where some communities are at grave risk of prejudice, discrimination, and violent exclusion.[10] Instead race and racialization—defined here as processes through which social inequality is rationalized as natural, inheritable, and enduring—help explain why and how police malign particular communities (not all religious groups are racialized or represented in similar ways) in relation to the antisodomy law.[11] Building on Ania Loomba's argument that religion is neither a preracial form of difference nor racism's latest iteration but has been central to the development of its modern formations across the globe, this approach shifts attention to sexuality and race thinking (after Arendt) in *post*colonial India.[12]

While hijras may also be seen as a religious-cultural community, they are not typically placed alongside Hindus, Muslims, and other religious groups, and their genealogy is more directly framed in terms of criminality—as characteristically transgressive and predisposed to crime—which echoes in the discussion groups among Delhi Police. Mindful that hijras have long been interpellated by the antisodomy statute, this chapter seeks to explore the logics of policing that name disparate communities—Muslims, hijras, and even Sikhs—in the same breath and to analyze the play of culture and nature through which the antisodomy law facilitates the reach of policing well beyond its scope.

Internal Sovereignty and Legacies of Violence

Nothing identifies the state with coercion and violence more overtly than the police and the military. The distinctions between them are not always easily drawn, but my particular interest in this chapter is the institution of the civilian police located within a larger strategy of state-based governance and charged with maintaining "internal sovereignty." Defining *sovereignty* as the ability and the will to employ overwhelming violence and to decide on life and death, Thomas Blom Hansen and Finn Stepputat argue for the need to understand sovereignty as a cultural construction and emphasize its internal aspects, secured through the exercise of violence over bodies and populations.[13] As I see it, civilian police, charged with the maintenance of law and order, are crucial to the safeguarding of internal sovereignty, which explains why they are also among the most flawed and reviled of state institutions in India.

In postcolonial India antipathy to the police occurs not only among the vulnerable but also among the middle and upper classes, and the view that police abuse the law—through corruption, bribery, lack of responsiveness to public grievances—is commonly shared and supported by documentation. A study by People's Watch across nine states and forty-eight districts in India estimates that 1.8 million people are tortured by the police each year.[14] Ordinary citizens and members of marginalized communities—the indigent, Dalits, scheduled castes, and hijras, among others—frequently do not report crimes committed against them for fear of police retribution. A Human Rights Watch report underscores the following areas of concern: police failure to investigate crimes, arrest on false charges and illegal detention, torture and ill treatment, and extrajudicial killings.[15] Widespread aversion to the police also breeds contempt for the institution, and they are routinely characterized as ineffectual and incompetent, as is often the case in Hindi films (Bollywood). In a particularly ironic moment during fieldwork, a Hindi film was playing on a TV in the lobby of an office where I was waiting to meet a state official, and security personnel and I watched the stock scene of a group of policemen unsuccessfully chasing the hero, further signifying the lack of complex understandings.

INSTITUTIONAL HISTORIES

Tracing historical and cultural legacies of the police in India, Kirpal Dhillon describes an institution that remains a product of colonial policies and practices and antiquated juridical systems.[16] Forged by the Indian Police Act of 1861 and the Indian Evidence Act of 1872, the police, David Arnold suggests, was the outcome of techniques of control developed in order to strengthen the colonial state's control over the indigenous society and mirrored the structures of another British colonial force, the royal Irish constabulary.[17] He further notes that institutional hierarchy was distinctively racial as relatively few European officers occupied the highest positions out of an entrenched distrust of Indians and a low opinion of their abilities and character. At the same time, recruitment policies disaggregated people into convenient stereotypes of "martial races," or "Brahmans," giving preference to some groups over others and recruiting from the "low castes" only when others were unavailable for recruitment.[18] Drawn from subaltern groups, the rank and file of the police were paid little and had poor working conditions and no prospects of upward mobility compared to the Europeans or the inspectorate drawn from the Indian middle classes.[19] The failure of adequate supervision, petty corruption, illegal extraction, and predatory acts became institutionalized and further alienated the constabulary from subaltern communities. From its start, the role of the police was to impose and maintain law and order, not to provide service and security to their communities, and they were accountable to the masters and not to the communities, patterns that endure to date.

Although police reforms have occurred in postcolonial India, they have been incremental, not sweeping, leaving intact colonial structural flaws relating to accountability, autonomy, and inequity.[20] The lasting colonial legacy has ensured that the police protect and defend the establishment, the wealthy and the powerful, the locally influential, while typically remaining indifferent and frequently oppressive to the communities they watch (over). Systemic alienation of the police from the communities where they enforce the law and maintain order remains essentially unchanged, and, if anything, people's mistrust of the police may have deepened. Furthermore civilian police still do not operate as an autonomous unit answerable to the community, despite efforts at fostering police and community ties in cities like Mumbai; rather the police are subject to the state-level political executive. While the police also exist at the national level (such as the Central Reserve Police Force, the Border Security Force, the Intelligence Bureau, the National Security Guards), the civilian police fall under the authority and purview of state governance, creating a two-tier system of policing.[21] The chain of hierarchy and accountability of the civilian police ends with the state executive branch via a civilian district magistrate and the state police chief, thereby making police at the local or district level responsible to the political wing of government rather than the law or communities they serve. The Delhi Police motto—"With you, For you, Always"—aims at bridging these divides, inviting the trust of the public and fostering a community-oriented police force, but without structural reforms addressing autonomy from political leadership, accountability to communities, and inequities within the institution, this motto falls significantly short of its promise.

The bulk of the police force, its constables and head constables, continue to live at the edge of poverty, working long hours in arduous conditions not unlike their predecessors in colonial times.[22] In Delhi police constables perform twelve-hour beats daily, make between Rs 3,200 and 4,000 ($72–110) per month, are statutorily required to be available twenty-four hours a day, have no fixed days off, and often return home to their families no more than three days a week, sleeping at the station instead.[23] Ventures into the restricted areas of Delhi Police stations during fieldwork revealed large rooms with a row of simple beds and personal items stowed beside them. Human Rights Watch reports even more dire working conditions in other cases.[24] In 2008 there were an estimated 79,000 Delhi police, of which 7 percent were women.[25] Most officers are from the Hindu ethnic community of Jats from the neighboring state of Haryana. The institution is controlled by the Union Ministry of Home Affairs and is headed by the police commissioner. In Delhi there are three special commissioners of police, seventeen joint commissioners, seven additional commissioners, seventy-four deputy commissioners, and 272 assistant commissioners of police. All senior police officers are graduates of the elite Indian Police Service and have no experience with hands-on policing. They take highly competitive entrance exams with a selection rate of less than half a percent and start their careers by heading a police district.[26] The Delhi Police are divided into eleven districts and 177 individual police stations, known as *thanas* in Hindi. Thanas are headed by inspectors, who are university graduates, whereas constables are recruited locally and given training that ill prepares them to respond to the needs of the communities they police.

Colonial and postcolonial contexts are marked by continuities as well as differences, and it is important not to exaggerate either. The end of colonialism and a dynamic postcolonial context notwithstanding, the rank and file of the police still stand at the threshold of state and society and embody the paradox of being both state agents and subalterns, while practicing the enforcement of law in flawed ways. And, although Hansen and Stepputat argue that colonial forms of sovereignty are more spectral, fragmented, and racial, their traces are still discernible in the responses by members of the Delhi Police to my discussion questions.[27]

The "Nature" of Unnatural Sex

On June 10, 2005, I accompany Manjeet, an outreach worker for Naz Foundation, the NGO that filed the challenge to Section 377 in the Delhi High Court in 2001, to a police station in South Delhi. Similar to programs aimed at creating awareness among police on sexuality-related issues in nations such as Kenya, Nepal, and the United States, Manjeet conducts HIV/AIDS informational and sensitization programs at police stations in Delhi. After going through the basics of HIV and AIDS, what causes HIV infection, and how to prevent it, Manjeet turns the group over to me for a discussion that lasts over an hour. I step to the front of the room to face twenty-five police constables, introduce myself as a teacher and researcher in the area of sexuality, and say that I am interested in what they know about Section 377 of the Indian Penal Code and how they enforce it.

"It's to do with unnatural sex," "Any kind of unnatural sex involving animals, dead bodies," chime a few constables. "In the case of an old man trying to have sex with a young girl." They speak about Section 377 easily and participate in the ensuing discussion on the criminal law.

I ask the twenty-five constables for cases that they have encountered related to Section 377. The examples pour fast and freely. An old man raped a young boy and he came to the police; a Muslim couple, where the wife did not want anal sex and filed a complaint against the husband. "It happens more among Mohammedans," one constable asserts informatively, casually in Hindi. Manjeet, a turban-wearing Sikh, reproves the constable immediately, saying firmly but kindly that such remarks shouldn't be made about any community ("Kisi community ke bare main aisa nahin kehna chahiye"). Without missing a beat, the constable responds, "Your community is the second one where it happens the most" ("Uske baad apki community main sabse zyada hota hai"). Laughter explodes among the constables; none of them challenges either statement. The constable adds in English, "Don't mind, please," and then in Hindi, "I say what I have seen."

The twenty-five constables in the room are seated in neat rows on either side of a center aisle, and Manjeet and I take turns standing in front of the desk at the head of the room. The spacious though not large room is comfortably filled. A cooler, a machine that works on a combination of air and water, brings relief from Delhi's dry heat while creating a background din, and the drawn window curtains shield the room from the midday heat. A few posters are tacked to the walls: one in English on sexual harassment, one in Hindi advocating against dowry, and in the back of the room a fading image of a once-resplendent Madonna and the baby Jesus. The dull cream color of the walls, the sun-bleached curtains, and the posters give the room a drab, worn appearance. In contrast, the constables are neatly attired in their khaki uniforms. All male, their years of service in the police range from six to thirty-two. These policemen have served and continue to serve the beats—in the streets, the parks, the neighborhoods. Our discussion is primarily in Hindi, liberally peppered with words, phrases, and sentences in English.

The constable's assertion that "unnatural sex" happens more among Muslims and Sikhs is a stunning displacement of sexuality and criminality onto religious-cultural groups. It is preceded by examples of what constitutes unnatural sex: nonnormative and unnatural sexual practices. The point that such practices occur primarily among Muslims and Sikhs suggests powerful sentiments among the police that are not simply about homophobia but about the fear and (pleasure of) hatred of particular minority religious-cultural communities. Missing from these initial examples is any mention of same-sex sexual activity among adult women or men, making the glib association between unnatural sex and Muslims that was reinforced time and time again in conversations with police constables in Delhi all the more disturbing. The use of the term *Mohammedans* rather than *Muslims* deepens the distance between the constable and those to whom he refers, for *Mohammedans* was a term used by the British to describe the followers of Islam and is still commonplace in Delhi, along with *Muslims* (in English and Hindi) and *Musselman* (in Hindi). The scathing connotations of the constable's statement are exacerbated by the laughter of his colleagues.

Manjeet's timely intervention is rebuffed immediately by the constable. The term *community* that echoes in their exchange, as in the Hindi-English phrase *apki community* (your community), is partially derived from the term *communal* in the Indian context. Had Manjeet and the constables spoken entirely in Hindi, they would have likely used the term *quam* (translated as *community* or *nation*). The *Oxford English Dictionary* notes the particular association of community and the communal within the South Asian context, wherein community is shaped by religious and ethnic difference and intercommunal strife.[28] Sudipta Kaviraj draws a distinction between fuzzy and enumerated communities, the ones that are not territorially based—caste, religion—and the ones that are both about numerical strength and territory, such as nations.[29] The exchanges on community between Manjeet and the constable are condensed narratives of the history of the postcolonial Indian nation within which religious communities became enumerated, consolidated despite their "fuzzy boundaries," and grist for the discourse of communalism. Muslim and Sikh communities in India have indistinct boundaries and are characterized by internal religious, linguistic, caste, geographic, gender, and class differences, much like Hindus—right-wing attempts at homogenizing Hinduism notwithstanding.[30] Still, dominant and minority religious-cultural communities are seen as the basis for struggles around political, economic, and cultural resources.

That these ideologies and sentiments are not limited to constables became clear in the group discussion with those higher up the chain of command, the middle rung of the police, where more than forty-five heads of police stations and police inspectors gathered for a training session on gender sensitization and gender justice on July 13, 2005, at the lecture hall Teen Murti Traffic Lines in New Delhi. The program was managed by the joint commissioner of police, women's crime cell, who invited me to conduct a segment of the training session in an administrative building of the Delhi Police.

As I enter the nondescript room, painted in a fading grayish white, some forty-five members of the police including two women are seated at tables. It is set up like a classroom, and I face them from a platform at the front of the room with a blackboard behind me. Unlike the constables, most of the men and women are dressed in civilian clothes and hold at least a bachelor's-level degree; like the previous group discussion, we speak in a mix of Hindi and English. To highlight the role of culture and history in constructing gender as unequal difference, I lead a discussion on the meaning of the normative categories of woman and man. The discussion is lively and the issues of how gender categories exercise constraints on personhood, conduct, roles, occupations, and so on are thoughtfully received, although punctuated with emphatic beliefs about women's responsibility in monitoring our bodies and selves.

As the discussion turns to same-sex sexualities and Section 377, many of the male police repeatedly and emphatically insist that most crimes are committed by Muslims. As a group they are resolute in their belief that most crimes under Section 377 and indeed most crimes in general are committed by Muslims. Some are quiet, but others assert, "Most unnatural sex crimes are committed by the Muslim community"; "I have seen that this happens more among Muslim people"; "Most complaints on 377 are about these people." No one disagrees. One of the two women openly concurs in Hindi, "Madam, I too have seen this." Non-Hindu-identified officers listen quietly to these vehement charges against a minority group, perhaps cognizant of its explosiveness (one Sikh man wears a turban). I present the counterargument that Muslims do not and could not account for the bulk of crimes in a country that is more than 84 percent Hindu. Some remain quiet; others disagree. Eventually the discussion tapers off inconclusively and unsatisfactorily, some officers obviously restless as the allotted time comes to an end.

The question is how to account for this insistent displacement of unnatural sex or sexual crimes committed under Section 377 onto Muslims in particular, and to a lesser extent onto Sikhs, by the Delhi Police. How to explain the consistent association between what are seen as abnormal sexual practices and religious-cultural groups?

RACIALIZED COMMUNALISMS

In the Indian context, these remarks by the Delhi Police are likely to be ascribed to communalism; that is to say, the mostly male Hindu police are prejudiced against Muslim and Sikh communities. Rooted in British colonial administrative politics and coming into usage by the 1920s, the term *communalism* continues to be widely used in India to represent religion-based sectarian differences as well as mutual prejudices and hostilities and symbolizes loyalty to one's community over nation and an impediment to patriotism. The primary challenge facing Indian nationalism, it is believed, are communalism's various iterations: intercommunal strife, competition for resources, politicization of religion, violence, perceived Muslim and Sikh loyalty to faith over nation, dissidence in Kashmir, and (Muslim) terrorism. But what is crucial and relevant to the discussion here is that communalism is seen as both cause and effect of historically and socially entrenched attitudes of prejudice and discrimination between religious communities. Since the majority of Delhi Police are ethnically and religiously distinct Hindu Jats from the neighboring state of Haryana, their prejudicial associations of (homo) sexual crimes with Muslims and Sikhs could be seen as communalist.

Its history and continued significance notwithstanding, the discourse of communalism is increasingly inadequate to account for such responses by state agents or citizens who are members of a majoritarian religious community and an ethnic community with the political clout to be heavily recruited into the Delhi Police. Gyanendra Pandey notes that the term *communalism* persists despite its declining relevance in the Indian context because it serves as a shared language for discussion but also because of intellectual inertia.[31] It must be why terms such as *riot*, *communal riot*, and *communal violence* are repeatedly put in scare quotes, for typically Muslims, Christians, Sikhs, and Dalits are the ones who are grievously hurt by majoritarian Hindu groups with the implicit and explicit collusion of state institutions and agents.[32] In the past few decades riots and mutual conflict and hostility have expanded to genocide, pogroms, forcible conversions to Hinduism, and torching and looting of the property of minority religious communities (alongside intercaste, interethnic, and gender-based violence).

Neither does the term *communalism* help explain the institutionalization of socioeconomic inequalities and discrimination that are captured, for example, by the Sachar Committee report, "Social, Economic and Educational Status of the Muslim Community in India." Documenting the widespread and disproportionate gaps in educational attainment, income, bank credit, and high-level government jobs across thirteen Indian states, the report also identifies widespread perceptions among Muslim communities of prejudice and discrimination toward them.[33] Increasingly, in lieu of communalism, the politics of religion and religious hierarchies is represented in the lexicon of *majorities and minorities*, and riots have come to be partially replaced by the lexicon of *pogroms and genocide*. As Rustom Bharucha writes, it is difficult to seek academic solace in communalism while the exclusion of Muslims escalates from a racism of domination to a racism of extermination.[34]

Needed here is a theory of racialization in India's present to locate the insistence by members of the Delhi Police that unnatural sex crimes are mostly committed by Muslims and, to a lesser extent, Sikhs. The problem, though, is that race and racialization as categories and processes are typically reserved for the colonial context in India. Despite Indrani Chatterjee's critical examination of racial hierarchies in precolonial India and Loomba's useful theorizing of religious and caste differences as racialized processes in India's present, the accepted approach, if not articulated belief, is that race ought to be reserved for the colonial context and that it does not belong analytically within the contemporary Indian context, for racial difference has been primarily conceptualized as colonial difference between Europeans and Indians, between whites and browns.[35]

Stated simply, the reluctance to use the analytics of racialization in India's present is because Hindus and religious minority groups are not phenotypically different. Curiously, select groups self-characterize as racially distinct—for example, some Hindu fundamentalists and some Sikh political leaders—but in general race and racialization appear to have no analytical purchase in a phenotypically mixed national context.[36] This, despite the intertwined genealogies of race and communalism in the Indian context, for as Pandey reasons, race was part of the same colonial and naturalized taxonomies out of which came communalism.[37] It was not unusual to identify "martial races," the British colonial belief that some groups were naturally, inherently more effective for combat, which resulted in the recruitment of Sikhs for positions in the military and the police in the northern part of the territory and Muslims in the southern part.[38] The lexicon of race, then, inflected not only the transactions of the rulers and the ruled but also the distinctions among religious-cultural communities that were in the process of being consolidated.

If communalism is distinctively or exceptionally South Asian, then race has a Euro-American provenance. The conceptual genealogy of race is drawn largely from the Atlantic slave trade and early colonial encounters in the Americas. Even though there are multiple trajectories of race, racial classifications, and racial discourses, race in its Euro-American genealogy has come to be about somatic differences; as Paul Gilroy argues, it has been about the discourses and practices of color, face, hair, skin, and more.[39] In her critical intervention, however, Loomba questions these conflations of race with body that amplify Euro-American histories into universal definitions of race.[40] Further, to see racialized difference as written on the body is to engage a particular genealogy of race thinking and racisms and lose sight of the collective insistence of critical scholars that race is not grounded in apparently somatic differences but in cultural discourses that produce the body as the site of unequal difference. Constituting race and racisms across a variety of cultural settings are discourses of *unequal and naturally occurring differences* that are seen as "natural" and "transmissible"; put differently, race and racializations are wrought from cultural and historical regimes of classification that rationalize forms of inequalities on the basis of natural, extracultural difference. Needed, then, are multiple genealogies of race and racializations, and the trajectory that I am considering here is not intelligible through what Gilroy calls a politics of the chromatic and optical, but through cultural discourses of blood, psyche, and sinew.[41]

RACIALIZATIONS OF BLOOD, PSYCHE, AND SINEW

Responses by members of the Delhi Police may seem to be about cultural difference, but they are in fact about discourses of nature and naturalized disparities—putatively inherent in communities and reproducible from one generation to another—that are widely pervasive in Hindu majoritarian discourses. Muslims are consistently cast as both alien outsiders, the descendants of Mughal invaders who proselytized Islam, as well as internal outsiders, the marginalized caste Hindus who converted to Islam. As the largest religious-cultural minority (approximately 13 percent of the population), Muslims are widely (mis)represented through a complex web of discourses of "blood" (read: nature or biology), "psyche" or religious-emotional essence, and "sinew" or physicality and prowess. Sustained by notions of fanaticism as a natural extension of the faith, differences in hygiene and diet (especially meat eating), and hypersexuality (polygamy, high population growth rates, and excessive sexual appetites, especially for Hindu women), Muslims are seen as innately physically and psychically different. It is not unusual to hear Hindu sentiments in places like Delhi that capture this troubling mix of culture and nature, community and inheritability in phrases such as *Unki to Quam hi aise hai* (This is the nature of their community).[42]

Discourses of sexuality give greater potency to such racialized projections of communal difference, for if the myth of the "over-sexed Muslim man and his over-fertile Muslim wife/wives" or falsehoods about the Muslim growth rate echo among majoritarian Hindus and other minority groups,[43] the circumcised penis circulates as the embodiment of a community and its otherness. Analogically invoking Frantz Fanon's critique of how black male bodies are reduced to the penis, Bharucha notes that in the hate literature on Muslims in India, the circumcised penis is equated with an unclean body, polygamy, and lasciviousness.[44] Paola

Bacchetta extends this argument to suggest that Hindu nationalists assign queer gender and sexuality to all who are "others" of the Hindu nation, but especially Indian Muslims, who are cast as hypermasculine and hypersexual, sexually violent as well as sexually deviant.[45] However, these racialized projections of "queer" sexuality, nonnormative and excessive, are not limited to the political core of Hindu nationalism but resonate more widely in the majoritarian populace.

That constables and their seniors would share and echo some of these commonplace associations between Indian Muslims and sexual deviance may not be unexpected but is nonetheless disturbing. The concern that those who are duty bound to protect all equally hold such deep-seated racialized prejudices is further exacerbated by the low numbers of Muslims across all ranks of police in much of the nation as well as Delhi. For example, Omar Khalidi observes that after many Muslim rank-and-file police opted to migrate to Pakistan in 1947, depleting the Delhi force, no effort was made to recruit Muslims for decades thereafter.[46] As a result by 1991 the Delhi Police were a mere 2.3 percent Muslim.[47] In her compelling writing on the role of the police in the violence in Gujarat, Teesta Setalvad asserts that the small number of Muslim police officers and those from the lower ranks are systematically denied positions that entail directly managing law and order, especially heading police stations and districts.[48] The combination of flawed structures of accountability and forms of racism internalized within its ranks has driven police complicity with Hindu majoritarian groups during pogroms and genocide against Muslim communities. Indeed the evidence for repeated police failure to protect Muslim and Sikh groups under threat, either by inaction or active participation in violence, is overwhelming.[49] Although Khalidi's study is an important reminder that police can be led to prevent and stall violence against minorities, the constables reveal entrenched racialized beliefs about the sexual nature and conduct of religious minorities.

The racialized attitudes and beliefs about criminality and unnatural sex conveyed by the constable and implicitly endorsed by his colleagues in the first discussion, and more broadly endorsed in the second discussion, are not simply factors of group dynamics but appear to be more pervasive. During my trip to another police station to gather FIRs on Section 377, a constable followed me into the Records Room, dusty and cramped with a couple of tables, several chairs, and metal shelves stacked with files and ledgers. I sat across from another constable at an adjoining table, the first constable politely asked what I was doing. When I explained my interest in seeing the FIRs on Section 377, he said without solicitation or hesitation that it's a crime mostly committed by Muslims. Unable to let it pass, I used the authority of evidence to say that the data do not support this claim and cited the twelve FIRs I had already gathered, which seemed to primarily incriminate Hindus; nine out of the twelve were Hindu names, while only two names appeared to be Muslim and one was likely Sikh. Joined sporadically by the constable at the adjoining table, what followed was an argument about those who commit crimes under Section 377 that tapered off when neither of us was able to alter the other's views. Perhaps most ironic, while I, a feminist scholar, clung to evidence, the first constable insisted that his belief was rooted in his *experience* of policing! This highlights two interrelated points: first, that the group discussions are not anomalies in terms of the racialization of crimes under Section 377; second, that although Muslims were slandered across instances of fieldwork, the group discussion with the constables was the only time in which Sikhs were maligned. The racialization of Sikhs in India's past and present is qualitatively and historically different compared to Muslims, and even though it reverberates at the national level, it is also peculiarly a product of Delhi as the site of bloody, calculated vengeance.

SIKHS: RACIALIZED FLUCTUATIONS FROM "ULTRANATIONALIST TO ANTINATIONALIST"

The 1984 pogrom against Sikhs in Delhi was a turning point in dominant representations of Sikhs from ultranationalist to antinationalist in ways that resonate among the Delhi Police. In their introduction to *The Delhi Riots: Three Days in the Life of a Nation*, Uma Chakravarti and Nandita Haskar suggest that the pogrom produced a new minority, but its creation had been under way long before 1984. In contrast to the web of colonial and postcolonial histories constructing differences and hierarchies between Hindus and Muslims, Sikhs struggled to forge a community religiously and politically distinct from Hinduism and Hindus during the late colonial period.[50] Sikh leaders' aspirations for a separate Sikh state federated to either India or Pakistan at the time of partition in 1947 were not realized, but a political struggle for a linguistically defined, Punjabi-speaking state followed. Brian Keith Axel explains that the notion of a sovereign Sikh nation-state first emerged in the Sikh diaspora in the

1970s and was embraced after the watershed of 1984, when a massive military offensive violated Sikhism's most revered site, the Golden Temple, or Harmandir Sahib.[51] In retaliation two Sikh bodyguards assassinated Prime Minister Indira Gandhi on October 31, 1984, unleashing three days of brutal, orchestrated violence against Sikh communities by majoritarian Hindu political leaders with the participation of party Hindu henchmen, petty criminals, and even upper-caste and Dalit neighbors in some cases, and the complicity of the police. Afterward, until the end of the 1990s, a protracted struggle to constitute a sovereign Sikh state was brutally suppressed by military and police violence, and Sikhs were recast in the national imaginary as an antinational minority, terrorists, and religious separatists.

In her fieldwork in Delhi during and in the aftermath of the 1984 pogrom, Veena Das details the changing self-representations of Sikhs and dominant Hindu depictions of them.[52] Das suggests that in 1981–84, during civil obedience campaigns led by Sikh leaders, Sikhs increasingly described themselves as a distinct race, whose history was written in the blood of martyrs and who were unambiguously masculine, militant Sikh literature portrayed Hindus as essentially effeminate, cunning, and weak. These categories were reversed in the imaginaries of majoritarian Hindus. Das crystallizes Hindu understandings of Sikh traits in circulation at the time: that Sikhs are loyal only to their religion, fanatical to the point of madness, capable of betraying the closest trust, snake-like in that they will bite the hand that feeds them, naturally aggressive, attracted to violence, and incapable of observing normal social constraints. Much like the genocide against Muslims in Gujarat, the terror inflicted against Sikhs was methodically executed and the police either deliberately did not intervene while the murderous violence raged for three days or, in some cases, reportedly participated in it. The compilation of interviews in the book *The Delhi Riots: Three Days in the Life of a Nation* is replete with accounts of the ways police refused to stop the victimization of Sikhs.

Delhi Police involvement in the 1984 pogrom and the broader shift in dominant perceptions and the strengthening of these racist stereotypes of Sikhs appears to have left an imprint on the constables in this group discussion. Once again cultural discourses are intensified by institutional imbalances, namely the declining representation of Sikhs in the Delhi Police. Historically Sikhs served in the military and police in numbers much higher than their share of the population (which is approximately 2 percent); in 1991 they constituted an impressive 21 percent of the Delhi Police.[53] However, since 1984 their numbers have been dwindling dramatically, as confirmed by the National Minorities Commission, with rumors of a ban against Sikh recruitment, according to Khalidi. Indeed in my numerous visits to police stations and police headquarters in Delhi, I was hard-pressed to find turban-wearing Sikhs. As Khalidi also confirms, the rank and file of Delhi Police is constituted largely by Haryana (Hindu) Jats. The constables' responses in the group discussion indicate their ambivalence toward Sikhs due to national and regional histories that go unchecked by the skewed numbers in the Delhi Police force.

After the group discussions and other instances in which the police pointed to Muslims as the culprits of crimes under Section 377, I returned to the Delhi Police Headquarters to meet one of the senior officials for the third time with the intention of making him aware of the pervasive associations of sexual crimes with Muslims, and to a lesser extent Sikhs, among constables as well as the middle-rung police I encountered. But the official, one of only two turban-wearing Sikhs I encountered among Delhi Police, who had previously been helpful by authorizing the release of data to me, vigorously dismissed my concerns. "A few bad apples in the police force" was how he explained away what I sought to call to his attention. My point is not to argue for a monolithic view of the police or the reproduction of racializations but to underscore the queering of racialized religious minorities and the insistence on their association with criminality that so quickly rise to the surface in discussions among Delhi Police constables on Section 377. The extent to which these ideologies and sentiments are shared and acted upon during routine policing and the handling of complaints remains a matter for further investigation, but the fact that the police officers and rank and file who intervened on behalf of the victims in Gujarat in 2002 and Delhi in 1984 were exceptional is a reason to not be overly optimistic.[54] Still, in their responses to how Section 377 is used, participants of both discussion groups emphasized the letter of the law, denying violence in some cases while openly defending it in others.

> I ask the constables in the group discussion about when and under what circumstances they use Section 377. The responses come swiftly and almost unanimously. "Only when there is a formal complaint"; "When a formal complaint is lodged and after the medical examination, then Section 377 may be used." I probe deeper, asking whether they use it when two men or two women are strolling in a park, whether it is used even when both parties consent to sex. "It's when there is no consent that we do something about it and only then"; "377 is used even when consent is there"; "It's mostly due to a complaint being lodged and due to sex in public places"; "It doesn't come up when both parties consent, since no complaint is filed"; "We would not stop [threaten or arrest on charges of suspicion] two men or a young man and a woman in a park."

The constables easily summarize the guidelines for enforcing Section 377—the filing of a formal complaint and a medical examination—implying that men consenting to same-sex sexual activity (in private) would be practically exempt from the force of this law. At odds with documented police abuse especially of young men suspected of being sexually dissident,[55] these responses also do not address the fact that laws regulating public sex are hardly neutral, for a couple arrested for heterosexual public sex would likely be charged under public nuisance or public indecency laws, not the harsher punitive measure of Section 377. Almost lost in the din, one constable's response that the law is used regardless of consent—"even when consent is there"—speaks to instances of police responding to or taking what they see as preventative action against male-to-male sexual activity in public areas, such as parks, near urinals, and other cruising areas, which itself is partly a result of Delhi's high population density and lack of privacy in indigent, working-class, and even middle-class households.

Despite the troubling reports of police abuse and one constable's caution that consent is immaterial to the antisodomy law, other police officials also denied violence against same-sex sexualities. When I first tried to delve into these allegations with the presiding New Delhi Police commissioner in June 2003, the interview was terminated within a few minutes since he wasn't aware of the Naz Foundation writ or its status, even though the Delhi Police were named as respondents (chapter 2). What did get his attention, however, was the issue of police abuse, which he vehemently denied, insisting that the institution's role is merely to enforce the law, a point that would be hotly disputed by those who bear the brunt of this enforcement. The position that the police merely enforce the law was repeated almost to the letter two years later, in June 2005, by the New Delhi commissioner of police, who said, "We come into the picture only if there is something repugnant to the law. We enforce the law." Even as it is possible that the constables and other police I encountered in my fieldwork were not personally violent toward same-sex sexualities, all denied using (extralegal) violence to enforce the law.

In sharp contrast, police violence was openly and unapologetically endorsed in the case of hijras. While the association between religious-cultural minorities and unnatural sex crimes was suggested in the two discussion groups, it is not clear whether these members of the police are more likely to target Muslims or Sikhs in maintaining sexual and social order. But such ambiguities were nowhere in evidence regarding hijras, whom the constables target them on the grounds that "they have sex in public places"; "they do it for money—for Rs. 50, Rs. 200 to 300" (approximately $1, $4–6). They tell me to see for myself: near the domestic airport, hijras attract clients and then rob them of their clothes and their money. In the second discussion group the more senior police men and women added, "They are criminals"; "They rob and steal from their clients"; "They are up to no good. It is our responsibility [to stop them]"; "They do wrong. They solicit sex."

Perhaps the association between hijras and the antisodomy law is not unexpected, not least because one of the earliest cases (1884) under the statute had to do with a hijra, Khairati, who was charged without a complaint or evidence (chapter 3). More surprising is the vehemence and openness with which some police in Delhi alluded to and justified the targeting of hijras. Saying that this is "how hijras are," the constables described the need for "preventative" policing—stopping hijras and demanding to know what they were doing, labeling them troublemakers and keeping an eye on them, and using violence as necessary. Anticipating complaints about police inaction from those they refer to as "people like me" (*aap jaise log*), the senior members suggest that constables are being proactive by policing hijras. Representing hijras as "antipolice," these members of the Delhi Police force see no difficulty in flexibly enforcing the antisodomy statute even when there are no complaints, victims of crime, or evidence of wrongdoing.

Yet, given the requirements for registering crime under Section 377, noted by the constables, policing often relies more formally on other legal provisions, most notably the Immoral Traffic Prevention Act (ITPA) of 1956. Aimed at curbing sex work, ITPA was amended in 1986 to be gender-neutral, thereby encompassing hijras and other non-woman sex workers. Although the law does not actually criminalize sex work or sex workers, its enforcement is primarily targeted at soliciting sex in public places, making hijras, sex workers, and others vulnerable. Despite the fact that hijras are heavily dependent on sex work and vulnerable to sexual violence from thugs, goons, *and* the police due to their extreme social marginalization, Section 377, ITPA, and other provisions are being stretched, bent, and rationalized by constables and their senior representatives in the interests of public morality and social order.

Represented in police accounts is not just the association between hijras and sexual transgression but also hijras' inherent tendency toward crime in general, a view that derives from the colonial era. Overlaying the past of the antisodomy statute and hijras is their classification in the Criminal Tribes Act, first introduced in the northern provinces in 1871 of the colonial territory and then throughout British India by 1911. Mapping its history, Meena Radhakrishna writes that its underlying purpose was to suppress the "hereditary criminal" groups, for the problem of crime was seen as intrinsic to native society.[56] Amended in 1897 to include eunuchs and hijras, every aspect of their lives was criminalized and subject to surveillance and harassment by the police, according to Arvind Narrain, and the local government was required to maintain a register of the names and residences of eunuchs, "deemed to include all members of the male sex who admit themselves, or on medical inspection clearly appear, to be impotent," who might be "reasonably" suspected of kidnapping or castrating children, or might be charged under Section 377 of the Indian Penal Code.[57]

Even though hijras were eventually declassified as a criminal community, the associations between same-sex sexual practices and a tendency toward crime as a group continue to endure among the members of the Delhi Police. Hijras were forged out of the same overarching colonial taxonomic discourses that homogenized people as Muslims, Sikhs, Brahmans, and Dalits, among others, but setting them apart are what Narrain describes as colonial administrators' perceptions that hijras have an innate tendency toward licentiousness leading to sexual non-conformity and criminality.[58] Delhi Police members' justifications for targeting hijras also track closely with colonial standards for enforcing the Criminal Tribes Act, which were as low as "reason to believe" that the community was criminal, making the Act amenable to indiscriminate use.[59] By rehearsing conjoined histories of same-sex sexual practices and petty crime, such as theft, police responses do not distinguish between enforcing Section 377 and policing other forms of crime putatively committed by hijras. Rather their responses allude to the ways the antisodomy law may be used to regulate acts and transgressions that lie well outside its scope or, put differently, the extent to which the statute might bolster and justify policing.

Fractures of Heteronormativity

I ask the constables whether Section 377 should change. Several say unequivocally, "Sex between men or between women is wrong"; "This is against our culture." They raise concerns: "If 377 is removed it will increase homosexual behavior"; "What will happen to the population if everyone is doing unnatural sex, especially in the next hundred years?" But there is more. One constable says that the law should change: "Each person has a right to sexual satisfaction" ("Har ek ko sexual satisfaction ka adhika'r hai"); "This law is wrong in the case of two adults who consent to sex. This law should change"; "This law should be changed as now we are free from colonialism"; "There should be a difference between forced and consensual sex." The discussion and disagreement continue.

The constables have much to say on the future of Section 377, but they are not of one opinion. Several insist that same-sex sexual activity is inherently wrong, echoing what Monique Wittig has described as securing sex within a heterosexual matrix. Other constables reference cultural integrity, saying that these sexual practices are against "our culture," as does the same constable who racialized crimes reported under Section 377, and still others imply that the law should reflect the cultural injunctions against same-sex sexualities. Some raise concerns about the social implications of decriminalizing same-sex sexual activity: increased homosexual behavior and, not least, a decline in the population as a result—ironic, given the national count of more than one billion people.

But others disagree. One constable turns toward his colleagues who oppose the law to resolutely say that the law is wrong when applied to two consenting adults and it should therefore change. Invoking the colonial past and postcolonial present, another constable sees Section 377 as a burden of colonial history that ought to removed, making law and culture compatible once again. The distinction between consensual and coerced sex turns out to be important for some constables as they consider the possibility of retaining Section 377 only in cases of coercive sex. The discussion is lively and lasts for a while.

Perhaps most notable is the constable who says in Hindi that each person has a right to "sexual satisfaction," a phrase he says in English. Elsewhere I have discussed the relevance of English in enabling a language of sexuality among the urban middle and upper classes, and the constable's social class notwithstanding, the phrase *sexual satisfaction* allows him to capture the need for sexual gratification or fulfillment that everyone shares.[60] As he says, "each person" (*Har ek*) has this need or desire for sexual satisfaction, framing it within a language of rights (*adhika'r* in Hindi).[61] While this may appear to resonate within a sexual rights framework, best described by Diane Richardson as the result of heterosexist understandings of sexual activity and sexual pleasure giving way by the 1980s to the idiom of sexual identities, the constable's response could be interpreted differently.[62] Rather than reflecting a transnationally circulating grammar of gay rights, it may well be reflecting regional histories of sexuality and social class in which the rural and urban elite, especially the landed gentry and the nobility, were considered to be entitled to pleasure and desire, regardless of the object choice.[63] Chatterjee reads the presence of same-sex desire within the context of master-slave relations in precolonial India, while Lawrence Cohen underscores the presence of more than one register of the sodomite and the gay in India's present, where desire exists outside the aesthetic of middle-class urban life.[64] The disputed rights-bearing homosexual subject therefore may not simply be accommodated within a transnational model of sexual citizenship but may be about the amplification of regional and class-based genealogies of same-sex desire.

Muslims', Sikhs', and hijras' associations with sexual perversion was not openly or implicitly contested in the two group discussions, but both groups did debate who may be entitled to sexual satisfaction and endowed with the ability to consent unfettered by a colonial law. Undoubtedly some constables believed that same-sex consensual sexual practices among adults are wrong or go against the grain of Indian cultural orientation, and they expressed their dissent accordingly. Yet it also became increasingly clear that the subject who may or may not be emancipated by changes to Section 377 was not necessarily the maligned religious-cultural minorities or the gender-queers. By the time the discussion moved to the possibility of changes to Section 377, the subject who may or may not be granted the right to act on same-sex desire no longer seemed to be the same. Taken together, the excerpts suggest that while there may be some leeway in the policing of adult consenting same-sex sexual subjects, there is little tractability in the regulation of racialized queers and gender-queers; indeed the antisodomy statute may be used to enhance and justify governance in order to maintain social order.

Ruminations

Analyzing perceptions about the antisodomy law among the Delhi Police confirms the subjectivities of juridical practices of governance. Parallel to the inconsistencies between a law partly designed to persecute the sodomite and its expansive use to prosecute sexual violence on children, aggravated sexual assault on women, and more, policing related to the antisodomy law also yields an unexpectedly complex picture. In the examples of crime falling under Section 377's ambit, constables identify potential examples—sex involving animals, old men trying to have sex with children, a wife filing a complaint against her husband—that do not easily align with homosexuality, or heterosexuality, for that matter. It is documented that police persecute same-sex sexualities, but whether Section 377 is its primary channel is uncertain.

Police responses associate the antisodomy law or the injunction against unnatural sex more closely with religious-cultural minorities, especially Muslims, which is to say, a law may be intended for one purpose, but law enforcement practices invoke something else altogether. Not surprisingly the constables take the position that they enforce the law as it is written, and they deny any deliberate targeting of same-sex sexualities under Section 377, since it requires the filing of a complaint. At the same time, they tightly link unnatural sex to non-Hindu subjects: the constable's claims that unnatural sex is more frequent among Muslims goes unchallenged by his peers, and a follow-up claim about Sikhs is endorsed with laughter. The question I posed initially was about the kinds of crimes committed under Section 377, but the discussion among the constables seamlessly shifted to the "who"—namely Muslims and Sikhs—and this racialized pejorative queering of religious-cultural minorities was partly repeated in the second discussion group with the more senior officials.

Identifying the race thinking implicit in the police responses helps explain the subjectivities of policing and the endemic forms of prejudice that so quickly rise to the forefront in discussions on the antisodomy law, even though race cannot be "epidermalized" in India quite as it is the United States, Western Europe, South Africa, and elsewhere.[65] Sharing his concerns about the occlusion of race among Indians in an unusual exchange with Amitav Ghosh, Dipesh Chakrabarty perceptively notes that racisms among Indians are often silenced, and accounts of "communalist" behavior are often difficult to distinguish from what elsewhere is called racism.[66] The takeaway from the police responses is not the need to overturn a cultural and academic history that pivots around the term *communalism* but to come to grips with its racialized connotations—rearticulating the relationship between culture and nature to be attentive to the invidiousness of that which is inscribed on the body but also to cultural discourses that purport to be about innateness, inheritability, and sexuality.[67]

The police discussions also gesture toward the flexible uses of Section 377 in conjunction with other provisions to capaciously target hijras, while bolstering law enforcement as an essential means to protect the social and sexual order. Unstinting and unapologetic about their derogatory perceptions of hijras, seen as inherently criminal due to their gender nonconformity, members of the Delhi Police justify preventative actions and brute force against them. That Section 377 but also ITPA and other laws may be used to this purpose became amply evident, for example, when police in Chennai arrested three Aravanis (the regional term for hijras) and eight men who have sex with men (MSM) based on allegations that they would routinely cruise for sex and money in a public park.[68] Entrapped merely on the basis of their shared identities, the Aravanis and MSM were not booked under Section 377 but under Section 8b of the ITPA, since its bar is much lower and its gender-neutral language facilitates the policing of a range of queer subjects.[69]

A focus on the intensity with which crime under Section 377 is recorded, the extent to which it is prosecuted in the higher courts, and its routine enforcement provides a thoroughgoing view of biopolitical and juridical practices that mediate the relationship between sexuality and state. The antisodomy law's history and uses bring into view not only the profound irrationalities and passions of governance practices but also the complexities and counterintuitions of how regulating sexuality helps secure agencies and institutions constituting the state, such as NCRB, courts, and police. Each of these lenses complicates assumptions about Section 377's detrimental effects on same-sex sexualities by indicating that the violence and harassment may be enacted not primarily through Section 377 but by juridical mechanisms; that Section 377 is part of a corpus of other provisions that, despite appearances, is likely affecting a host of other social subjects and sexual practices beyond the scope of same-sex consensual sex among adults; and that these biopolitical and juridical mechanisms deriving from the antisodomy law are helping reaffirm the indispensability of law, law enforcement, and number-crunching agencies. Going forward, these insights anticipate the difficulties of a struggle for social justice that pivots around the state, a narrowly conceived subject, and a focus on a specific law.

PART THREE

OPPOSING LAW, CONTESTING GOVERNANCE

CHAPTER 5

PIVOTING TOWARD THE STATE

Phase One of the Struggle against Section 377

By filing its challenge to the antisodomy law in the High Court of Delhi, Naz Foundation became the protagonist of an unparalleled struggle to decriminalize homosexuality in India, rendering New Delhi the epicenter and the state the antagonist.[1] Naz Foundation worked closely with the Lawyers' Collective to undo the criminalization of same-sex sexualities in a context facing what then appeared to be an HIV/AIDS pandemic. Even though the Lawyers' Collective was headquartered in Mumbai, where the writ petition was scripted, and the Mumbai High Court had been a possible contender, the reach for justice gradually came to be centered in the capital city. Initially not widely known in Delhi or beyond, the writ progressively drew support from around the country but also early criticism that law and the state were being seen as the avenues for justice. As the legal process unfolded, though, the criticism gave way to robust support for undoing Section 377 and the battle lines solidified around the state.

In its early stages the Naz Foundation writ set into motion a tussle between sexuality and the state, or more precisely a confrontation between sexuality rights activists and the government and other state units, mediated by the judiciary. Over time the cast of characters and their positions changed, often dramatically; for instance, the government's position shifted from being firmly opposed to decriminalization to implicitly supporting it in the Supreme Court after 2009, and, after initially dismissing the Naz Foundation writ on a technicality, the Delhi High Court went so far as to decriminalize homosexuality. Yet the limitations of a struggle encumbered by the histories, procedures, and imperatives of law persisted.

First, the Naz Foundation writ had to hinge on a narrow legal strategy aimed at showing the unconstitutionality of the antisodomy law, thereby letting it bear all the weight of injustice and discrimination against sexual and gender minorities. Implicitly recognizing the unintended uses of the law, the writ sought to unhook the criminalization of same-sex sexualities from the prosecution of child sexual violence and sexual assault against women. The writ asked for Section 377 to be "read down" so as to exclude adult consensual same-sexual activity from its purview. It became incumbent to prove that Section 377 violated constitutional principles, while anchoring rights and protections for same-sex sexualities to the legal outcome.

Second, institutional parameters also shaped the nuances of the writ by influencing its angle and arguments—what would be persuasive to the justices, effectively reason with the government, and conform to legal precedence. Third, Section 377 had to become the lightning rod of institutionalized injustice. Criticisms of the antisodomy law were already in circulation, for a writ also filed in Delhi High Court by the AIDS Bhedbhav Virodhi Andolan (ABVA) in 1994 had sought its repeal, and trailblazers such as the Mumbai-based gay activist Ashok Row Kavi had previously called for the removal of this colonial relic. Other criticisms had taken the form of signature campaigns to undo the law—in the cities of Mumbai, Kolkota, and Patna—but it was in the aftermath of the Naz Foundation legal challenge that Section 377 became the flashpoint and decriminalizing homosexuality the priority in the struggle for justice for same-sex sexualities.[2]

A central task of this chapter is to sort through the entanglements of a historic effort that was circumscribed by its pivot to the state. A critical account of the Naz Foundation undertaking and the subsequent legal proceedings is still to be written; this chapter focuses on the first phase, the period between 2001 and roughly 2006, to tell the story of the writ, how its orientation to the state shaped its rationale and limitations, the basis for its support as well as criticisms, and its evolution into a national-level campaign. Beginning with the Naz Foundation initiative, the chapter arcs through the legal proceedings, the growing campaign against Section 377 fueled by the writ's dismissal in Delhi High Court in 2004 on a mere technicality, Naz Foundation's appeal to the Supreme

Court, and the subsequent apex court ruling in 2006 directing the lower court to decide the case on its merits. It draws on fieldwork at Naz Foundation and the Lawyers' Collective, as well as interviews with sexuality rights activists and visits to organizations across five major cities: Bengaluru, Chennai, Kolkata, Mumbai, and New Delhi.

More conceptually this chapter uncovers sexuality's significance to the state, surfacing as it did in the transactions between Naz Foundation–led efforts to decriminalize homosexuality and state units, especially the government. Particularly revealing were the inconsistencies of the government's legal response filed in Delhi High Court in 2003 (and its later rejoinder to Naz Foundation's appeal to the Supreme Court) that nonetheless cohered to help shore up the imperatives of the state and governance by regulating sexuality. Based on my fieldwork at the Ministry of Home Affairs, the state unit responsible for filing the government's legal response, this chapter looks beyond the reply's inflammatory rhetorics and seeming confusions to uncover the mechanisms through which it was crafted. Illuminating the biases and ideologies riving the government's response, I analyze how the perils and excesses of sexuality were purposefully invoked to preserve the integrity of state institutions and justify state intervention.

Engaging the Manichaean State: The Naz Foundation Writ

Founded in 1994 by its director, Anjali Gopalan, Naz Foundation India Trust is an NGO focusing on HIV/AIDS prevention and treatment as well as other matters of sexual health.[3] Since its inception, Naz Foundation has sought external funding—from the MacArthur and Ford foundations in the United States, the Lotteries Commission in the United Kingdom (now known as Community Fund), and the Standard Chartered Bank—to maintain distance from Indian state agencies even though units such as the National AIDS Control Organization (NACO) and its regional counterparts rely heavily on NGOs to do HIV/AIDS-related outreach work.[4] As Anjali Gopalan explains, Section 377 presented an impediment to this work; police would frequently use it as an alibi to harass Naz Foundation staff and state officials refused to distribute condoms in prison on account of it, leaving little choice but to seek legal recourse with assistance from the Lawyers' Collective HIV/AIDS Unit.[5]

The Lawyers' Collective was established in 1981 under the stewardship of the project director, Anand Grover, subsequent to a Supreme Court ruling that expanded access to the courts and led to the widespread use of the kind of public interest litigation represented by the Naz Foundation writ.[6] Inspired by his rapport with Dominic D'Souza, an activist who was incarcerated under the Goa Public Health (Amendment) Act of 1986 for being HIV-positive, Grover says that the experience made him aware of the import of sexuality and human rights, ultimately leading to the creation of the HIV/AIDS Unit in 1997 in Mumbai with financial support from the European Community. According to Grover, the Lawyers' Collective HIV/AIDS unit was interested in legal action against Section 377 mostly because it criminalizes particular forms of sexual practices and undermines HIV prevention efforts.[7]

The collaboration between Naz Foundation and the Lawyers' Collective may have been close over the years, but its history is sometimes recounted differently. Shaleen Rakesh, who was initially the Naz Foundation representative in Delhi High Court, suggests that they approached the Lawyers' Collective because of its efforts in the area of HIV/AIDS: "I think that we had actually initiated it in the sense that we had been looking at Section 377 as a major obstacle for our ability to do the work that we do. And, for that reason we were exploring what we need to do to challenge Section 377. We had absolutely no idea whether we need[ed] to go to court or whether we should go to Parliament, whether it should be a writ petition, whether there should be like a media advocacy campaign of some sort."[8] Seeing it otherwise, Vivek Diwan, who was an advocate with the Lawyers' Collective, suggests that as a unit devoted to legal advocacy it was the Lawyers' Collective that identified the need to challenge Section 377 and Naz Foundation as the petitioner.[9]

How Delhi came to be the site of the legal challenge to Section 377 is also understood differently, for Rakesh implies that the writ was filed in Delhi High Court because Naz Foundation was the petitioner, while Grover suggests that the writ was filed in Delhi High Court because the previous challenge to the antisodomy law by ABVA was thought to still be pending. Filed under the leadership of the activist Siddharth Gautam and in the aftermath of the public controversy over the distribution of condoms to prisoners in Delhi's largest and most infamous prison, Tihar Jail, the ABVA writ sought a complete repeal of the antisodomy law.[10] In fact the judges ordered that the two petitions to be considered together, until it was learned that the Delhi High Court had dismissed the ABVA writ a few months earlier, on March 22, 2001, due to nonprosecution. Grover notes that it would have been easier and more strategic to enter the writ in Bombay High Court, which is generally regarded as more liberal.

Submitted to Delhi High Court on December 6, 2001, the Naz Foundation writ was drafted primarily by the advocate Sharanjeet Parmar, in consultation with others at the Lawyers' Collective, including Aditya Bondyopadhyay, and framed as a public interest litigation (PIL). Referring to such writs as social action litigation, Upendra Baxi distinguishes between Euro-American histories of PIL and the post-Emergency context of India, when Justices P. N. Bhagwati and V. R. Krishna Iyer helped relax the rules to provide better and cheaper access to the courts, especially for the rural poor and the socially marginalized.[11] Indeed the Indian Supreme Court's guidelines allow as little as a letter to serve as a PIL under what are considered egregious circumstances affecting the vulnerable, including issues related to bonded labor, child neglect, police harassment and death in custody, atrocities against women, torture of persons belonging to socially and economically disadvantaged groups, and more, as long as they entail a matter of fundamental rights and are of public interest.[12]

Since the guidelines stipulate that a PIL may be entered on behalf of disadvantaged people who are unable to access the court or may involve issues of public importance, the issue of *locus standi*, or legal standing before the court, is flexibly treated. Rather than being filed only by an aggrieved party, a PIL might be filed by anyone on matters related to public injury, thereby opening the door for organizations such as Naz Foundation to challenge the constitutionality of Section 377. Further, since the writ was framed from the standpoint of the antisodomy law's harmful effects on consenting same-sex adults and matters of public health, it could also meet the bar of public interest.

Additionally the Naz Foundation writ could be filed as a PIL because of the changing cultural context in which it took shape (and which it helped change further through the course of the legal campaign). By 2001 gay, lesbian, and same-sex desire–oriented groups and organizations had mushroomed across the metropoles and the second-tier cities, and two works of gay and lesbian literature, *Yaarana: Gay Writing from India* and *Facing the Mirror: Lesbian Writing from India*, emerged to displace a dubious collection of journalistic writing on homosexuality.[13] The English-language media routinely carried mostly puerile stories on gay men, hijras, and homosexuality, and leading magazines published dubious "sex surveys" that included questions of same-sex desire. But the greatest public attention occurred as a result of the controversy over Deepa Mehta's film *Fire* and the vandalizing of theaters in Mumbai by members of the right-wing group Shiv Sena as well as the countermovements, especially the Campaign for Lesbian Rights, that heightened discourses and anxieties about same-sex desire while also thrusting them into the limelight.[14]

Nothing helped set the stage for the Naz Foundation writ more than the intensifying fears about HIV/AIDS, for India was in the grips of a health crisis of possibly epic proportions.[15] While the Naz Foundation writ was being drafted, NACO and individual state-based AIDS control societies were implementing the National AIDS Control Programme and targeting specific populations, including women sex workers, injecting drug users, and truck drivers, but especially males who have sex with males (MSM) and hijras. NGOs such as Naz Foundation, Humsafar Trust (Mumbai), and Sahodaran (Chennai) expanded the reach of state governance by delivering services, but they also sought to protect sexual and gender minorities by fostering awareness of HIV/AIDS and safer sex practices. Yet, as Lawrence Cohen has shown, at the same time they were producing a grammar of "indigenous" and "elite" sexual identities in ways that came to haunt the Naz Foundation writ (more on this in chapter 6).[16]

Along with the increasing focus on same-sex sexualities as public health hazards, the precarious position of HIV/AIDS-oriented organizations affected the climate in which the Naz Foundation writ was filed. Mere months before the writ was filed, police in the northern city of Lucknow arrested several men who were outreach workers for the NGO Bharosa Trust. The offices of Bharosa Trust and its affiliate, Naz Foundational International (not related to the NGO Naz Foundation), were raided, material was confiscated, and outreach workers were imprisoned for more than a month, charged, among other counts, under Section 377. Autonomous groups, organizations, and individuals throughout the country rallied in support of Bharosa Trust and Naz Foundational International, and the gathering concerns about Section 377 were amplified by the Naz Foundation writ.

STRATEGIC ENCOUNTERS WITH THE MANICHAEAN STATE

No encounter with the state remains impervious to its imaginations, and the Naz Foundation writ was no different in this regard from similar legal challenges that see the state as capable of withholding and conferring rights, continuing wrongs or making right. The Naz Foundation writ usefully dehomogenized the state into its constituent parts, naming among its respondents national-level state institutions and agencies housed in New Delhi—the Union of India, including the Ministries of Home Affairs, Health Welfare, and Social Welfare, and NACO—and regional-level institutions: the Government of National Capital Territory of Delhi, the police commissioner of New Delhi, and the Delhi State AIDS Control Society. Despite its emphasis on the discrepancies between state institutions such as NACO that work with same-sex sexualities and the antisodomy law that criminalizes them, it held firmly to a Manichaean view of the state.[17]

Also at play was the widely held belief that law may be the last bastion of intervention into an otherwise impregnable state and, in contrast to the intractability of politicians and the police, courts are the most likely arbiters of justice. Repeating this commonly held view, Gopalan told me that although state bureaucracy and the government can be regressive and inefficient, the Indian courts have been progressive. According to Rakesh, the legislature was not considered a viable option for repealing Section 377 without the support necessary to introduce a bill and debate and vote on it favorably; this resulted in the choice of the High Court of Delhi.[18]

Shaped by the discourses and logics of law, the writ took a threefold strategy. First, anticipating the argument that Section 377 also pertained to sexual assault on children and women, it disengaged the criminalization of homosexuality by asking the court to exclude private adult consensual sex from the purview of Section 377, leaving the rest of it intact. Second, the writ hinged on the unconstitutionality of Section 377 and assumed the burden of proving how the law violated the fundamental rights of same-sex sexualities guaranteed by the Constitution, especially by Article 14 (equality before the law), Article 15 (prohibition of sex discrimination, argued to include sexual orientation), Article 19 (fundamental liberties), and Article 21 (right to life and privacy).[19]

Third, using the twin concepts of ordered liberty and individual autonomy, the Naz Foundation writ reprised the well-known position that, privacy is about the right to be left alone, arguing that this right is violated by Section 377.[20] Citing Indian case law and foreign jurisprudence, the Naz Foundation writ argued that private consensual sexual relations lie at the core of intimacy and are therefore included in the right to privacy: "No aspect of one's life may be said to be more private or intimate than that of sexual relations. Individual choices concerning sexual conduct, preference in particular, are easily at the core of the 'private space' in which people indeed decide how they become and remain 'themselves.'"[21] Giving privacy a spatial twist, the Naz Foundation writ pled that only adult consensual same-sex sexual activity conducted *in private* would be exempt from Section 377's purview. Understood both abstractly and literally, privacy in this sense was used to emphasize that what occurs between consenting adults in private spaces ought not to be of concern to the state, while anticipating judges' concerns that decriminalizing homosexuality would also license sex in public. Thus in one of the early court hearings (January 28, 2002) Grover asked that the word *private* be inserted in the final entreaty to the judge, "for a declaration that Section 377 of the Indian Penal Code, to the extent it is applicable to and penalizes sexual acts in *private* between consenting adults, is violative of Articles 14, 15, 19 (1)(a–d) and 21 of the Constitution of India."[22]

If the Naz Foundation intervention had to conform to law's parameters, then it also had to be persuasive in the courts, resulting in a public health approach. Concurrent with the HIV/AIDS crisis and the unprecedented scrutiny on same-sex sexualities, the writ underscored the need to protect public interests by promoting, respecting, and protecting the human rights of the vulnerable, especially the gay/MSM communities, and effectively checking the spread of HIV/AIDS infections. Arguing that Section 377 drives same-sex sexual activity underground, it reasoned that the law not only imperils gay men and MSM but also jeopardizes the well-being of their wives and partners and, in turn, the public: "It is submitted that Section 377 serves as a serious impediment to successful public health interventions. Social non-acceptance of sexuality minorities denies them the liberty to court or have relationships openly, thus driving them underground, limiting their choice and restricting their freedom to have safe-sex; which thereby increases the spread of HIV/AIDS. Having been driven underground, safe sex campaigns aimed at the MSM and gay community are extremely difficult to implement."[23] Seeking to align the decriminalization of homosexuality with state interests, the writ gambled that the courts and the government were much more likely to be sympathetic if the issues were framed by the epidemiology of HIV/AIDS. But it was a strategy not without consequences, for the writ implicitly yoked decriminalizing homosexuality to more effective governance; that is, narrowing Section 377 would allow the state to better regulate gay men and MSM in the interests of public health.

The language and the logic of the writ resonated in two broad ways among sexuality rights organizations and individuals in the years after it was filed in Delhi High Court: it helped amplify wide-ranging criticisms of Section 377, and the writ itself drew strong criticism. By 2005, when I met with individuals and organizational representatives across the five metropoles (Bangalore, Chennai, Kolkata, Mumbai, and New Delhi), the need to counter Section 377's impact on consenting same-sex sexualities had crystallized. There was consensus on the material harm of Section 377 as well as its oppressive symbolism, for it was noted that the code is a barrier to the rights and recognition of same-sex sexual subjects insofar as it inherently criminalizes them. What also resonated was the Naz Foundation writ's argument that as a colonial product of Christian morality, the antisodomy law is inconsistent with a more diverse and tolerant Indian cultural history. Similarly it was strongly believed that Section 377 has no place in a modern society that recognizes diversity, and the writ's argument that the statute is at odds with international law (Article 12 of the Universal Declaration of Human Rights and Article 8 of the European Convention for the Protection of Human Rights and Fundamental Freedoms), to which the Indian state is a signatory, was also echoed.

Another criticism of Section 377 emphasized its instrumentality to the state because it pitted sexual orientation against children's rights, as noted by the representative of Haq: Center for Child's Rights, based in New Delhi. Dr. Ramakrishnan, a member of the Chennai-based Solidarity and Action against the HIV Infection in India, observed that family members and acquaintances frequently cite Section 377 as justification for stigmatization, and others underscored that the law also accounts for discrimination in the workplace, housing, and other aspects of daily life. Even though it was acknowledged in the formal and informal discussions that Section 377 was not the only inspiration for homophobic practices, it was seen as an ongoing threat. Most compelling, Abha, a member of the Delhi-based group Jagori, underscored the fear among minority sexualities simply because of the law, which is likely why the arrests in the city of Lucknow in 2001 were repeatedly cited in the interviews and discussions.[24] Not surprisingly, then, the state's arbitrary (mis) use of the law remained the most pressing point of concern among the supporters of the Naz Foundation legal challenge.

CONCERNS, CRITICISMS, AND QUESTIONS ABOUT ORIENTING TO THE STATE

Section 377 may have emerged as the lightning rod of institutionalized injustice following the arrests in Lucknow and the filing of the Naz Foundation writ, but building a campaign around it initially drew only equivocal support from sexuality rights–oriented organizations and individuals.[25] The most incisive concerns hinged on the lack of a substantial critique of the state, as was captured by Pramada Menon, a feminist and queer-rights activist based in New Delhi, in her interview. Noting that laws are meant to uphold and not deny rights, she said, "We need to start questioning the state. Section 377 needed to be questioned, but we need to hold the state accountable. . . . The state needs to be accountable to us."[26] Advancing this line of thought, members of LABIA, an autonomous feminist group in Mumbai, asserted that decriminalizing homosexuality would not lessen the role of the state in regulating the lives of homosexuals but in fact give it greater reach and power.

Other critics honed in on the limitations of law as an instrument of social justice, echoing long-standing concerns of Srimati Basu, Nivedita Menon, and other feminists.[27] Conveying their ambivalence in interviews and group discussions about the impact of law, these detractors wondered whether sexual and gender minorities would face less stigma and harshness at the more intimate level of the family even if homosexuality were to be decriminalized, a point that was also expressed among those who remained staunchly supportive of the Naz Foundation writ. For example, in their discussion group Naz Foundation outreach members hoped that undoing Section 377 would bring relief from police abuse but also noted that it was unlikely to mitigate the atrocities committed within the family. A representative of Jagori stated that Naz Foundation's focus on decriminalization articulated what sexuality rights groups and organizations do *not* want rather than offering ways of lessening cultural and social homophobia that are not focused on the juridical aspects of the state.

The writ's appeasement of the state in place of a fundamental rights-based challenge to Section 377 was a related worry articulated by feminist and sexuality rights–based groups. Early on, members of LABIA observed that a health-based approach does not sufficiently unsettle the structural and institutional underpinnings of heterosexism, and they questioned the lack of emphasis on a civil rights approach in the petition. Sharing these concerns, representatives of Saheli, a Delhi-based autonomous feminist group, noted that for all its strategic emphasis on public health, the writ would not be able to build an adequate case for the recognition of civil liberties and fundamental rights, the assurance of equal citizenship, and protection from discrimination. And, not least, critics accused the writ of placating the state by introducing the rider of privacy, essentially leaving sex in public to the harsh effects of Section 377 even though heterosexual activity in public carries a far lesser punishment. Their concern was that the writ ignored the implications of social class and feminist cautions that private zones, even the proverbially intimate bedroom, ought not to be inherently protected. The crucial distinctions between strategies that reinforce the power of the state and those that aim to undermine it were thus articulated in these initial criticisms of the Naz Foundation writ.

If Naz Foundation's orientation to the state and law were points of contention, the organization's single-handedness posed another problem. By working more or less independently, Naz Foundation had assumed the primary responsibility for reforming Section 377 and lost an opportunity to mobilize a social movement that could shift public awareness and the social climate in which courts work. Members of Saheli saw law not as a mechanism of social change but a platform to foster awareness and stage political protest, making Section 377 an avenue for disseminating information, bringing awareness, and altering social attitudes toward homosexuality and gender minorities. The concern was that, regardless of the legal outcome, the process by which the petition was filed would not enable a broader social movement that would be crucial for long-term gains for sexual minorities. For this reason, Deepti and Laxmi, representatives of Saheli, emphasized the differences between the ABVA and Naz Foundation writs: ABVA was a nonfunded group committed to forging coalitions and, in turn, a broader movement for sexuality rights that exceeded the decriminalization of sodomy.[28]

Another area of consideration, and a frequently mentioned point, was the lack of consultation in the process leading up to Naz Foundation's petitioning the Delhi High Court. Discussion participants described the process ABVA used as democratic and inclusive, for the group had led a demonstration against police harassment and torture of gays and lesbians and widely circulated a letter inviting participation and solidarity from a wide range of constituents, while in contrast Naz Foundation was criticized for operating autonomously and excluding constituencies outside of Delhi. This allegation was disputed by Rakesh, who identified three consultative meetings over the three-year period when the writ was being drafted, and a memorandum shows that one such meeting was held on May 16, 2000, by the Lawyers' Collective and was attended by members of fifteen Delhi-based groups.[29] Capturing the strategies and options discussed at the meeting, the memorandum recommended that the Lawyers' Collective broaden the consultative process to include other cities and that the draft of the writ be circulated especially among groups working on sexual health issues, as a result of which two additional meetings were held outside of Delhi, in Bangalore (2000) and Mumbai (2001).[30]

Seeing these efforts as mostly superficial and insufficient, many individuals and representatives of organizations continued to echo concerns about the single-handedness of an initiative of national relevance and great import, particularly if it were to result in an unfavorable judgment, jeopardizing a fresh challenge to the law for a significant length of time. Participants repeatedly criticized Naz Foundation for not making a greater effort to include other funded and nonfunded groups, inform them, and dialogue with them on issues of critical political importance to a wide range of groups and communities. Sappho, a support group for lesbian, bisexual, and transgender women in Kolkata, pointed out that they become aware of the Naz Foundation's legal challenge to Section 377 well after the fact, for they had no knowledge about the petition prior to its filing, hearing only vague reports about its being under preparation. Others felt that no concerted attempts were made to address the concerns and questions that were raised about the petition that remained essentially limited to one organization and one city.

An informal coalition of lesbian, gay, bisexual, hijra, sexual rights, transgender rights, kothi, MSM, and HIV/AIDS groups circulated a letter registering their protest against Naz Foundation shortly after the petition was filed in Delhi High Court.[31] Signed by thirteen groups based in Bangalore, Chennai, Hyderabad, Kolkata, Mumbai, and Pune, the letter faulted Naz Foundation and the Lawyers' Collective for initiating a legal campaign without their involvement despite their long-standing work and commitment to the repeal of Section 377, registered their dissent against the legal challenge, and demanded copies of the writ petition and related documents, while urging a more inclusive tack. In his written response, Grover, lead counsel on the writ, stressed that the process had been open and inclusive and refuted charges that information had been withheld by the Lawyers' Collective.[32] Clarifying the distinction between a campaign and a writ petition challenging laws, he explained that, unlike processes for legislative amendments or the drafting of bills, the legal process cannot be open and exhaustively consultative, and he kept the focus on the law by inviting groups to support the Naz Foundation petition through formal interventions in the courts.

Most of the concerns and criticisms of the Naz Foundation writ stayed out of public view, with either strong or tacit support expressed in the media. Newspapers mostly published updates on the legal process in the months and first couple of years following the petition and interviews with Rakesh and others, alongside the usual fare of titillating stories on same-sex sexuality, including gay parties, discotheques, and "coming out" narratives, among others. Some sexuality rights activists wrote articles strongly supporting the decriminalization of homosexuality, even as others withheld public approval, a situation that changed dramatically with the government's first response, filed in Delhi High Court in 2003. Press coverage of the struggle to decriminalize homosexuality exploded as a result, and the criticisms of the Naz Foundation writ gave way to a rallying cry for sexual justice from the state.

The Imperatives of Governing Sexuality: Legal Proceedings and the State's Response

Between December 2001 and September 2004, the Naz Foundation writ was listed in the Delhi High Court fourteen times. However, while the court listings and orders issued are documented, court proceedings are typically not made available, unlike in U.S. courts, for example.[33] Nothing substantial transpired on some of the dates when the writ was listed, whereas other hearings were relevant and turned out to be decisive. On January 28, 2002, the Lawyers' Collective informed the court about the pending ABVA petition, as a result of which the presiding justices ordered the two writs to be considered together, though it was later discovered that the ABVA writ had been previously dismissed.

Two interventions hostile to the Naz Foundation PIL were filed, the first on behalf of the organization Joint Action Counsel Kannur (JACK), which was founded by Puroshothanam Mulloli in the 1970s but came into public visibility in the aftermath of the HIV/AIDS crisis.[34] Taking the position that HIV/AIDS was manufactured by multinationals to forge a single global economy, Mulloli and his partner, Anju Singh, were especially critical of Naz Foundation and the grounds on which they were challenging the constitutional validity of Section 377.[35] Arguing that Naz Foundation could not seek to test the validity of the law without reporting any specific injury as an organization, the JACK affidavit questioned Naz Foundation's locus standi to file a PIL, while making the farfetched claims that Naz Foundation is part of an international network of market forces using the decriminalization of homosexuality as an avenue for establishing and legalizing the sex industry.[36] Suggesting that sexual acts between consenting adults "are not always natural, normal or permissible under the law" just because they are consensual, the affidavit ironically took the position that Section 377 was helping prevent the spread of HIV (even though JACK sees HIV as a corporate invention).[37]

In one crucial moment, amid a series of uneventful hearings, the presiding judges ordered that the chief justice of the Delhi High Court should preside over subsequent hearings, which is why, after many twists and turns, the 2009 Delhi High Court decision was crafted partly by Chief Justice Shah.[38] The more definitive moment in the Naz Foundation–led struggle against Section 377 finally came on September 6, 2003, when, after significant delay and repeated injunctions from the court, the government filed its response to the writ. As became evident over the next year, it had a polarizing effect: it swayed the first decision of the Delhi High Court, furnished in September 2004, against the Naz Foundation writ, while precipitating widespread support for the writ among sexuality rights groups and organizations throughout the country and consolidating a struggle against the state.

THE GOVERNMENT REPLIES

In a nutshell, the government's response (Counter Affidavit on Behalf of Respondent No. 5 in the matter of Civil Writ Petition 7455/2001) did not support the Naz Foundation writ to modify Section 377.[39] Early responses to the government's reply dismissed it as homophobic and contradictory, if not, as some critics insisted, confused. For example, in his essay "Getting the State out of the Bedroom," Rakesh Shukla argues that the response was on shaky legal grounds and lacked substantive arguments while buttressing social prejudice.[40] Numerous other responses, published in English-language print media and posted in listservs, sought to systematically demolish the government's reply, questioning its linking of homosexuality with crime and defense of sanctions against homosexuality on the grounds of Indian morality and culture. Though such criticisms are useful, they stop short of more complex and layered analyses of sexuality's relevance to the state.

The government's reply began by casting doubt on Naz Foundation's locus standi on the grounds that only those whose rights are directly affected by the law can question its constitutionality. Arguing that consent is irrelevant to acts considered unlawful, it took the stance that "no person can license another to commit a crime."[41] Further, denying that there was evidence indicating acceptance of same-sex sexual practices in precolonial India, it claimed that social disapproval of homosexuality continued to be strong enough to warrant its criminalization. Citing the Law Commission of India's 42nd Report as evidence, the government's response noted that even if homosexuality was now tolerated in the United States and the United Kingdom, Section 377 reflects the prevailing values and mores of Indian society.

For all its defense of the imperative to criminalize homosexuality, the reply was also laced with conciliatory logic. Emphasizing that Section 377 is used mostly to punish child sexual abuse and to fill a lacuna in rape laws, it argued that Section 377 had been rarely used to penalize homosexuality, that the law was always applied to the particulars of a case, and that courts used contemporary meanings to consider whether an offense fell within the ambit of Section 377. Maintaining that the law was used only when a victim filed a complaint, it countered that for all practical purposes private consensual or homosexual activity was excluded from prosecution under Section 377, further foregrounding the ambivalent, inconsistent nature of the government's reply. Closer investigation, however, cautions against reading these apparent confusions as signs of either an incompetent state or the condescension of power and point instead to the subjectivities of state structures and procedures through which such statements are crafted.

SUBJECTIVITIES OF STATE MECHANISMS: MINISTRY OF HOME AFFAIRS

The Judicial Division of the Ministry of Home Affairs (or Home Ministry) oversees matters related to the Indian Penal Code or the Criminal Procedure Code whenever there is a question of amending or interpreting a law, which is why it also responds to writs like the one by Naz Foundation that challenge the constitutionality of a law and names the government of India among the defendants. Thus what is interpreted to be the government's response or the state's response is in fact the position of one division of one ministry, under the leadership of the home secretary and home minister. While the home minister is a political appointee of the government in power, bureaucrats staff the middle and upper layers of the Judicial Division of the Home Ministry, often for no more than one year.

It turns out that typically junior-level bureaucrats draft the government's response after some discussion within the department; in this case a desk officer and a deputy secretary crafted the government's writs, including the one filed in September 2003. The director and the joint secretary review the draft, making comments and notes. When the joint secretary considers it appropriate, the draft is shared with the home minister. The interviews with the directors of the Judicial Division and a joint secretary confirm that as bureaucrats in the hierarchy of the department review the response in the making, they will leave their notes and comments in the folder, and they can also record their dissent, if any, to aspects of the statement.[42] The final approval of the response comes from the minister, who may ask for it to be significantly modified or even reversed.

Inconsistencies in the government's reply are partly the result of subjective opinions on the challenge to Section 377 that prevailed in the Ministry of Home Affairs. My interviews with the two directors, the desk officer, and the deputy secretary at the Judicial Division confirmed that the decision to not support the Naz Foundation writ was endorsed by the home minister. However, as Director G. Venkatesh acknowledged, all members of the unit did not share the view that homosexuality should be criminalized, but, as he put it, they were afraid to be seen promoting this view, even as he cautiously expressed his support for the decriminalization of homosexuality in our meeting.[43] Likely, then, the seeming confusions and equivocations of the government's reply were the product of the varying views of state bureaucrats and the political appointees who had input, and its unwieldiness was the result of successive edits, inflammatory comments, and caveats that worked nonetheless to preserve the state through its dominion over sexuality.

REGULATING SEXUALITY, PRESERVING THE STATE

Underpinning the assortment of excuses for why Section 377 should not be modified in the government's affidavit were discourses of sexuality as an object of regulation and affirmations of the state as a crucial source of governance. The government's reply was notable for the way it produced sexuality, for example when it incited the perils of sexual practices that could be unleashed by the overturning of Section 377:

> A perusal of cases decided under Section 377 . . . shows that it has only been applied on the complaint of a victim and there are no instances of its being used arbitrarily or being applied to cases of assault where bodily harm is intended and/or caused and the deletion of the said section can *well open flood gates of delinquent behavior and be misconstrued as providing unbridled licence for the same*. Sections like Section 377 are intend[ed] to apply to situations not covered by other provisions of the Penal Code and there is neither occasion nor necessity for declaration of the said section unconstitutional [emphasis added].[44]

It is unclear from the response why the deletion (or really, modification) of the statute would unleash the "flood gates of delinquent behavior" or be misconstrued as "providing unbridled licence," but there is little ambiguity about the picture of sexuality's excesses.

If the inflammatory language was used to invoke the dangers of sexuality, then upholding Section 377 was used to endorse the role of law and the state: "While the Government cannot police morality, in a civil society criminal law has to express and reflect public morality and concerns about harm to the society at large. If this is not observed, whatever little respect of law is left would disappear, as law would have lost its legitimacy."[45] In other words, law's very legitimacy comes to rest on the continued criminalization of homosexuality. The response repeatedly endorses the state's role in protecting public safety, health, and morals.

The indispensability of the state in safeguarding against the ills of sexuality was reiterated more than once in my meetings with state officials, including another director of the Judicial Division, Kamala Bhasin, some two years after the government filed its reply. Since she had not been in this position for long, and in fact seemed to know little about the Naz Foundation writ, she turned to the folder in her possession—roughly four inches thick, green in color, and tied with a jute cord. Peering into the folder in the relative dark of her office as a result of the electric cuts on a hot summer afternoon, she said, "Internally, some felt that Indian society is laid back, resistant to change. Naz is asking for unnatural sex, promiscuity, and society is resisting. It is like sati; Indian society was resistant to change, and it would not have been abolished had the law not been changed. But unnatural sex is a reality; we cannot simply put it down. It's very internal to human beings and will come up one way or another. But higher authorities felt that there is no demand in Indian society for change. Naz is only one organization, and change will lead to promiscuity. And society is not demanding change, society is not ready for it."[46]

That sex, particularly same-sex sexual practices, is a reality that cannot be repressed and therefore must be managed by law in the interests of a society unprepared for it was reiterated frequently. In another revealing moment, the more senior joint secretary of the Judicial Division had this to say when pressed on the matter of Section 377: "I will quote philosophy. In our thought, the sexual act should have dignity, elegance to it, should be between male and female, should go by the order of nature—in animals as well [we] see the same thing. Why should there be any deviation from the order? When the first Law Commission was formed in 1832, it was decided that unnatural sex should be an offense. But what is happening now is that human nature is volatile and wants to express all kinds of fantasies. The question is whether individuals should be allowed to fantasize at the cost of society."[47] The discursive productions of same-sex sexuality as unnatural, deviant, and volatile are notable in this response, as are the functions of law in protecting the natural and social order. Sexuality may be repeatedly invoked as an object of regulation but in ways that serve the imperatives of the state.

Shifting Landscapes: Gathering Mobilizations and Legal Wranglings

Exactly a year after the government's reply, the first phase of the struggle to decriminalize homosexuality came to an abrupt end with the Delhi High Court ruling on September 2, 2004, dismissing the Naz Foundation writ. Echoing the government's stance, the court turned it down on the grounds that Naz Foundation did not have the necessary locus standi. Choosing to not treat the Naz Foundation writ as a PIL, the justices of Delhi High Court brusquely wrote, "In this petition we find there is no cause of action as no prosecution is pending against the petitioner. Just for the sake of testing the legislation, a petition cannot be filed."[48] Citing a 1972 decision, *Vijay Kumar Mundra v. Union of India and Others*, before the liberalization of PILs discussed earlier, the court took the position that Naz Foundation was not aggrieved by the law and dismissed the writ as merely an "academic challenge."

The Delhi High Court ruling further galvanized the broad support for the Naz Foundation writ that had emerged in the aftermath of the government's response. The government's reply, its stance, inflammatory language, and seemingly confused reasoning had the unintended but useful effect of drawing the ire of sexuality-rights activists, including those who had previously expressed reservations about the writ. Although lending support to the writ and efforts to repeal Section 377 were not the same until then, the government's reply helped turn them into common cause and ignited a struggle for justice that was subsequently waged on city streets, on the Internet and television, and in print media. Fueling this incipient legal-political mobilization, the Delhi High Court's dismissal of the Naz Foundation PIL helped consolidate it into a national campaign and solidify opposition to the state.

Once the Lawyers' Collective appeal (Review Petition 384 of 2004) to the Delhi High Court ruling was rejected on November 3, 2004, national consultation meetings were organized to collectively strategize on the next steps. Deliberations about strategy had already started to take place informally among activists and on Internet-based discussion groups, especially LGBT-India@yahoo.com, as well as formally in meetings in Delhi (September 13 and 16, 2003) and Mumbai (September 28, 2003).[49] In sharp contrast to the circumstances in which the Naz Foundation writ was first filed, the Lawyers' Collective organized consultative meetings in Mumbai (March 10, 2004) and Bangalore (June 13, 2004), wherein a broad range of constituencies considered ways of shoring up the legal challenge by demonstrating to the Delhi High Court that the Naz Foundation writ was widely supported and documenting the harmful impact of Section 377 on gender and sexual minorities. Although all of this was preempted by the Delhi High Court's dismissal of the writ, these forums facilitated a process of collective decision making about whether the court's ruling ought to be appealed in the Supreme Court, not least because, as Vivek Diwan of the Lawyers' Collective suggested, the Naz Foundation writ entailed questions of fundamental rights.[50]

However, the decision to seek recourse from the apex court was neither inevitable nor without risks and was the result of three meetings consecutively organized in Mumbai (October 24, 2004), Bangalore (December 12–13, 2004), and then again in Mumbai (January 9, 2005).[51] At the first meeting three main options were identified in anticipation of the Delhi High Court's rejection of the appeal to reconsider its dismissal of the writ and then subsequently deliberated upon: (1) to not pursue the case any further, (2) to ask the Supreme Court to direct the Delhi High Court to reconsider its decision on the mere technicality of locus standi, and (3) to file writs against Section 377 in other high courts.[52]

The first alternative, to drop the case, which was seen as equivalent to doing nothing, was never seriously discussed, and while the third possibility, to file new writs in other high courts, was considered, the discussion came to rest primarily on the second and most viable option: to file what is known as a special leave petition (SLP) to appeal of the court's ruling in the Supreme Court.[53] This was not without significant risk, for had the apex court rejected the SLP, it would have effectively ended the legal campaign to decriminalize homosexuality for the foreseeable future. A second and equally significant risk was that the Supreme Court would deliver a binding judgment on the merits of the Naz Foundation writ, thereby bringing the entire legal process to a definitive end. While some contributors at the second Mumbai meeting supported the proposal, others were strongly opposed due to the risks of an adverse judgment from the apex court. Even though no vote was taken, support was overwhelmingly in favor of filing an appeal in the Supreme Court, and since such appeals need to be submitted within ninety days of the high court's ruling, the Lawyers' Collective entered a petition on February 17, 2005.[54]

The Supreme Court Steps In

Following legal procedures, the Lawyers' Collective filed an appeal (SLP, Civil, No: 7217–7218 of 2005) with the Supreme Court of India, challenging the high court's 2004 dismissal of the Naz Foundation writ.[55] A relatively brief document, the Naz Foundation SLP highlighted two questions for the apex court's consideration: whether the Delhi High Court was right to dismiss the Naz Foundation writ on the grounds that it was not personally aggrieved and whether the constitutionality of Section 377 is merely academic, especially given its salience to MSM and, in turn, public health. Put differently, the appeal to the Supreme Court hinged on the arguments that the Naz Foundation writ should be legitimately seen as a PIL and that Naz Foundation had the locus standi to file such a constitutional challenge. Countering the Delhi High Court's reliance on a 1972 decision (*Vijay Kumar Mundhra v. Union of India*) to reject the Naz Foundation writ as a PIL, the SLP specified that the ruling decision occurred prior to the liberalization of PILs and cited later higher court decisions to argue that courts have allowed organizations to intervene, especially when socially or economically disadvantaged groups, such as MSM, cannot move the courts on their own behalf.

On the related argument of locus standi, the SLP underscored Naz Foundation's history and orientation as an organization and its bona fide interest in the constitutionality of Section 377 given the law's impact on its HIV/AIDS-related work and outreach among sexual minorities vulnerable to the law. Citing a series of such decisions from the higher courts, the SLP emphasized instances when individuals and organizations not personally affected may challenge constitutional violations; for example the Supreme Court allowed a public interest group, People's Union for Civil Liberties, to challenge the constitutional validity of the Prevention of Terrorism Act of 2002.[56] Arguing that the lower court had dismissed the Naz Foundation PIL on a mere technicality, the SLP asked the justices simply to "remand the matter back to the Hon'ble Delhi High Court and direct it to hear the matter on merits."[57]

As a respondent, the government was required to file a reply to the Naz Foundation appeal. Compared to its earlier delays and equivocations, the reaction was swifter and more combative.[58] Reiterating its stance that the Naz Foundation writ could not be seen as a PIL, it argued that the Delhi High Court was indeed right in dismissing the writ as merely academic, for no specific evidence had been offered to support the claims that the criminalization of homosexuality was hampering the organization's work and that third parties, such as Naz Foundation, could not invoke the courts to enforce the fundamental rights of the accused in matters pertaining to criminal law. Upholding the state's obligation to regulate sexuality, this round of the government's reply noted, "Even if it is assumed that the rights of sexual minorities emanate from a perceived right to privacy, it is submitted that the right to privacy cannot be extended to defeat public morality, which must prevail over the exercise of any private right."[59]

Departing from its 2003 iteration in the high court, the government's reply in the Supreme Court sought to reassert the imperatives of governing sexuality by limiting the role of the judiciary. Taking the stance that courts have no jurisdiction over prohibited acts, it argued, "It is essential[ly] a matter of legislative policy and there are no judicially manageable standards by which to assess as to whether a particular act should be made an offence or not."[60] Seeking to safeguard institutional reach over sexuality, the government's statement threw into question the right of the judiciary to review and decide whether particular acts should constitute offenses. Invoking the recommendations of the 172nd Law Commission to widen the scope of the rape laws, make them gender-neutral, and delete Section 377, the response argued that any changes to Section 377 ought to be directed by the legislature and not by a judiciary acting beyond the scope of its authority, thereby protecting the domain of the state.

As it turned out, the Supreme Court justices did *not* agree with the government's statement, and a year later the justices ruled in favor of the appeal, instructing the Delhi High Court to reconsider the Naz Foundation writ on its merits. In a succinct order passed on February 3, 2006, the justices wrote:

> The challenge in the writ petition before the High Court was to the constitutional validity of Section 377 of the Indian Penal Code, 1860. The High Court, without examining that issue, dismissed the writ petition by the impugned order observing that there is no case of action in favour of the appellant as the petition cannot be filed to test the validity of the Legislation and, therefore, it cannot be entertained to examine the academic challenge to the constitutionality of the provision.

> We are, however, not examining the issue on merits but are of the view that the matter does require consideration and is not of a nature which could have been dismissed on the ground afore-stated. In this view, we set aside the impugned judgment and order of the High Court and remit Writ Petition (C) No. 7455 of 2001 for its fresh decision by the High Court.[61]

Directing the Delhi High Court to reconsider the Naz Foundation writ, the Supreme Court justices also invited the general public to weigh in on the possibility of decriminalizing homosexuality.

Provisional Thoughts on an Unfolding History

By challenging Section 377 in the Delhi High Court, the Naz Foundation writ furthered what had been set in motion by ABVA. Despite their differences and the less than enthusiastic support for the Naz Foundation pleas, the two writs shared a focus on HIV/AIDS and the demand to decriminalize homosexuality. Yet the Naz Foundation legal challenge made far more headway than ABVA's due to changes in the broader cultural context—public health concerns about HIV/AIDS, greater state scrutiny of sexual and gender minorities, but also increasing visibility as a result of English-language media, including film, television, and print media—to say nothing of differences in access to resources. Unlike ABVA, an autonomous nonfunded group, Naz Foundation and the Lawyers' Collective had access to external funding for legal advocacy, which allowed them to pursue a long legal process.

Naz Foundation did not pursue broad-based endorsement but proceeded single-handedly on a matter of collective significance and social justice for sexual minorities. Most cogently articulated by autonomous feminist-oriented organizations, these criticisms echoed Nivedita Menon's insight that renouncing law may not be an option, but it diverts ethical and emancipatory impulses.[62] Resonating with Srimati Basu's caution that the turn to law can have both uncertain and mixed results, critics of the Naz Foundation writ petition saw law, at best, as a tool to foster public awareness of social injustices and mount political campaigns.[63] Shaleen Rakesh, the initial Naz Foundation representative to the Delhi High Court, noted that political mobilization had always been a component of the strategy regardless of the legal outcome, but it could not be realized initially as a result of the exclusion of constituencies in and outside of Delhi.[64]

Even as the Naz Foundation plea sought to move the courts, its critical impulses were already blunted, to paraphrase Derrida, by having to subject itself to the very force of law.[65] In the legal struggle against the antisodomy statute, the state became an icon of power's egregiousness (as well as beneficence) that, ironically, structured the contestation itself. Amplifying anxieties swirling around law, the Naz Foundation strategy reinforced the view that Section 377 was the primary instrument of the state's symbolic and material persecution of the homosexual as sodomite. Ignoring the more complex histories and possibilities related to the exercise of the law, and the possibilities that same-sex sexualities are not the only ones impacted by it, Section 377 was made to carry the weight of showing how same-sex sexualities are unfairly targeted. Unable to mount an offensive deriving from the ensemble of laws, practices, policies, and discourses—vagrancy laws, policies against sex work, views of hijras as criminals, among others—through which sexual and gender minorities bear the brunt of governance, the initiative was beholden to procedural constraints and strategies that would likely have a successful outcome.

Arguing that the state has no compelling interest in criminalizing consensual same-sex sexual activity among adults in private, the Naz Foundation petition relied on the HIV/AIDS crisis and individual and public health concerns to be persuasive to the court. In effect the writ took the position that it would be in the collective interest to stop the spread of HIV/AIDS by decriminalizing homosexuality, and that it would make for more effective governance. Further, the process of filing the writ prevented Naz Foundation from rallying other constituents into a collective struggle, but it also had to avoid being seen as politicizing the challenge against Section 377, for that would have prejudiced the judges against the merits of the plea.[66]

Naz Foundation's interpellation of state agencies and institutions triggered affirmations of the state and its reach over the perils inherent to sexuality. A closer look at the specifics of the government's first substantial writ in the Delhi High Court and the mechanisms through which it was developed by the Judicial Division of the Home Ministry offers a fuller view of the subjectivities that color what Sudipta Kaviraj has aptly called "the state of great reach."[67] It invites a fresh understanding of the ways both of the government's replies—the one submitted to the Delhi High Court in 2003 and the one submitted to the apex court in 2005—produced sexuality as essentially disorderly and given to excess in ways that require the tempering effects of the state on behalf of the public.

But such positions, as well as the Delhi High Court's dismissal of the Naz Foundation writ in 2004, also had the unintended effect of rendering the antisodomy law the flashpoint for a national legal and political countercampaign. The early reservations of several sexuality rights–groups based in Bangalore, Chennai, Mumbai, and New Delhi against the Naz Foundation petition gave way to a collective struggle to decriminalize homosexuality as a sign of social justice for sexual and gender minorities. Inasmuch as there appeared to be little choice but to rally behind the Naz Foundation–led pivot to the state, Section 377 also became a platform from which to influence public attitudes and launch awareness regarding same-sex sexualities. It was at this moment that the National Coalition of Sexuality Rights formed in Bangalore, and Voices against Section 377, the coalition that was to impact the next phase of the struggle to decriminalize homosexuality, emerged in Delhi.

CHAPTER 6

STATE VERSUS SEXUALITY

Decriminalizing and Recriminalizing Homosexuality in the Postliberalized Context

Sometimes one needs to write pieces while breaking down into tears. That is the only way we can stay true to the fact that words are not enough to express our anguish and our disbelief but also our strength.
—Ponni, "Justice Will Prevail," Kafila, December 11, 2013

With these wrenching words, Ponni gave expression to the dismay and distress brought on by the Supreme Court judgment issued on December 11, 2013, effectively recriminalizing same-sex sexual activity.[1] Issued in response to petitions by a ragtag group of individuals and groups, the apex court's ruling was all the more jarring and unexpected, overturning as it did the historic 2009 Delhi High Court decision decriminalizing homosexuality. Although the previously named respondents, especially the government of India and regional and national state units, did not appeal the Delhi High Court ruling in favor of Naz Foundation, in an oddity of the Indian legal system the highest court allowed other opponents to intervene in the legal process, then, implicitly siding with them, it undercut the bid to undo the antisodomy law.

Through a lens sensitive to states' subjectivities, this chapter explores the contrasts between the two court rulings; they could not have been sharper, and not only in terms of their outcomes. While biases appear in both documents, the Supreme Court ruling is overtly skewed in terms of justices' affect and prejudices, and whereas the 2009 Delhi High Court decision is carefully crafted and extends constitutional rights to sexual and gender minorities, the Supreme Court version is sloppy, perhaps hastily written, and inconsistent in its legal reasoning.[2] Probing these differences from the perspective of sexuality's constitutive effects reveals the significant way in which the two judgments diverge: even as the Delhi High Court verdict sought to mitigate the power of the state, the highest court endeavored to safeguard state institutions and even expand governance through the regulation of sexuality.

Comparing the two texts also leads to the surprising insight that these are conflicting reactions to the imperatives of sexuality, state, and governance in postliberalized India. Building on critical commentaries on the extant sociopolitical context, this chapter considers the ways neoliberal modalities helped imagine a reduced role of the state and advance an individualized, assimilationist, and transnational rights regime, as such enabling the Delhi High Court's decision to overturn the antisodomy law. Parsing the historic as well as flawed aspects of the judgment, I investigate the cornerstones of the first ruling, namely principles of privacy, equality, and constitutional morality, from the angle of the complexities of governance and the antisodomy law developed in the preceding chapters; Section 377 is not the only law governing homosexuality, and same-sex sexualities are not the only ones affected by it. The Supreme Court 2013 pronouncement was also shaped by the imperatives of postliberalization. Considering the justices' views on the need to uphold the antisodomy law in a context of rapid social change, I show that reaffirming the state and prolonging governance through legislative intrusions seems more important than ever before.

Delving into the second phase of the struggle to decriminalize homosexuality, in 2006–13, this chapter picks up the threads after the Supreme Court's 2006 directive returned the Naz Foundation writ to the Delhi High Court, instructing it to reassess the plea on its merits. Setting the stage for the 2009 Delhi High Court decision decriminalizing homosexuality, the discussion highlights the influential impact of Voices against Section 377, a coalition of Delhi-based groups that emerged in 2004 following the government's inflammatory legal reply filed in the Delhi High Court.[3] Juxtaposing the two legal texts, I account for how they could offer substantially different visions of the intersections of sexuality, state, and nation before going on to place them within the postliberalization context and analyze their limitations.

The Delhi High Court Redux

Much changed after the Supreme Court's 2006 injunction to the Delhi High Court to reconsider the Naz Foundation writ on the basis of its merits; the struggle morphed from a legal initiative led primarily by a single organization to nationally coordinated political campaigns to decriminalize homosexuality. Taking their measure, Sophia, a member of several Delhi-based groups—CREA, Anjuman, Nigah, and Voices against Section 377—expressed her enthusiasm at the broad-based coalition against Section 377, while anticipating its regrettable fragmentation after the decriminalization of homosexuality.[4] Among the coalitions to emerge was the Million Voices Campaign, aimed at documenting sexual diversity as well as opposition to Section 377 on pieces of cloth to be quilted together. In the city of Bangaluru, the sexuality rights organization Sangama coordinated the National Campaign for Sexuality Rights to forge a coalition of more than fifty organizations united against Section 377.[5] Mumbai-based organizations, including Humsafar Trust and LABIA, came together on August 16, 2005, following India's fifty-eighth Independence Day to inform and educate the public about Section 377.

Underlying the numerous coalitions, public demonstrations and rallies, open letters to officials, articles, press releases, and interviews were two interrelated legal-political strategies. Section 377 and the Naz Foundation writ were being used as platforms to inform and change public discourse on same-sex sexualities regardless of the eventual legal outcome, a process that was facilitated by the English-language media. Until 2003 efforts to decriminalize homosexuality mostly occurred outside the media, but this changed dramatically after the government's reply became public; then the legal process began to be routinely reported, along with articles intended to have an informative bent, even if that wasn't always apparent to the critical eye.[6] Proliferating images of sexual and gender minorities at queer pride parades that were becoming an annual feature around the country, the media helped shape a climate in which homosexuality was a part of public discourse that exceeded a focus on HIV/AIDS.[7] Furthermore, since the Delhi High Court justices had partly dismissed the Naz Foundation writ in 2004 due to lack of evidence of public opinion favoring the decriminalization of homosexuality, the other priority was to showcase the widespread support in favor of modifying Section 377. These efforts resulted in numerous public demonstrations organized in cities around the country, as well as a friendly intervention filed by the Delhi-based coalition Voices against Section 377, which provided the scaffolding for the momentous ruling *Naz Foundation v. Government of NCT of Delhi and Others.*

THE INTERMEDIARY: VOICES AGAINST SECTION 377

Drafted by the Bangalore-based Alternate Law Forum, Voices against Section 377 (hereafter Voices) filed an intervention supporting the Naz Foundation writ in November 2006 and was represented in the Delhi High Court by the lawyers Shyam Divan, Arvind Narrain, and others.[8] Although the Voices petition paralleled Naz Foundation's constitutional challenge to Section 377—for violating the fundamental rights to equality, freedom of expression, dignity, privacy, and liberty—it also exceeded the scope of the earlier writ in ways that reverberated powerfully in the 2009 Delhi High Court judgment. Making the Voices plea distinctive was the fact that it was filed on behalf of a coalition that cut across homosexual and heterosexual lines, giving it broader legitimacy.[9] Demonstrating a range of activities, expertise, and experience related to LGBT issues and more, including combating violence and discrimination, child rights, and sexual education, it positioned the coalition as "represent[ing] a substantive body of public opinion which favours the decriminalization of consensual homosexual sex between adults."[10] The writ thus sought to persuade the Delhi High Court justices that decriminalizing homosexuality was of interest and import not only to same-sex sexualities but to a broader public of all sexual and gender persuasions.

Unlike the Naz Foundation's strategic emphasis on public health and effective governance, Voices provided the Delhi High Court with a twofold conceptual critique of Section 377. First, the Voices writ argued that the law impacted all adults, regardless of their sexual orientation, but affected sexual minorities in particular by being the cause of brutal human rights violations, an obstacle to equal citizenship for a significant section of the population, and an impediment to the self-worth of those persons who identify as LGBT. Emphasizing Section 377's hindrances to self-expression and personhood, the Voices writ stated:

> The history of violation and abuse . . . has as its locus the virulent homophobia sanctioned by Sec 377. The harm inflicted by a provision such as Sec 377 . . . radiates out and affects the very personhood of

> LGBT people. Sexuality is an aspect of the human personality, which lies at the core of the individual. In the social climate fostered by Sec 377 it becomes difficult, if not impossible, to publicly own and express one's sexuality thereby silencing a core aspect of one's personhood. Sec 377 by its very existence chills the expression of one's sexuality and its presence directly relates to the sense of self, psychological well-being and self-esteem of LGBT persons. There are numerous psychological ill effects suffered by LGBT persons in India due to the extremely adverse social climate fostered by Sec 377.[11]

The Voices petition detailed the physical and psychological harm that resulted from Section 377, but more compellingly noted Section 377's stifling of a minority and marginalized group's expression. Drawing attention to the intangible but no less significant harm caused by silencing a core aspect of personhood, the writ further argued, "Sec. 377 . . . , which criminalizes and stigmatizes homosexuality renders LGBT persons invisible and silences them. It therefore acts as a structural limit that does not allow for the possibility of freely exercising one's rights of freedom of speech and expression."[12]

This scathing assessment of Section 377 was carefully supported with evidence of injury to sexual and gender minorities, which turned out to be most persuasive to the justices issuing the 2009 Delhi High Court verdict. *Naz Foundation v. Government of* NCT *of Delhi and Others* reproduced in detail instances of harm cited in the Voices writ, for example, the arbitrary arrest of outreach workers from Bharosa Trust in 2001 under Section 377 and in 2006 the unjust use of Section 377 in Bangalore to arrest four hijras even though they had committed no offence, as well as other examples of sexual violence against hijras, gay men, and lesbians.[13] The Naz Foundation petition had underlined the risks posed by Section 377 to all LGBT persons, keeping the emphasis on the violence experienced by MSM, but submitted little by way of supporting evidence. By calling attention to specific examples of sexual, physical, psychological, and emotional violence experienced by these groups, the Voices intervention offered a more evidentiary critique while also arguing that all LGBT persons are at potential risk due to Section 377, a point the justices affirmed in *Naz Foundation v. Government of* NCT *of Delhi and Others.*

Second, the Voices writ presented the court with a critique of state governance. Notwithstanding the paradox of seeking intervention from one arm of the state to limit another, it introduced the principle of constitutional morality to argue that the state did not have a compelling interest to abridge same-sex sexualities' constitutional rights to privacy, dignity, and autonomy. Constitutional morality was used to counter positions that homosexuality ought not to be decriminalized due to prevailing (notions of) public morality. At the same time, the petition showed that public opinion on homosexuality and indeed Indian culture itself was plural and dynamic; it cited changing attitudes and queer cultural traditions, such as the Aligal Thiruvizha festival derived from the Hindu epic *Mahabharata* and held annually in the southern state of Tamil Nadu, offering the Delhi High Court more ammunition to rule in favor of the Naz Foundation writ.

The gist of the Voices intervention lay in drawing parallels between the criminalization of same-sex sexualities and untouchability, caste discrimination, sati, and child marriage—all practices that have seen significant change in public opinion as a result of legislative intervention. By creating equivalences between gender and sexual minorities and those who have long been recognized by the courts as vulnerable—Dalits and other subjects of caste discrimination, widows, and others—it urged the justices to see same-sex sexualities as a minority in need of legislative protections by extending to them the rights to equality and prohibition from discrimination alongside the principles of privacy and constitutional morality. Together these rights and principles became the cornerstones of *Naz Foundation v. Government of NCT of Delhi and Others* and its litmus test.[14]

Divergent Outcomes: From Delhi High Court to the Supreme Court

Recalling the decisive moment on July 2, 2009, in the Delhi High Court when the justices decriminalized homosexuality, the emotional words of the scholar and activist Gautam Bhan evoked the profundity and power of the *Naz v. Government of NCT of Delhi and Others* ruling from the perspective of those most involved in the struggle against Section 377 and most impacted by it:

> Court one, item one on the Delhi High Court's cause list. Ten thirty in the morning on the 2nd of July. A high court pass secured by a few dozen activists each of whom was remembering moments from the

last decade of fighting Sec 377. It is these simple words and an electronic pass receipt that a movement lasting decades and a legal battle lasting eight years came down to. In the end, it was enough. When the judgment was read, you could feel the emotion in the room. Our tears flowed not just because we had "won." They came for the judgment that had set us free.[15]

Anticipation and optimism had been building for months and weeks even as many braced for an unfavorable outcome. On the day before the decision, Atul's excitement was palpable as he ended his email post, "Best of luck to all of us 'queers,' 'faggots' and 'dykes.'"[16] As the decision reverberated beyond the courtroom, the shock of relief gave way to joy and bursts of emotion among untold supporters within and outside of India, and images, interviews, editorials spread quickly, keeping the verdict in the print and digital media well after it was no longer front-page news.[17]

Naz v. Government was an extraordinary ruling. Issued by Chief Justice A. P. Shah and Justice S. Muralidhar, the judgment was crafted with the care and conscientiousness due a public document likely to set a precedent and is impressive not only for rupturing the legal discourse on homosexuality by modifying the 150-year-old colonial law but also for its substantive and detailed arguments. Despite favorable outcomes, judgments have been known to be deeply flawed and problematic in their reasoning, as feminist scholars have underscored, but *Naz v. Government* stands apart due to its principled reasoning.[18] Although Naz Foundation had petitioned the court to narrow Section 377, the court took the more radical stance of declaring it to be constitutionally invalid and reached beyond the writ's emphasis on public health and more efficient governance to reframe health as a right with freedoms and entitlements.[19]

The *Naz v. Government* ruling exceeded the Naz Foundation writ in large part due to the Voices intervention. This is not to suggest that the justices might have ruled against the Naz Foundation writ or not so unequivocally promoted the principles of equality and inclusiveness without the intervention of Voices, for that is a matter of speculation. Rather what is evident is that the Voices writ, as well as the legal counsel's arguments, persuaded the justices of the law's harmful effects on LGBT persons and provided the language and the tools with which to take a principled stance against it. The range of materials and references introduced by

Voices during the court proceedings—for example, the Yogyakarta Principles and case law from Fiji, Nepal, and the United States—gave heft to the ruling as it decriminalized private, consensual adult same-sex sexual activity and brought sexual minorities for the first time within the fold of constitutional rights and protections.[20]

Naz v. Government's triumph lies in its spirited emphasis on Articles 21 (protection of life and personal liberty), 14 (equality before the law), and 15 (prohibition of discrimination) and the accent on the principle of constitutional morality as the only litmus test of compelling state interest. Linking personal liberty to the elusive but important concept of dignity, the judges emphasized that the constitutional provision means acknowledging "the value and worth of all individuals as members of our society." Making the verdict truly unprecedented was their position that sexual orientation falls within the ambit of the private space of personhood. Potentially impacting not just sexual minorities but all manner of sexual orientations, sexual choice, and activity, they reason, "it [the constitutional protection of dignity] recognizes a person as a free being who develops his or her body and mind as he or she sees fit. At the root of dignity is the autonomy of private will and a person's freedom of choice or action."[21]

A related aspect of the ruling's significance was its creation of a legal standard for recognizing same-sex sexualities under Article 15 of the Constitution, which prohibits discrimination based on religion, race, caste, sex, or place of birth. Setting a precedent, the justices wrote, "The purpose underlying the fundamental right against sex discrimination is to prevent behaviour that treats people differently for reason of not being in conformity with generalization concerning 'normal' or 'natural' gender roles. Discrimination on the basis of sexual orientation is itself grounded in stereotypical judgments and generalization about the conduct of either sex."[22] The protection against discrimination shields individuals against abuses by the state and, as Arvind Narrain and Marcus Eldridge clarify, also from discrimination by another citizen, making it incumbent upon the police, for example, to intervene in such instances.[23]

Not least, the opinion affirmed judicial responsibility to uphold the principle of constitutional morality in order to protect the rights of sexual and gender minorities, regardless of public opinion. Taking a firm stance against the government's position challenging judicial authority, the justices argued that the "role of the judiciary can be described as one of protecting the counter majoritarian safeguards enumerated in the Constitution." Although they conceded that courts would normally defer to the legislature while conducting a judicial review of law, the justices endorsed that courts ought to exercise sovereign jurisdiction when matters of constitutional importance are involved, such as constitutionally entrenched human rights. Since rights fundamental to an individual's humanity—namely the right to personal liberty and equality—were at risk, they endeavored to safeguard them: "The role of the judiciary is to protect the fundamental rights. A modern democracy, while based on the principle of majority rule, implicitly recognizes the need to protect the fundamental rights of those who may dissent or deviate from the majoritarian view. It is the job of the judiciary to balance the principles ensuring that the government on the basis of number does not override fundamental rights."[24]

Taken together, these cornerstones of the *Naz v. Government* ruling vindicated an eight-year legal struggle for sexual justice that may have pivoted toward the state but had spilled onto the streets and into the media. The verdict helped brush aside any remaining differences and disagreements among the various sexuality rights constituencies and was collectively embraced as a monumental victory, inspiring numerous celebrations, commentaries, and efforts to inform and educate about its implications.[25]

The enthusiasm, though, gradually eroded in the following months due to reports of continued abuses toward sexual and gender minorities within and beyond the jurisdiction of the Delhi High Court and the realities of law's disconnect from social life that surfaced with the much publicized suicide of Dr. Siras, a language professor at the premier Aligarh Muslim University, who was targeted due to his sexual orientation.[26] Emerging criticisms and concerns about the limited implications of the Delhi High Court decree soon gave way to fresh apprehensions that it might well be overturned as numerous appellants sought legal redress from the Supreme Court, ironically remaking Naz Foundation from a plaintiff to a defendant. Finally, when the Supreme Court verdict was delivered, and despite the tenor of the hearings that had fueled anxieties about an unfavorable outcome, it still came as a tremendous and unexpected blow.

THE SUPREME COURT, 2013

Ominously describing the last official act of a retiring Supreme Court judge, Vikram Raghavan offers an inside view of the hours before *Suresh Kumar Koushal and Another v. Naz Foundation and Others* was delivered on December 11, 2013, upholding the validity of Section 377: "On Wednesday morning, Justice Ganpat Singh Singhvi donned his black robes one last time. The judge with a smiling face had a busy day ahead of him. After hearing several cases, he would attend a late-afternoon retirement party on the Supreme Court's lawns. But Singhvi's first appointment was in the Chief Justice's Court. Retiring judges spend their final day in that majestic chamber. There, a large crowd eagerly awaited Singhvi. They had gathered to hear his widely anticipated last judgment."[27]

Dashing the hopes and aspirations of sexuality rights activists and a legion of supporters, *Koushal v. Naz* was shocking not just because of the Delhi High Court's earlier ruling decriminalizing homosexuality but also because of the considerably greater visibility of sexual and gender minorities at regional and national levels in the preceding years. Speaking amid the firestorm of anger, protest, and dissent contrasting sharply with the celebrations and sentiments following the lower court's overturning of Section 377, Gautam Bhan said, "We are quite stunned. We didn't expect this. Every trend—in everyday life, in court and jurisprudence—was pointing in the opposite direction."[28]

Koushal v. Naz was delivered in response to special leave petitions, much like the one Naz Foundation filed in 2005, asking the Supreme Court to reconsider the lower court's decriminalization of homosexuality. Notably the appeals did not come from the government or the regional and national state agencies that were the focus of the original Naz Foundation writ but from a motley collection of individuals and organizations, such as Suresh Kumar Koushal, Krantikati Manuvadi Morcha Party, Utkal Christian Council, and the All India Muslim Personal Law Board. With the exception of two opponents, B. P. Singhal and JACK, these had not been part of the legal process thus far. Although the justices also entertained fresh interventions in favor of decriminalization—Voices against Section 377, Nivedita Menon and a number of other academics, and parents of LGBT children, among others—they did so without placing the burden on appellants to explain why the Supreme Court should accept pleas interfering in the lower court's judgment or how they were affected by it.

In direct contrast to *Naz v. Government*'s accent on judicial obligations to protect the rights of minorities, the principle driving the Supreme Court judgment was judicial restraint, leading to its arguable conclusion that the lower court had wrongly exceeded its jurisdiction by decriminalizing homosexuality. Confirming that courts have an absolute right to review legislation, the verdict nonetheless argued that justices should declare laws unconstitutional or narrow them only in rare cases: "The Courts should accept an interpretation of constitutionality rather than one that would render the law unconstitutional. Declaring the law unconstitutional is one of the last resorts taken by the Courts."[29] Such an interpretation may be judicial prerogative, notwithstanding critics' point that the case law cited in *Koushal v. Naz* does not actually support its arguments, but what needs to be accounted for is why the ruling seems so intent on castigating the Delhi High Court justices and defending the criminalization of homosexuality.

The apex court's opinion found fault with *Naz v. Government* on the grounds that the Naz Foundation writ had not provided factual evidence supporting its constitutional challenge or its argument that Section 377 permits state-based discrimination of sexual minorities. This position could be reached only by purposefully ignoring the substantial evidence first submitted by Voices in 2006 and added to by others during the Supreme Court proceedings. Drawing a false comparison of numbers—that sexual minorities are but a "minuscule fraction" of the population and relatively few cases have been prosecuted under Section 377 over a 150-year period—the justices used biopolitical logic to refute the interpretation that it violates Articles 14, 15, and 21. Whereas the Delhi High Court ruling implied that the law's small archive was a reason to undo a little-used statute and uphold the constitutional rights of sexual minorities, the Supreme Court justices used it to dismiss sexual minorities as too few to warrant protections (!) and ignored the law's wider potential impact across sexual orientations.

That *Koushal v. Naz* is a decree in search of arguments is perhaps nowhere more evident than in the discussion on Article 21, where it purports to take up the issue of rights to privacy, dignity, bodily integrity, and sexual choice, but in ways that are left unreconciled (or could even be understood as favoring the decriminalization of homosexuality). Quoting extensively from legal cases that confirm these fundamental rights, the judgment merely juxtaposes several citations, for example, one arguing that compelling state interest abridges women's right to terminate a pregnancy with another unequivocally confirming the right to live with dignity, without offering any interpretation or reasoning of how *Naz v. Government* is on the wrong side of these precedents. But then, abruptly noting that police may misuse Section 377 to harass, blackmail, and torture, and diverging sharply from the Delhi High Court's interpretations, it infers that the problem does not lie with the law itself.

Koushal v. Naz has invited much criticism not just because of the outcome but because its shoddiness and biases mark the tone and texture of this almost hundred-page text, belying law's putative objectivity. As legal scholars have usefully noted, the ruling has factual errors, quotes with missing legal citations, and several inconsistencies between how legal precedents are used even though their outcomes do not actually support the justices' interpretations.[30] These subjectivities also organize the structure, arguments, and language of the opinion in ways that were anticipated by the hearings, for in contrast to the unofficial transcripts of the Delhi High Court hearings (September–November 2008), the notes for the *Koushal v. Naz* proceedings (February–March 2012) frequently include observations on the odd nature of the justices' questions and affect.[31] These differences are the result of the sometimes overtly and sometimes implicitly editorial nature of the unofficial transcripts available for both hearings, but they also speak to the peculiarities of how the Supreme Court justices sought to educate themselves about homosexuality, the scope of the antisodomy law, and the differences between abnormal and unnatural sex. Further, it is not that the *Naz v. Government* transcripts do not record the justices' affect—their frustrations with the various parties, their personal opinions—but where those hearings are primarily focused on the histories, complexities, and nuances of the antisodomy law and the arguments pertaining to it, the Supreme Court proceedings lead a note-taker to write, "The justices are starting to enjoy the case. Ok, perhaps that's not a respectful way of putting it, but there's definitely a sense from today's report that they are getting interested in the issue and also intrigued by some of the more bizarre aspects of S.377."[32]

Almost half of *Koushal v. Naz* is devoted to reviewing the appeals and positions of the various litigating parties, but its more substantial discussion begins with an overview of the relevant sections of the penal code. In an odd move, the judgment juxtaposes the now amended Sections

375 and 376 with the antisodomy law, while failing to address how this law is no longer necessary to prosecute aggravated sexual assault that exceeds the scope of rape. (Also completely neglected is any mention of the provisions specifically addressing sexual violence against children, passed only months before, that further reduce the onus on the law.)[33] More peculiarly it sees fit to introduce *Black's Law Dictionary* definitions of *buggery*, *carnal*, *carnal knowledge*, and *nature* that, along with a cursory and incomplete review of the history and case law of Section 377, allows for the following deduction: "It is true that the theory that the sexual intercourse is only meant for the purpose of conception is an outdated theory. But, at the same time it could be said without any hesitation or contradiction that the orifice of mouth is not, according to nature, meant for sexual or carnal intercourse. Viewing from that aspect, it could be said that this act of putting a male-organ in the mouth of a victim for the purposes of satisfying sexual appetite would be an act of carnal intercourse against the order of nature."[34]

Revealing as this language is about the justices' personal biases, it also indicates their affect by registering, as Pratiksha Baxi incisively notes, "the shudder of disgust that grips the judicial body" as they weigh in on the antisodomy law.[35] These judicial dispositions and passions confirm the thoroughly subjective aspects of law and facilitate more critical understandings of the two texts and the complexities of sexuality, juridicality, and the state underlying their differences. *Koushal v. Naz* may have elicited much criticism, in contrast to the mostly laudatory readings of *Naz v. Government*, but there is more room for deeper and more nuanced analyses of both texts and their limitations.

Competing Visions, Shared Contexts

In a nutshell, *Naz v. Government* attempted to mitigate state regulation of same-sex sexualities, thereby decriminalizing homosexuality and arguably reducing the state's influence, whereas *Koushal v. Naz* represented an effort to reinforce the state through its continuing control over sexuality. The Delhi High Court ruling may have unwittingly reaffirmed and even expanded aspects of the state—the relevance of the constitutional charter and the role of the judiciary—but it did endeavor to remove consenting same-sex sexual practices from being subject to the institutional reach of law. It may have offset decriminalization by bringing sexual minorities under the law's rights and protections in new ways, and yet it is hard to ignore the symbolic and material implications of declaring the antisodomy law invalid for same-sex consenting adult sexual activity. Further, insofar as the antisodomy statute became the symbol of state and social injustice, its undoing did matter, despite the complexities of Section 377. Thus at least in one meaningful and unparalleled way the Delhi High Court justices tried to curb governance, diminishing, in effect, the prospect of the state.

Koushal v. Naz's withering criticisms of the Delhi High Court ruling and its interpretations, however, are most fruitfully understood as an attempt to reinforce the state and, more specifically, the legislature's purview over sexuality, which also explains why the court seemed so concerned about overstepping judicial boundaries. Defending the legislature's role over the making and amending of laws, *Koushal v. Naz* reasoned that lawmakers best understand the needs of the people, a position that is particularly difficult to sustain for a colonial relic authorized by a body that was hardly representative of the people it was governing. Begging a thoughtful consideration of the antisodomy law, the justices sought refuge in the inaccurate assertions that Parliament had repeatedly refused to reconsider Section 377 even though the Indian Penal Code had been amended some thirty times since independence, most recently in 2013 to incorporate changes in sexual assault laws, and the 172nd Law Commission Report had recommended its deletion. On the contrary, the antisodomy statue had not repeatedly come up for debate, which was one reason ABVA and Naz Foundation sought recourse in the high court, nor did it feature prominently in debates on modifications to rape laws, which explains why the justices offered no specific evidence to support their reading of the legislature's disposition.[36]

Beyond merely shoring up the role of the legislature in general, the ruling governs matters of same-sex sexualities in particular. Not content to weigh in on the merits of the lower court's verdict, *Koushal v. Naz* is generative on matters of same-sex sexuality, drawing sharp distinctions between those "who indulge in carnal intercourse in the ordinary course" and those "who indulge in carnal intercourse against the order of nature." Even though the apex court justices argued that Section 377 does not discriminate against any group of people, they defined sexual minorities as a separate class of people. Despite the crucial fact that the government, acting on behalf of the various state agencies first named as respondents in the Naz Foundation writ petition, chose not to appeal the Delhi High Court ruling, the matter was turned over to the legislature for further deliberation. The most crucial player in the legal process, the Home Ministry, entered an affidavit on March 1, 2012, on behalf of the government, stating that it was not contesting the decriminalization of homosexuality, yet the justices were reluctant to undo the antisodomy law and at pains to uphold the regulation of same-sex sexualities as the preserve of the state. Concluding, "Notwithstanding this verdict, the competent legislature shall be free to consider the desirability and propriety of deleting Section 377 from the statute book or amend the same as per the suggestion made by the Attorney General," they allow for modifications in the antisodomy statute, but not without implying the importance of the state and its mechanisms of governance.

Alongside other recent changes in laws related to managing sexuality, the impulse to preserve legislative aspects of the state and prolong governance is evident. Legislative changes have resulted in more capacious definitions of sexual assault, a wider understanding of sexual violence—including acid attacks on women and stalking—and harsher punishment. The Protection of Children from Sexual Offences Act of 2012 represents even greater state intervention and governance for it introduced laws that are specific to children, explicitly criminalizing sexual assault and other offenses against them, including sexual harassment, pornography, and abetting in such crimes, and also details criminal procedures and the setting up of special courts. A hard-won victory by children's rights activists, the upshot of this Act may well prove to be useful, but it is part of a broader trend toward more legislation that is being reinforced by the Supreme Court justices' decision to not decriminalize homosexuality. Indeed while the judgment makes a passing reference to the Criminal Law (Amendment) Act of 2013, it does not include so much as a nod to the Protection of Children from Sexual Offences Act and uses the antisodomy law to endorse the legislature and legislative action.

The paradox is that mitigating rather than reaffirming state regulation of same-sex sexualities is traceable to the same postliberalization context, where law assumes ever greater prominence in mediating conflict.[37] Indeed "law struggles," through which ordinary people or groups pin their aspirations on new and better-enforced laws in the postliberalization context, are what predisposed Naz Foundation to focus on Section 377 as the starting point of a movement for sexual justice.[38] Seen through the prism of sexuality, these law struggles help identify the ways ongoing economic and political changes—especially trends toward the gradual undoing of the developmental state as a means of social redistribution, privatization of infrastructure, greater access to transnational finance, the rise of NGOs—allow justices to alternatively reduce and reinforce the state.[39] But more attention to the judgments' sociopolitical context encourages analyses of how, despite its praiseworthy attempt to attenuate governance, the *Naz Foundation* opinion is constrained by neoliberal logics and *Koushal v. Naz* is understood as a forward-looking endorsement of the arguably beleaguered state.

NEOLIBERAL LOGICS AND THEIR LIMITS

Naz v. Government could in fact imagine a diminishing of the state by drawing on a neoliberal understanding of gay rights that, particularly in the context of India, has gained currency in the shadow of the HIV/AIDS crisis and postliberalization policies. Vigorously challenged by critical scholars and activists as a universalizing, individualizing, and privatizing discourse emanating from the Euro-American West, often beginning with decriminalization and geared toward assimilation and inclusion, this rights regime hinges on the relationship between the individual and the state, typically mediated by law, while sidestepping the urgencies of economic, cultural, and social justice.[40] Equally important, it obscures colonial histories, for this version of gay rights is not simply exported to postcolonial contexts such as India but gets uniquely associated with issues of national modernity and progress in ways that were previously indexed by "women and development."[41] Advanced by the Naz Foundation writ and embraced by the *Naz v. Government* ruling, this approach called for the retrenchment of the state from the lives of sexual minorities, but just as not all women were seen as symbols of modernizing states, not all disenfranchised groups and communities were equally included in the vision of a plural democratic nation—an analysis that becomes increasingly evident through careful consideration of *Naz v. Government*.

FAULT LINES OF PRIVACY

As discussed in chapter 5, the Naz Foundation writ introduced the idea that privacy—in the sense of personal liberty and autonomy—is integral to the sanctity of personhood and that consenting same-sex sexual activity conducted in private spaces ought to be free from the state's intrusions, arguments that subsequently became a cornerstone of *Naz v. Government*. Deriving from the Voices writ's discussion of privacy as including the right to make decisions related to the intimate aspects of life, the justices went on to offer a nuanced and robust understanding of the discursive aspects of privacy as a fundamental right due to sexual and gender minorities. Persuaded that sexual orientation should be a matter of privacy, personal liberty, and autonomy, they defined it as a "private space in which man may become and remain himself."[42] They ceded that the Indian Constitution does not offer a specific right to privacy, citing earlier decisions in Indian case law that provide for the "right to be left alone" and allow for the abridging of personal rights only if compelling state interest can be shown.[43] Noting these landmark decisions as well as U.S. jurisprudence, they summarized:

> The sphere of privacy allows persons to develop human relations without interference from the outside community or from the State. The exercise of autonomy enables an individual to attain fulfillment, grow in self-esteem, build relationships of his or her choice and fulfill all legitimate goals that he or she may set. In the Indian Constitution, the right to live with dignity and the right of privacy both are recognised as dimensions of Article 21. Section 377 . . . denies a person's dignity and criminalises his or her core identity solely on account of his or her sexuality and thus violates Article 21 of the Constitution.[44]

The judgment relied heavily on the Voices intervention to present an understanding of privacy not as a matter of private places but more broadly about self-autonomy and personhood, in ways that would have had considerable ramifications for Indian jurisprudence.[45] Yet in the last instance the judgment narrowed decriminalization to same-sex sexual activity in *private spaces*, leaving same-sex sexual activity in nonprivate spaces still prosecutable under Section 377 (rather than falling under the scope of indecency laws and such similar to heterosexual activity in public). More important, it raised questions about the limitations of using privacy to safeguard rights, a point that resonates with Katherine M. Franke's critique that the U.S. Supreme Court territorialized the right to intimacy within the bedroom and strengthened a de-radicalized and domesticated vision of sexual rights among gay communities with the *Lawrence v. Texas* decision.[46]

Much like *Lawrence v. Texas*, the rider of privacy papers over pertinent gender and class differences among queer groups.[47] As Ponni, a member of the Delhi-based groups Anjuman and Nigah, suggested in her interview, Section 377 does not impact all queer groups equally or in the same way, and the Naz Foundation writ does not spell out clearly how the law impacts those who are differently gendered, for even if women do not cruise in public parks, they are affected by Section 377.[48] Even though MSM and other socially disadvantaged groups were the basis on which the Naz Foundation writ moved the Delhi High Court, working-class gay men and MSM are the ones least likely to have access to the privacy of a home or a hotel, leaving them exposed to the threat of Section 377.[49] In fact sexual contact, especially among working-class, non-English-speaking males, kothis, and hijras, frequently occurs in public settings such as parks and urinals, which adds to their vulnerability from the police and cancels privacy in the sense of safety from intrusion.[50]

Thus self-responsibilization (after Nikolas Rose), or in this case having to assume the burden of ensuring one's personal liberty, mediates the decriminalization of homosexuality in the *Naz v. Government* judgment, in keeping with concerns about the neoliberal (mis)uses of empowerment especially among vulnerable communities.[51] Mindful of the implications of this approach, the Voices intervention deliberately omitted the privacy clause and some closely involved with the Naz Foundation writ regretted including it, but ultimately the ruling could not and did not sidestep a contradiction haunting the legal process: the initial focus may have been on working-class gay men and MSM, but privileged gay men would likely have been the chief beneficiaries had homosexuality been decriminalized.

CONSTITUTIONAL MORALITIES AND THE HAZARDS OF INDIVIDUALISM

Constitutional morality, a concept introduced by the Voice writ and borrowed from the framer of the Indian Constitution and Dalit activist Dr. B. R. Ambedkar, was used in the *Naz v. Government* verdict as a bulwark against claims of public morality. Public morality was used repeatedly, most notably in the government's 2003 response in the Delhi High Court to oppose the Naz Foundation bid on the grounds that Indian society disapproves of homosexuality enough to criminalize it and attitudes in India have not sufficiently changed to justify the modification of Section 377. In another hostile intervention, this one filed in 2006 by B. P. Singhal, an individual who positioned himself as an able representative of the "Indian masses," the argument was that public morality was strongly opposed to homosexuality for it represented a threat to the sanctity of the family and the nation.[52]

Offering the principle of constitutional morality, first invoked by Ambedkar in a speech delivered on November 4, 1948, to enshrine the independent nation as a liberal democracy, the 2006 Voices writ countered arguments of public morality by arguing, "In fact there is a large body of opinion which favours the reading down of [Sec] 377, on the precise grounds that Sec 377 is an affront to a constitutional morality based on the protection of rights."[53] Reasoning that public morality is an inadequate reason to curtail the rights to dignity, autonomy, and, for that matter, privacy, the Voices intervention called on the justices to affirm and uphold the secular and constitutional principles on which liberal democracies are based.[54] Persuaded by these arguments, the justices firmly contradicted the government's position that public morality is grounds for restricting fundamental rights: "Popular morality, as distinct from a constitutional morality derived from constitutional values, is based on shifting and subjecting notions of right and wrong. If there is any type of 'morality' that can pass the test of compelling state interest, it must be 'constitutional' morality and not public morality. This aspect of constitutional morality was strongly insisted upon by Dr. Ambedkar in the Constituent Assembly."[55]

But the concept of constitutional morality is also profoundly tied to the sanctity of the individual over the collective in ways that do not travel well across time. Ambedkar may have used it to defend the Draft Constitution against criticism that it was based on a Western model and give primacy to the individual over what he called village republics—dens of provincialism and communalism that were ruining India—declaring, "I am glad that the Draft Constitution has discarded the village and adopted the individual as its unit."[56] Yet whereas individualism may have promised liberation over the forms of caste, religious, and gender oppressions wielded at the community level in the years following independence, it looks suspect in the context of postliberalization. Rather than offering protections and rights to the marginalized, it results in an uneven distribution of justice by working in favor of those who are already advantaged—as is clear in the earlier discussion on privacy.

Furthermore individualism's potentials have not been realized in preventing ongoing caste-, communal, and gender-based violence, and it is unlikely to shield most sexual and gender minorities who are persecuted not as individuals but as members of communities, especially under laws with much lower thresholds than Section 377's. In other words, the violence of law and law enforcement and forms of social stigma are profoundly attached to what are perceived as pejorative characteristics common to a group—hijras, kothis, gays, and others—in ways that I gestured to in chapter 2 and made starkly evident in chapter 4 (when police inflict preemptive violence on hijras or entrap them simply because of their identity). In his reflections on intensified policing of hijras in the city of Bangalore in the aftermath of the *Naz v. Government* judgment, Arvind Narrain suggests that the most crucial lesson to be drawn is that decriminalizing the antisodomy law has little impact on the most vulnerable gender and sexual minorities.[57]

PITFALLS OF EQUALITY

Naz v. Government was exalted as both sign and effect of a liberal democratic national state for upholding the values of a democratic nation and equal citizenship and providing a pathway for additional constitutional protections to all vulnerable minorities, including Muslims, Christians, women, tribals, Dalits, and disabled persons.[58] The legal scholars Lawrence Liang and Siddharth Narrain compared it to *Roe v. Wade* and *Brown v. Board of Education* to suggest that the ruling will likely have an impact well beyond its apparent legal scope.[59] Laying the foundations for the principles of equal rights and citizenship endorsed in the ruling, the Voices writ implored the justices to place same-sex sexualities on par with Dalits, religious-cultural communities, and other minorities already afforded constitutional protections, a view then reinforced by the justices' position that courts ought to take the lead on behalf of sexual minorities much as they had done by abolishing forms of discrimination such as untouchability, caste discrimination, sati, and child marriage.

Although the principles of equality and inclusion are held to be among the most promising and perhaps far-reaching aspects of the *Naz v. Government* judgment, they are tempered by the disconnect between formal equality and extant inequality that has been a long-standing feminist concern.[60] Further, if formal equality cannot ensure justice, then the equivalences between sexual minorities and other groups implied in the judgment are no guarantee that all minorities will be seen as emblems of national modernity.[61] Noting that the term *minority* is restricted to religious groups in official terminology, Zoya Hassan cautions that despite discourses of religious pluralism, constitutional bindings of equality have not translated into the lives of Muslim communities.[62] The gravest issue is that demands for equality for religious-cultural groups are historically and presently constructed as a threat to the national fabric and, especially in the case of Muslim communities, seen as antimodern and somehow more prone to sexual deviance. At issue, then, is not only the gap between equality's formal provisions and its substantial absences but also the frequently heard concerns that some religious-cultural minorities are not deserving of inclusion, and the reverse logic that equality for some religious-cultural minorities (read: special treatment) undermines the integrity of the modern democratic nation. Thus *Naz v. Government* is not immune from cautions that neoliberal logics distinguish between citizens—those who contribute the essentials of enterprise and modernity—and populations who are seen as unworthy of the privileges of citizenship.[63]

SEXUALITY AND THE SEEMINGLY IMPERILED STATE

After December 11, 2013, the lower court judgment's pronouncements became moot but all the more heroic because of the apex court's reinstatement of the antisodomy law. Seen in light of this binding decision, the regional high court's reliance on neoliberal logics, with all of their flaws and biases, seems far more palatable and preferable to the draconian alternative that reaffirms the criminalization of homosexuality. However, despite the disturbing outcome, deeply flawed reasoning, and endorsement of an archaic law in contradistinction to the lower court, the Supreme Court's position does not represent a throwback to the past but, parallel to the lower court's opinion, an urgency of the present and the path ahead, a view that is amply reflected in the text and also anticipated in the hearings for *Koushal v. Naz*.

Throughout the hearings the justices emphasized the changing nature of Indian society, especially in response to appellants' claims that same-sex sexual activity is against the natural order of things, and pointed instead to new technologies such as blood and sperm donation and in vitro fertilization. They underscored the mutability of words such as *unnatural* a number of times during the hearings, and also, according to the unofficial transcripts, sought to analyze the relevance of Section 377 in the modern context. The senior justice and the author of the fateful verdict took a dynamic view of sexuality, noting that same-sex sexual activities were recognized in India and represented in art well before the advent of the British and the colonial law. Continuing this thread, the judgment sought neither to restore India to an ageless past nor to consign it to an unchanging present, thus raising the question of how to contextualize its unequivocal stance on criminalizing homosexuality.

Quoting at length from a precedent on capital punishment, the justices underscored the imperatives of staying on a path best suited to India. Highlighting the differences between what are characterized as social conditions as well as general intellectual levels across India and the West, they argued that India cannot risk "experiments" such as abolishing capital punishment or, by extension, the antisodomy statute. Further raising the specter of following Western sexual mores, this time by turning to a previous ruling upholding the customs of arranged marriage, they cautioned against circumstances when legal changes elsewhere are "blindly followed in this country without a critical examination of those principles and their applicability to the conditions, social norms and attitudes existing in this country."[64] Thus the injunction against homosexuality may be a Western import, but, according to the justices, its continued criminalization by the state in a context overrun by Coca-Cola and fashion parades even at the village level is best suited to India.[65] In other words, where *Naz v. Government* responded to the dynamics of sexuality, political economy, and nation in the present moment by decriminalizing homosexuality, *Koushal v. Naz* found a reason to recriminalize it.

Fragments

Naz Foundation's legal challenge to Section 377 gradually coalesced into a political campaign for decriminalizing homosexuality that, as a result of the twists and turns in the courtrooms, has precipitated a nascent sexuality rights movement in India. This shift in mobilization, kindled by the government's reply to the Delhi High Court in 2003 and fueled by the court's dismissal of the Naz Foundation writ in 2004, meant collectively embracing a struggle whose flashpoint was the antisodomy statute. If that meant becoming complicit with law, in the sense of what Gayatri Chakravorty Spivak has described as folded togetherness, which is to say breathing new life into Section 377 to show its detrimental effects on same-sex sexualities, it also enabled broader critiques of law and governance, signaled by the Voices intervention in the Delhi High Court in 2006.[66]

While transnational flows of a liberal gay rights approach, particularly resonant in the wake of the HIV/AIDS crisis and liberalization policies in the Indian context, informed the Naz Foundation writ, the Voices intervention was driven by a more radical and instructive vision of queer politics, reflected in the words of its primary author, Arvind Narrain: "A queer vision is not merely about equal rights for LGBT persons but about loosening up the rigid structures of caste, gender, and compulsory sexuality. It is about questioning notions of purity, muddying rigid boundaries and opening up a space for those at the margins of hegemonic structures which make up our society. What a queer vision also calls for is an open-ended political project which has the capacity to be self-reflexive and take on new concerns."[67] And whereas the Naz Foundation writ focused narrowly on law and was shaped by what Jacques Rancière has called the partition of the perceptible, that is, the internal frontiers created within marginalized groups for fear that some among them would weaken the arguments for equal rights, the Voices intervention sought to use the courts to mount a vision of rights and protections due sexual minorities that exceeded decriminalization.[68] Yet both these writs are also fruitfully understood as products of their time, marking shifts in a political consciousness that was forged in an unfolding legal campaign.[69] Many of those closely associated with the Naz Foundation writ came to ally themselves more firmly with Voices' vision, blurring ideological lines. But it is also true that these two writs reflect enduring differences in a common political struggle between a discourse of gay rights and what might be called a discourse of the disadvantaged, whereby justice for sexual minorities is entwined with other social equities, including caste, class, religion, and gender.

Issued at their crosshairs, the *Naz v. Government* verdict was both historic and unfinished. Building on what was initiated by the Naz Foundation intervention and advanced through the Voices plea, the justices reduced the reach of governance by decriminalizing homosexuality. A closer analysis of the text, however, shows that it could not sidestep the structural constraints plaguing the quest for reform, pivoting around one law and one putative subject. Unable to contain the differences of social class and gender expression that mediate the antisodomy law's effects on same-sex sexualities, the ruling circumscribed the rights of sexual minorities through the principle of privacy. Since Section 377 and a host of other laws, policies, and practices of governance affect hijras, kothis, and others collectively, the individualized rhetoric of constitutional morality would likely also have fallen short of its promise. And, ignoring the antisodomy law's potential impact on religious-cultural minorities, the ruling raises the question of whether some sexual minorities can portend the possibility of postcolonial progress while other minority groups are ignored by modernity.

In contrast to the more nuanced interpretations encouraged by *Naz v. Government*, *Koushal v. Naz* has little to recommend it, not only because the outcome is on the wrong side of history but because of the reasoning through which it arrives at this position. The lower court used the antisodomy law to bring sexual minorities into the fold of Indian gay history, but the apex court's ruling sought to reaffirm the history and structures of governance that pertain to and extend beyond the scope of this law. The antisodomy law may not have been used much, and sexual and gender minorities may nonetheless have been implicated by it, but that was not reason enough for the Supreme Court to deliver justice or weigh in on the side of the lower court. Revealing a remarkable sense of discomfort with same-sex sexual practices in the hearings as well as the decision, the justices ignored the spirit of *Naz v. Government* to fault it for overstepping judicial restraints, even though the same qualms did not seem to apply in other cases on which the senior judge ruled.[70] Insisting that the judiciary must modify laws only in the rarest of cases, they opened the door for further legislative intrusions, which is all the more concerning since they believe that the legislature has thus far shown no interest in decriminalizing homosexuality. Amplifying legislative activity related to sexual violence, such as the Criminal Law (Amendment) Act and the Protection of Children from Sexual Offences Act (which could make Section 377 defunct), they charged the legislature with the task of determining the interests of a nation amid rapid changes that are filtering down "even" to the village level, thereby endorsing the sanctity of the state and miscarrying sexual justice.

AFTERLIVES

Uncovering sexuality's constitutive effects on states through struggles playing out in the Indian context is the central charge of this book. Denaturalizing the image of a measured monolithic entity, it suggests that the mandate to regulate sexuality helps reproduce states and that cares and considerations related to sexuality impact the spaces, discursive practices, and rationalities of governance. Spotlighting the more than decade-long struggle to decriminalize homosexuality through fieldwork conducted among state institutions, sexuality rights organizations, and activist networks, this investigation underscores sexuality's salience in shifting the grounding framework for understanding the state.

Coming to grips with sexuality's effects on states cautions against assumptions about the declining relevance of states as a result of neoliberal policies or transnational forms of governmentality. Indeed focusing on the antisodomy law and the shutting down of dance bars indicates the tenacity of sexual discourses, practices, and imaginations that continually breathe life into the idea of the state. State-based governance may be receding in some areas, but sexuality's putative threat to lineage and inheritance, marriage and family, work productivity, the socialization of children and their conduct, life and heath helps perform states ontologically as coherent, rational, asexual, and indispensable.

Pressing against ontologies of the state draws attention to the discursive practices that give it substance and force. Focusing on them during visits to NCRB yielded fresh insights into the potency of routinized bureaucratic procedures, how sexual concerns parse statistics and how they structure the agency's spaces and interpersonal relations. Similarly repeated calls to the Ministry of Home Affairs revealed that the government's responses to the Naz Foundation writ issued from the ideologies of sexuality embedded in institutional processes. Honing in on the forms and methods of governance exposed the inconsistencies that keep it supple and expansive. Recall, for instance, that Section 377 has been flexibly used to prosecute child sexual assault, and case law archives a steadily expanding interpretation of sexual offenses. Such a view also reveals that biopolitical, juridical, and neoliberal modalities do not supplant one another but continually and unevenly play out at various (blurred) levels of the state—in the streets and in regionally based policy, national discourses, institutional practices of national-level agencies that are nonetheless located in the neighborhoods of the capital city, and more.

At the same time, a close look at these subjective, sexualized practices of governance confirms that those marginalized on the basis of social class, caste, gender affiliation and expression, sexual orientation, religion, and, as will become clearer below, nationality are disproportionately affected. Speaking passionately, if pejoratively, Delhi police reveal that enforcing Section 377 more likely imperils the underclasses that they encounter on the streets and the beats, particularly the racialized and gendered minorities among them. These revelations also suggest the need to marshal more thoroughgoing appraisals of the state, accounting for the biases, desires, and passions of power as much in terms of sexuality as race, gender, social class, and caste.

Grappling with questions of states' desires from this perspective leads to the key findings of this book: that it is not one law or another but an entire corpus of laws, practices, policies, and discourses directed toward managing sexuality that helps produce states and that not only generic gay subjects are impacted by the antisodomy law, therefore complicating and implicating reform-oriented struggles for sexual justice. Such endeavors inevitably animate the sexual state by returning repeatedly to the judicial sphere as the more progressive arm of the state and, especially in the case of the efforts to decriminalize homosexuality, assuming Foucauldian histories of the homosexual subject. Seeking justice through litigious interventions and therefore working within the institutional parameters already set in place, these efforts were obligated to focus on only one law and an equally narrow understanding of who is impacted by it. Missing, then, was a broadly conceived strategy impaling governance by taking on the nexus of laws, policies, and practices, among them the law against castration that affects hijras, the Immoral Traffic (Prevention) Act, the abuses of policing against multiple constituencies, and more. Responding to such omissions, the coalition Voices against Section 377 took on some of the battles deferred by the Naz Foundation writ, establishing evidence of a more systemic pattern of institutional discrimination against same-sex sexualities.

In response the Delhi High Court ruling decriminalized homosexuality and rightly brought sexual minorities under constitutional protection but was subsequently overturned. The verdict can be seen as a symbolic diminishing of the state, except that its recourse to gay rights as a marker of India's successful transition into modernity left out those who are most vulnerable to the vagaries of law. Yet this ruling looks less dire in comparison to the Supreme Court decision recriminalizing homosexuality and, in effect, renewing Section 377 as the scene of the battle for sexual justice. Setting back expectations of a legal victory as a sign of and threshold to more gains due sexual minorities, the *Koushal v. Naz* ruling unequivocally upholds the role of the state, especially the legislature, at a moment when the nation and state appear to be flailing under economic and social liberalization.

The role of courts in advancing or mitigating the integrity and importance of states in the Indian context continues to unfold on more than one front. Months after the crushing *Koushal v. Naz* decision was issued, the Supreme Court delivered a breathtakingly different ruling, *National Legal Services Authority v. Union of India and others* (hereafter NALSA *v. Union*), impacting transgender persons, hijras, and other gender-based minorities in India.[1] Likewise issued by a bench of two justices, K. S. Radhakrishnan and A. K. Sikri, NALSA *v. Union* unequivocally confirmed the legal right to choose gender identity for those transitioning between male and female and, in an exceptional gesture, established that hijras and all those who do not subscribe to a binary frame could identify as third gender.[2] A relief, a victory, a bold judicial vision written in two parts seeking to correct society's moral failure to embrace different gender identities and expressions by extending social justice to those long oppressed and denied. Noteworthy about the judgment is that it distills gender from biological sex as well as sexual orientation to recognize a broad spectrum of trans/gender subjects and critically assesses a range of international conventions and foreign case law to conclude that gender identity and expression ought to be protected by the Indian Constitution. In further contrast to the ruling recriminalizing homosexuality, NALSA *v. Union* interprets the legal recognition of gender minorities within the ambit of the constitutional rights to equality before the law (Article 14), prohibition of discrimination based on sex (Article 15), freedom of speech and expression (Article 19), and protection of life and personal liberty (Article 21). What's more, it openly presses against *Koushal v. Naz*'s troubling logic of small minorities by noting that gender minorities may be numerically insignificant but are nonetheless entitled to their rights.

And yet, despite its substantial differences from *Koushal v. Naz* and the fact that it unambiguously seeks to deliver justice to transgender persons and other gender minorities, or really because of how the justice is to be delivered, NALSA *v. Union* too shores up the role of the state. Even though the justices see gender identity as part of the moral prelegal entitlements due all persons, its arbiters are regional- and national-level state agencies and institutions. These are the units charged with determining and implementing procedures for legal identity recognition, leading Aniruddha Dutta to express concern about haphazard, regionally varied procedures to come and the overall trend toward bureaucratic hurdles and requirements over simpler, community-based processes.[3]

In another twist the government of India or, more precisely, the national-level Ministry of Social Justice and Empowerment subsequently petitioned the Supreme Court seeking clarity and modification on certain aspects of NALSA *v. Union*, revealing in the process the complex ways governance proliferates. Asking for greater clarity on parsing transgender from third gender, rightly suggesting the deletion of references to the term *eunuch*, and aptly questioning the collapsing of lesbian, gay, and bisexual persons into the category of transgender, the writ also takes up the justices' sweeping directives that states have to go beyond legal gender identity recognition. These include extending affirmative action policies to gender minorities; providing them adequate and separate medical care, public toilets, and other facilities; introducing welfare initiatives; addressing their social vulnerability; and ensuring their social integration. Undoubtedly crucial, these interventions nonetheless raise the conundrum of the extent to which social justice is routinely filtered through the imagination of the state. Ironically the ministry's writ wonders at the practicality of extending caste-based affirmative action policies to transgender and third gender persons since, according to its logic, caste is fixed at birth! Clarifications and modifications by the apex court are pending at this time and administrative procedures continue. Perhaps this ruling will slowly bridge the gap between law and life, all the while enabling the expansion of governance.

Rather than legal outcomes, then, the lasting political gains of efforts to ensure justice to gender and sexual minorities lie in forging movements that in the case of decriminalizing homosexuality have (re) emerged from failures in the courts—the social and political firestorm that followed in the wake of *Koushal v. Naz*, public demonstrations, scathing op-eds, angry blogs, and interviews criticizing the apex court's decision, keeping it in the limelight for many months. A Global Day of Rage inspired outpourings against the legal outcome from within India and numerous cities and organizations elsewhere, and for the first time many political and elected officials expressed support for decriminalizing homosexuality. In a complete volte-face from its earlier position, the government, as well as Naz Foundation, Voices against Section 377, and other parties to the legal proceedings, filed a review petition asking the Supreme Court to reassess the decision on technical grounds. Dismissed without so much as a hearing, the review petition has been followed by a more rarely exercised option, the curative petition, that can be filed on the grounds that a ruling represents a gross miscarriage of justice.

Even as sexuality rights supporters pursue law to its last possibility, increased political visibility, an expanding grammar of rights and justice for same-sex sexualities, more attention (especially from the media), and additional spaces for political activism and cultural expression are among the palpable changes that have occurred alongside and as a result of the focus on Section 377. Such engagements are helping to overcome legal defeats and inspiring criticisms of legal victories represented by *NALSA v. Union* that promise dignity to trans/gender minorities while criminalizing same-sex sexual activity. Rather than shortsightedly focusing on one law or one subject, the best of these engagements are articulating broader visions for social justice that bring together the most vulnerable, whether on the basis of sex, gender and gender expression, racialization, sexual orientation, caste, religion, or social class.

The State's Many Sexual Lives: Issues of Sexual Violence

In the spirit of juxtaposing the struggle to decriminalize homosexuality alongside other contestations, I sift two additional sites through a critique of the sexual state: sexual violence and immigration. While I stay within the Indian context, these issues reverberate widely across other settings as well.

Since December 2012 demands for the government to address sexual violence in India have occupied public discourse at an unprecedented scale. Triggered by the sexual assaults on Nirbhaya, a twenty-three-year-old woman, by six men and her subsequent death, these protests are against the pervasive sexual violence that women in Delhi and elsewhere in the country endure because of region, caste, religion, class, and gender.[4] Yet it was the sexual assault on Nirbhaya by a group of unknown men that prompted demonstrations in Delhi. Even as details of the assault filled the newspapers and digital media, the rallies as well as the public discourses of which they were a part hinged largely on the state's role in preventing and punishing sexual assaults on women.

The thrust of the demands has been to argue for better governance in order to deter sexual crime against women and ensure greater accountability from state institutions, including the police, law, state-run hospitals, and elected officials implicated in the safety and security of women. Much ire is rightly directed at the police, for they often do not follow established guidelines when sexual assault is reported. Moralism and bigotry on the part of police officers—for example, the notion that respectable women ought not to report sexual assault—often make them reluctant to record crime reports and gather and report evidence properly and make them more likely to be punitive toward survivors of sexual assault. The need for improved legal protocol in trying cases of sexual violence galvanized the spirit of protest as well. A legal process that tries accusers rather than the accused and is marred by loopholes, pervasive judicial sexism, and a glacial pace compound state ineffectiveness in preventing and prosecuting sexual violence. For the most part demands were focused on better laws, improved law enforcement, and harsher punishments, including the death penalty or at least chemical castration. Such approaches, however, are likely to yield uneven or unsatisfactory results at best, for they encourage an enlargement of existing structures of governance rather than their overhaul. Accordingly sexual violence cannot be seen primarily as either a failure of the state or the unfortunate result of a lack of adequate governance. Instead state governance needs to be viewed through the lens of sexual violence.

"JUSTICE J. S. VERMA COMMITTEE REPORT"

More effective responses, of which the "Report of the Committee on Amendments to Criminal Law" is a case in point, have taken sexuality's significance to governance as a point of departure to issue more thoroughgoing critiques of the state rather than call for its expansion.[5] Better known as the "Justice J. S. Verma Committee Report," furnished by a committee of three—two retired justices, Leila Seth and J. S. Verma, and Gopal Subramanium—this 630-page document compellingly reframes the persistent split between state and sexuality.[6] A collective archive produced at the threshold of state and society, the report is the outcome of contributions from a variety of women's groups from around the country, including Kashmir and the Northeastern States under military imposition, lesbian and gay constituencies, children's rights activists, legal experts and intellectuals from within and outside of India, research and support provided by young lawyers and academics, and, not least, over seventy thousand responses solicited from the general public.

Although the committee was charged with suggesting amendments to criminal law that would make for speedier trials and enhanced punishment, the input from women's groups working at the forefront of sexual, caste-, political-, and military-based violence led to a more sweeping indictment of governance. In contrast to the populist demands for increased governance, the committee's report is critical of legislative expansion by taking the position that earlier interventions, such as the Protection of Women from Domestic Violence Act (2005), have had uneven consequences, failing to stop the disempowerment of women. Indeed the report indicts the very structures and practices of governance for not ensuring gender equality and, worse, contributing to ongoing sexual violence by discriminating on the basis of sex or gender. In lieu of reinforcing a dichotomy between state and society, the recommendations emerge at their dense intersections.

Taking institutional histories, practices, and policies as its point of departure, the "Justice J. S. Verma Committee Report" advocates for their overhaul. It devotes an entire chapter to police reforms, spanning the modernization of the force, a significant reorientation of the relationship between police and community, and measures aimed at the welfare of those who police. Elsewhere the report recommends a review of the Armed Forces Special Powers Act (1958) and similar provisions that allow military and paramilitary forces to commit sexual violence on women in areas under occupation—Chattisgarh, Kashmir, Northeastern States, among others. Most notably a chapter on electoral reforms takes issue with the procedures that allow candidates accused of, charged with, or convicted of some form of sexual violence to contest elections. In a context where almost a third of the members of Parliament faced criminal charges and where members of Parliament, members of legislative assemblies, and candidates enter the electoral process even though they have been charged with sexual violence or crimes against women, this indictment is overdue.

The report also expands the definition of sexual violence by seeing it as a consequence of a view in which women embody religious and caste groups. Exceeding the conventional view that only respectable heterosexual women are to be protected from sexual violence, it incorporates lesbian, gay, and transgender people within the purview of nondiscrimination and safeguards from sexual violence. The definition of sexual violence is further expanded beyond rape as coercive penile-vaginal penetration to include sexual harassment at work, sexual harassment in public places, acid attacks, stalking, sex trafficking, and, perhaps most significant, marital rape. Even more expansive is the link to the biopolitics of nationally skewed sex ratios, particularly egregious in the states of Haryana, Punjab, and Rajasthan, to underscore the mix of cultural practices and state ideologies and failures that contribute to women's vulnerabilities. Limited access to land rights, resources, social services, education, and employment are identified in the report as contributing to women's vulnerability and implicitly being forms of sexual violence themselves.

Building on the extensive work conducted by women's and children's rights groups as well as feminist scholarship, the report reverses the relationship between sexuality and governance. Rather than serving as a mere commentary on how state institutions should tackle the difficulties of sexual violence, the report implies and implicates a deeply subjective state and criticizes institutional exploitations of sexuality and gender. Thus, cutting across the putative divide between state and society, suggested remedies include the dismantling of extraconstitutional bodies of governance, such as the Khap Panchayats and the Katta Panchayats, through which sexual violence against women is frequently arbitrated at the village level.[7] In place of the death penalty or chemical castration, the report emphasizes the need for education starting early in the informal and formal school curriculum and also encompassing state institutions. State institutions are seen as having a role to play in the curbing of sexual violence, but the report asserts that such a role will not be effective without a holistic review of governance, the sociocultural, and the gender and sexual biases that mark these institutions

Yet the split between state and society is not so easily undone. The Criminal Law (Amendment) Act of 2013, inserting changes in the rape laws and criminal procedures, was hastily passed by Parliament and approved by the president even though it violates the spirit and recommendations of the "Justice Verma Committee Report." The Indian Penal Code was amended to punish police failure to register grievous hurt, the purview of harm was expanded to include acid attacks, definitions of sexual harassment were revised, the employment of trafficked persons was penalized, rape laws were modified to include sexual assault, a provision for gang rape was included, and, contrary to the "Justice Verma Committee Report," the death penalty was instated in cases where sexual assault leads to death or a "persistent vegetative state." But because the Act elides a review of governance, gender inequality, and structural factors contributing to sexual violence, the modifications will produce uneven results at best and will strengthen governance rather than overhaul it.[8] As Ratna Kapur notes, in its eagerness to "do something" the government has issued an ordinance that does nothing to further women's sexual autonomy and bodily integrity while expanding a security regime to further regulate sexual conduct.[9]

Stirring the Sexual State and Anti-Immigrant Discourses in Delhi

Security regimes are enacted through sites overtly identified with sexuality but also terrains that are less obviously so marked. To explore the broad-based relevance of a critique of the sexual state, I turn to discourses of migration. India's reputation as a nation of emigrants notwithstanding, I focus on it as a site of immigration from neighboring Bangladesh.[10]

In May 2001, just months before the Naz Foundation plea was filed, another public interest litigation, Civil Writ Petition No. 3170 of 2001, found its way to the Delhi High Court. On the surface the two writs had little to do with each other, not least because of the difference in focus, but much like the Naz Foundation writ, the petitioner Chetan Dutt a Delhi-based advocate, sought state intervention to criminalize and deport migrants and prevent further migration specifically from Bangladesh: "A petition by way of Public Interest Litigation seeking directions, orders or appropriate writs from this Hon'ble Court whereby the influx of illegal migrants from Bangladesh into the capital of India could be checked/stopped and effective steps taken to remove the illegal migrants already in Delhi."[11]

Dutt's emphasis on Delhi rehearsed earlier histories of anti-immigrant discourses that have played out most acutely in the nation's capital, even though it does not represent the highest concentration of immigrants from Bangladesh. As Sujata Ramachandran notes, by the early 1990s Bangladeshi migrants in Delhi were the target of political vitriol and the active use of state capacities for deportation, even though many had lived in the city's slums for more than two decades.[12] As a result of this politicization by Hindu right-wing organizations and the ruling Congress Party's capitulation to their political rhetoric, Operation Pushback (1992) forcibly deported thousands of Bengali Muslims to Bangladesh. A subsequent Action Plan vested authority in local police to identify and detain unauthorized migrants.[13] Dutt's writ sought judicial directives that would continue these earlier initiatives by requiring the police and other relevant state agencies and institutions to identify and deport migrants from Bangladesh, stalling further unauthorized cross-border movements.

Dutt's rationale for the writ was twofold: the stresses on the social fabric and social services, as well as risks to the security of Delhi and its residents. Consistent as his fears were with Hindu nationalist convergences on Muslims as imminent threats to national security and sovereignty, he subsumed them under the pressures on the city's social infrastructure from extralegal migration. Suggesting that Delhi was home to some three million unauthorized migrants from Bangladesh, the writ goes on to claim that such migrants have overburdened the city by creating slum dwellings serving as hubs for a variety of criminal activities, namely drugs, sex, pornography, contraband liquor, and illegal guns, impacting numerous neighborhoods. By overloading civic facilities, threatening law and order, creating more slum dwellings, encroaching on scarce open land, engaging in fraudulent political participation, draining precious resources, and making welfare schemes ineffective, these migrants, the writ maintains, jeopardize the well-being of the capital and its people.

Biopolitical rationalities and sexual anxieties drive the scant evidence on which anti-immigrant discourses are based. This evidence is quotes from fourteen articles published between April and May 2001 in the *Hindustan Times*, the *Pioneer*, *Times of India*, and the *Financial Times*. What is striking about these articles is their shared emphasis on how unauthorized migration from Bangladesh jeopardizes the well-being of Delhi's presumably authorized residents. These biopolitical logics—that the welfare of Delhi's population is at risk because of voter fraud, unauthorized slums, criminal activity, and violence—are fueled by attention to unauthorized migration's impact on local demographics and, implicitly, sexuality. As elaborated in chapter 2, demographic indices—births, deaths, population growth, fertility rates, among others—reflect the obligations of managing sexuality as much at the individual as the collective level. A *Hindustan Times* article, "Bangladesh Used Us as a Punching Bag," cited as evidence in the writ, suggests, "We are playing host to no less than 15 million illegal immigrant Bangladeshis. They are a drain on our resources apart from the fact that they have disturbed the demographic balance. But political parties are busy increasing their vote bank through their support."[14]

The sexual imperatives of anti-Bangladesh rhetorics were further amplified in a meeting with Dutt. Reluctant to meet with me at his office, he agreed to a neutral, nondescript location to discuss his motivations for petitioning the Delhi High Court. Describing unauthorized immigration from Bangladesh as "voluminous," Dutt had much to say about all the ways he thinks migrants are "eating into the major resources" and presenting "an economic load on public facilities." Racializing the migrants as inherently "antisociety" because of their involvement in crime and violence, low level of education, and immoral practices, Dutt further underscored their significant demographic impact especially in certain areas of the city. He contemptuously likened immigrants from Bangladesh to fungus that will continue to grow until checked. Bringing sexuality directly into the equation, he lamented immigrants' ostensible propensity to have many children: "India is trying to restrict birth rate, but they think that all offspring are God's gift. For them, the more they procreate the better [for they are able to make demands on existing resources]."[15]

A series of subsequent court orders by Delhi High Court justices in favor of Dutt's writ gives some measure of its success.[16] But it was fieldwork in the Foreigners Regional Registration Office, the state institution regulating temporary and long-term residence in New Delhi, that provided insight into why institutional concerns with sexuality are so easily activated. In our meeting the officer in charge of authorizing deportation of migrants highlighted numerous cases in which women from Bangladesh were being purchased as wives due to the skewed sex ratios in the proximate states of Haryana, Rajasthan, and Punjab. Casting the issue of unauthorized migration primarily in terms of the trafficking of women, the officer saw deportation as an act of intervention on behalf of the women from Bangladesh.[17] In another instance, Mumbai police detained some two hundred women from Bangladesh on account of their being allegedly trafficked as bar dancers. Despite feminist reports suggesting that the vast majority of women are not trafficked, nor are they foreigners (chapter 1), in this and other instances the state's ongoing preoccupation with sexuality echoed familiarly across different sites. By continually "doing something" about the perils of sexuality, whether in relation to dance bars, immigration, sexual violence, Section 377, or other social problems, the state is actively constituted and state governance enacted.

Even as struggles for justice hang in the balance, sexual states in their various iterations continue to thrive. Reformist struggles as well as sexually oriented forms of governance sustain these states, and their relevance applies not only to India but to myriad other settings grappling with similar issues as well as sex trafficking, sex education, state-related sex scandals, health and disease, demographics, and more. Indeed the insights derived from the Indian context open up new questions and lines of inquiry in settings such as the United States and Europe, reversing the wisdom that these are the theaters of knowledge production (rather than more accurately being seen as cases that are elevated to the status of theory). These takeaways also implicitly trouble the fact that state sexuality remains under theorized, asking why, for example, Margot Canaday's fine analysis of the expansion of the bureaucratic state and the regulation of homosexuality in the twentieth century becomes virtually unimaginable in the contemporary United States.[18]

Therefore I close by briefly extending the approach developed in this book to the Russian context, specifically to its infamous national law against the "propaganda of nontraditional sexual relations" passed by its parliament in 2013. Widely known in the international English-language press and social media as the ban against gay propaganda, this law was indicted as draconian, Russia's war on gays, and the unleashing of state homophobia. Coming mere months before the 2014 Winter Olympics in Sochi, it was primarily attributed to President Vladimir Putin's attempts to reaffirm traditional Russian cultural values in opposition to Western liberalism, symbolized by support for gay civil rights. While Putin was undoubtedly a key player in passing the law, the focus on him has been in lieu of a more systematic analysis of the Russian state leading to a thicker understanding of the legislation.

In her analysis Marie Mendras points to a fundamental paradox characterizing the national state in Russia, the illusion of strong centralized statism and the reality of dysfunctional institutions and practices and privatized concentrations of power, thereby paving the way for a different reading of the 2013 homophobic law.[19] This is to say, the edict can be more usefully seen as an attempt to reconcile this paradox and shore up the role and relevance of the national Russian state, a point that is also borne out Laurie Essig's history of Russian state intervention in sexuality.[20] In other words, understanding the anti–gay propaganda law as an instantiation of governance that helps strengthen the illusion of statism and centralized control directed toward the good of the nation enables new possibilities of critical inquiry. It would also be useful to place this injunction alongside the corpus of laws, policies, discourses, and practices regulating sexuality that help bolster the state—for instance, the decree prescribing imprisonment for offending religious feelings that was passed by the Russian parliament immediately after the edict against gay propaganda as a means to limit the feminist queer political protests of the group Pussy Riot. And it would help to be mindful of the various constituencies, especially the Russian Orthodox Church and state television figures, who supported the ban against gay propaganda while actively fanning the idea and indispensability of the state.[21]

Engaging sexual states in a variety of contexts and through a variety of sites means reexamining foundational assumptions about sexuality as an object of governance and reorienting toward thoroughgoing analyses of governance practices, laws, policies, and discourses. If we are serious about loosening the state's grip on sexuality, especially in the interests of disenfranchised subjects, then the imaginations of states and expressions of governance have to be front and center in our analytics, as do our complicities in preserving the state or preemptively declaring its demise. Future critical assessments would attend to the afterlives of sexual states that persist well beyond the specific lenses through which they manifest.

NOTES

Chapter 1

1. The Bharatiya Bar Girls Union emerged under the leadership of Varsha Kale, a union activist and not a bar dancer herself, following a public rally in 2004 to demonstrate against increasing state restrictions, police harassment, a greater share of customer tips, and more. See Agnes, "State Control and Sexual Morality"; Seshu, "Bar Girls Seek Rights."

2. Bunsha, "Morality Check in Mumbai."

3. Aretxaga, "The Sexual Games of the Body Politic"; Alexander, "Not Just (Any) Body Can be a Citizen; Cooper, "An Engaged State; Duggan, "Queering the State."

4. Mitchell argues that the state should be considered "not as an actual structure but as the powerful, apparently metaphysical effect of practices that make such structures appear to exist" ("Society, Economy, and State Effect," 89). In "Limits of the State" he argues that the boundaries between state and society are not self-evident but are discursively produced.

5. Even though the issue of dance bars did not play out only at the level of the regional state and over the course involved numerous local, regional, national, transnational actors and discourses of governance, its axis was tilted toward the regional state.

6. Uberoi, "Introduction," xvi.

7. For example, see John and Nair's useful discussion in the introduction to *A Question of Silence?*

8. The now considerable literature on nationalism and sexuality was inaugurated by Mosse, *Nationalism and Sexuality*. Relevant here is also Stoler's point in "Affective States" that nation is analytically privileged over state.

9. During partition some seventy-five thousand women were raped or abducted by men across religious-cultural lines, which was seen as a matter of national shame, and the recovery of women, a matter of national honor. In a matter of

months some twelve million people crossed the new borders, with Muslims migrating into Pakistan and Hindus and Sikhs arriving in India, leaving behind land, immovable assets, and livelihoods. It is estimated that one million people lost their lives in the bloodbath on both sides of the border. The wrenching of families and communities from their lives and homelands, intense bloodshed and hatred, and the violation of women continue to echo in the recesses of living memory. On the issue of how the hurt against women as was seen as a violation of the nation and how the recovery of women became a matter of national honor, see Butalia, *The Other Side of Silence*.

10. Das, *Life and Words*, 170. Elaborating on the postcolonial sexual contract in "Framing the Postcolonial Sexual Contract," Keating also draws attention to the racialized aspects of the fraternal order represented by the postcolonial Indian statistic.

On the details on how state institutions and procedures served as the instruments of recovering women and protecting national honor, see Menon and Bhasin's *Borders and Boundaries*. The authors detail the more than seventy amendments, the exhaustive parliamentary discussions on the Abducted Persons Act of 1949, and the virtually unlimited powers granted to police to recover abducted women. The Act was the result of an agreement between the Indian and Pakistani governments in 1947 and was renewed annually until 1957. It authorized an extensive network of state representatives, ideologies, and practices in the recovery of women, including the police, social workers, refugee camp officers, tribunals, courts, and central and provincial bureaucrats and politicians. At the same time, women thought to be abducted were denied rights, legal recourse, or the agency of choice and could be forcibly confined to the refugee camps.

11. For example, see Sunder Rajan, *Scandal of the State*, for an analysis on the limits of the state and (heterosexual) women's issues in India, ranging from Muslim child brides and compulsory sterilization to the Uniform Civil Code.

12. For a treatment of obscenity in relation to the moral fabric of the nation, see Bose, Introduction to *Translating Desire*. For an alternate emphasis on the state in managing issues related to obscenity, see Puri, "Forging Hetero-Collectives."

13. Also notable is that charges under obscenity law are typically coupled with other provisions of the Indian Penal Code: religious offenses, inciting harm against a group, creating public mischief, Indecent Representation of Women (Prohibition) Act of 1986.

14. Sundar, "The Rule of Law and the Rule of Property."

15. There exists a considerable body of poststructuralist literature on the state that owes much to the combined influences of Corrigan and Sayer's approach to the state as cultural production (*The Great Arch*), Abrams's demystification of the state into both a system *and* an idea ("Notes on the Difficulty of Studying the State"), and Foucault's reflections on governmentality ("Governmentality"; "Subject and Power").

16. Critical ethnographies on states have usefully focused on the mechanisms through which states are produced and enacted. See, for example, Ferguson and Gupta, "Spatializing States"; Gupta, *Red Tape*; Gupta, "Blurred Boundaries"; Ong, *Flexible Citizenship*; Scott, *Seeing Like a State*. Also see the essays in the following volumes: Hansen and Stepputat, *States of Imagination*; Joseph and Nugent, *Everyday Forms of State Formation*; Steinmetz, *State/Culture*. For feminist discussions highlighting questions of sexuality and pedestrian aspects of governance, see Stoler's contributions, particularly, *Race and the Education of Desire*; *Carnal Knowledge and Imperial Power*; *Haunted by Empire*. Also see Weston, "A Political Ecology of 'Unnatural Offences.'"

17. On the significance of theorizing the political and subjective aspects of the state, see Rose, *States of Fantasy*. Stoler's "Affective States" also usefully lays the groundwork for thinking through the role of affect, sentimentality, and such, propelling (colonial) state governance.

18. For a particularly useful discussion on the affects of law, see the introduction to Brown and Halley, *Left Legalism / Left Critique*. Also relevant here are the contributions of Nair, *Women and Law in Colonial India*; Agnes, *Law and Gender Inequality*; Basu, *She Comes to Take Her Rights*; Menon, *Recovering Subversion*; Parker, "Observations on the Historical Destruction of Separate Legal Regimes."

19. Alexander, "Not Just (Any) Body Can Be a Citizen"; Alexander, "Redrafting Morality"; Alexander, *Pedagogies of Crossing*; Aretxaga, "The Sexual Games of the Body Politic"; Cooper, "An Engaged State," 257–58. For a more detailed engagement with feminist thought, sexuality, and governance, see Puri, "States' Sexualities."

20. A path for a structural understanding of sexuality was explicitly laid by Foucault in *History of Sexuality* and further developed by Sedgwick in *Between Men*. It is analogous to a structural understanding of gender (see, for example, S. Charusheela's discussion of economic structures as "bearers of gender"). Seen in terms of states, a structural understanding of sexuality is also parallel to Goldberg's notion of racial states developed in the eponymous book, *The Racial State*. For more specific explorations of the state from a non-identitarian view of sexuality, see Povinelli's contributions, especially "Disturbing Sexuality"; "Sex Acts and Sovereignty"; *The Empire of Love*.

21. Examples of the prominent theories of the biopolitical that ignore the relevance of sexuality are Agamben, *Homo Sacer*; Hardt and Negri, *Empire*; Hardt and Negri, *Multitude*. For useful exceptions, see Stoler, *Race and the Education of Desire*; Puar, *Terrorist Assemblages*. Nikolas Rose (*Powers of Freedom*) is perhaps the most well-known example among scholars taking the view that the state is increasingly obsolete and analysis of governance must tend to the complexities of governance, be they in the realm of personal relationships, family, the national domestic, biomedicine, or media, among others. For sexuality studies scholarship on neoliberalism pivoting away from the state, consult Berlant, *The Queen of America Goes to Washington City*; Duggan, *Twilight of Equality?*; Richardson, "Desiring Sameness?"

22. For excellent examples documenting ordinary people's views of states, see Navaro-Yashin, *Faces of the State*; Gupta, "Blurred Boundaries."

23. In *The Nervous System*, Taussig argues that marginalized groups fetishize the state, a point that I think has to be moderated. See especially the chapter "Maleficium: State Fetishism."

24. Noted by Wittig in *The Straight Mind*, this point has been developed by scholars such as Peterson, "Political Identities/Nationalism as Heterosexism." For useful analyses of states that are nonetheless developed around the dualities of homosexuality and heterosexuality, see Duggan, "Queering the State" and, more recently, Canaday, *The Straight State*.

25. For this reason, I have previously emphasized the idea of sexuality respectability (*Woman, Body, Desire*). Also see Geeta Patel's notion of the heteroproper in the Indian context ("Advertisements, Proprietary Heterosexuality, and Hundis").

26. On file with the author. My gratitude to Flavia Agnes for sharing it with me.

27. Bill No. 60 of 2005, 1–2.

28. SNDT-FAOW, "Backgrounds and Working Conditions of Women Working as Dancers in Dance Bars"; SNDT-FAOW, "After the Ban." Also see Anandhi's reflections on these research studies as well as the intense debates among the feminist researchers and activists that were provoked by the results, "Feminist Contributions from the Margins."

29. Along with the SNDT-FAOW study "Backgrounds and Working Conditions of Women Working as Dancers in Dance Bars," see Pandit, "Gendered Subaltern Sexuality and the State"; Gopal, "Caste, Sexuality and Labour."

30. See the second study by SNDT-FAOW, "After the Ban" on this point. Also see Agnes, "Hypocritical Morality"; Pandit, "Gendered Subaltern Sexuality and the State."

31. Agnes, "State Control and Sexual Morality"; Gopal, "Caste, Sexuality and Labour"; Makhija, "Bar Dancers, Morality and the Indian Law"; Pandit "Gendered Subaltern Sexuality and the State."

32. For the full text of the judgment, see *Indian Hotel and Restaurants . . . v. The State of Maharashtra*, Bombay High Court, April 12, 2006, http://www.lawyerscollective.org/wp-content/uploads/2013/05/Bombay-High-Court-judgment-12.4.2006.pdf.

33. The text of the judgment can be found at Civil Appeal No. 2705 of 2006, Supreme Court of India, http://judis.nic.in/supremecourt/imgs1.aspx?filename=40565.

34. "Maharashtra Firm on Decision to Ban Dance Bars: R. R. Patil," *Times of India*, September 7, 2013, accessed November 15, 2013, http://timesofindia.indiatimes.com/city/mumbai/Maharashtra-firm-on-decision-to-ban-dance-bars-RR-Patil/articleshow/22380404.cms.

35. "Maharashtra Firm on Decision to Ban Dance Bars."

36. For informed and informative histories of dance bars, see Agnes, "State Control and Sexual Morality"; Pandit, "Gendered Subaltern Sexuality and the State."

37. The elaborate licensing system that developed between 1947 and 1990 is euphemistically referred to as the *license raj* (or license rule). As Agnes notes in "State Control and Sexual Morality," the thicket of licenses was coupled with the *hafta raj*, or the rule of bribery.

38. For a particularly useful overview of the state after liberalization, see the Gupta and Sivaramakrishnan, "Introduction."

39. Joseph, "Neoliberal Reforms and Democracy in India."

40. Banerjee-Guha, "Neoliberalising the 'Urban'." Also see Prakash, *Mumbai Fables*.

41. Agnes, "State Control and Sexual Morality." Agnes has been the legal representative for the bar dancers' union.

42. Agnes, "State Control and Sexual Morality."

43. See Agnes, "State Control and Sexual Morality"; Pandit, "Gendered Subaltern Sexuality and the State." Mazarella also takes the position in "'A Different Kind of Flesh'" that the dance bars represented vernacular entertainment forms and were seen as an irritant to the cultural politics of globalization. In contrast, Kotiswaran in "Labours in Vice or Virtue?" repudiates a neoliberal framework in analyzing dance bars.

44. Joseph, "Neoliberal Reforms and Democracy in India," 3215; also see Fernandes and Heller, "Hegemonic Aspirations" for a useful discussion on this point.

45. In contrast to the view that the state is retreating, I take the position that it is reconfiguring. States have expanded responsibilities in ensuring a suitable climate for capital investment, providing infrastructure, and regulating public sector organizations, even as they are being "hollowed out" in some respects. For useful discussions on these points and critiques of the erosion of the state in post-liberalizing India, see Gupta and Sivaramakrishnan, "Introduction"; Gupta, *Red Tape*; Sharma and Gupta, "Introduction."

46. Gupta and Sivaramakrishnan, "Introduction," 1.

47. Mehta, *Maximum City*, 286.

48. Gurbir Singh, "Patil's Tarannum Googly for Bar Girls." *Economic Times*, September 19, 2005, accessed November 15, 2013, http://articles.economictimes.indiatimes.com/2005–09–19/news/27483882_1_bar-girls-deepa-bar-chandni-bar.

49. On the interface of U.S.-led antitrafficking and Maharashtra state discourses, see SNDT-FAOW, "Backgrounds and Working Conditions of Women Working as Dancers in Dance Bars." For a discussion on the human rights discourses resonating in the state's edict, see Makhija, "Bar Dancers, Morality and the Indian Law."

Chapter 2

1. For a useful discussion on the impact of routinized practices, see Nayan Shah's analysis of the governance of public health in San Francisco that historically worked to bolster popular racisms with the credibility of science and the authority of the state, *Contagious Divides*.

2. Agamben, *Homo Sacer*; Giroux, *Stormy Weather*; Hardt and Negri, *Empire*; Hardt and Negri, *Multitude*; Mbembe, "Necropolitics"; Ong, "Making the Biopolitical Subject"; Gupta, *Red Tape*.

3. On this point, see "Spatializing States," Ferguson and Gupta's discussion of how popular and academic discourses sustain visions of the state as "above" family, local community, and society and as "encompassing" these circles of affiliation.

4. Among others, see Aretxaga, *States of Terror*; Das, *Life and Words*; Fuller and Bénéï, *The Everyday State and Society in Modern India*; Gupta, *Red Tape*; Navaro-Yashin, *Faces of the State*; Rudolph and Jacobsen, *Experiencing the State*; Oldenburg, "Face to Face with the Indian State"; Tarlo, *Unsettling Memories*.

5. Gupta, "Blurred Boundaries," 376; Stevens, *Reproducing the State*. For a particularly useful discussion of the importance of ethnography among state institutions, see Oldenburg's ethnography of a district in the Indian state of Uttar Pradesh, "Face to Face with the Indian State."

6. All names of officials at the NCRB are pseudonyms.

7. In the introduction to their collection, *States of Imagination*, Hansen and Stepputat provide a particularly useful discussion on imaginations of the state as constitutive of it. This also resonates with Abrams's demystification of the state into a system *and* an idea in "Notes on the Difficulty of Studying the State."

8. NCRB, "Empowering Indian Police with IT."

9. Fuller and Harriss, "For an Anthropology of the Modern Indian State," 9.

10. Chatterjee, "Introduction." A few scholars writing on the state in India from a critical and useful perspective are worth mentioning here: Sugata Bose, Partha Chatterjee, Akhil Gupta, Ayesha Jalal, Sunil Khilnani, Rajeswari Sunderajan, and Emma Tarlo.

11. Kaviraj, introduction to *Politics in India*; Nandy, *The Romance of the State and the Fate of Dissent in the Tropics*; Gupta, "Blurred Boundaries," 389.

12. Weber, *Economy and Society*, especially 54–56, 956–1005.

13. Stoler, "Affective States," 9.

14. Aretxaga, "The Sexual Games of the Body Politic," 22, 4.

15. Grosz, "Bodies-Cities."

16. Along with Henri Lefebvre, other scholars have usefully examined the junctures of state and space. The list includes Neil Brenner, Bob Jessop, Martin Jones, and Gordon Macleod.

17. Lefebvre, "Space and State," 94.

18. On this point, see Lefebvre, "Space and State," 87.

19. Tarlo, *Unsettling Memories*, 75.

20. The language of the Immoral Traffic (Prevention) Act is not gender specific and it allows for the arrest of male-bodied or nonnormative gender and sexual minorities, a point to which I return in chapter 6. The full text of this Act is available at "Immoral Traffic (Prevention) Act." Delhi Department of Social Welfare, accessed January 11, 2008, http://indiankanoon.org/doc/69064674/.

21. National Crime Records Bureau, *Crime in India*.

22. The point is that crime affects women differently based on their social class, where they live, whether they are religious or ethnic minorities, or live in areas that are under military occupation.

23. "Crime against Women: Violence Within and Without," *Hindu*, September 1, 2002, accessed July 25, 2007, http://www.hindu.com/thehindu/mag/2002/09/01/stories/2002090100020400.htm. The People's Union for Civil Liberties, a self-funded human rights watchdog group, issues critical reports and numbers of crime against women; see "Crimes against Women," PUCL *Bulletin*, March 2006, accessed July 25, 2007, http://www.pucl.org/Topics/Gender/2006/crimes.html.

24. Hacking, "Biopower and the Avalanche of Printed Numbers," 281; also see Hacking, "How Should We Do the History of Statistics?"

25. Rose, "Governing by Numbers," 676.

26. Smith, "Rule-by-Records and Rule-by-Reports," 158.

27. Appadurai, "Number in the Colonial Imagination," 323.

28. For Hacking's useful discussion on the origins of statistics as moral science, especially in France, see "How Should We Do the History of Statistics?" 182. Extrapolating from Sanjay Nigam's work, Appadurai addresses the differences in the use of statistical measures in the colonies ("Number in the Colonial Imagination," 318).

29. Nigam, "Disciplining and Policing the 'criminals by Birth.'"

30. Appadurai, "Number in the Colonial Imagination," 319.

31. In their overview of the constructionist approach to social problems Holstein and Miller underscore, "They are the interpretive processes that constitute what come to be seen as oppressive, intolerable, or unjust conditions like crime, poverty, and homelessness" (*Reconsidering Social Constructionism*, 6).

32. On this point, see U. Kalpagam, "The Colonial State and Statistical Knowledge."

33. Consider here Gyan Prakash's discussion of colonial governmentality, which, he argues, set off bureaucratic expansion, rationalization, the use of statistics, and the constitution of a population identified by the challenges of health, productivity, sanitation, disease, and more (*Another Reason*, especially chapter 5).

34. Also a pseudonym.

35. More recently the rape law has been expanded to include sexual assault, a point that I take up more fully in the conclusion.

36. Scott, *Seeing Like a State.*

37. Spector and Kitsuse, "Introduction to the Transaction Edition," in *Constructing Social Problems*, ix–x.

38. Grewal, *Transnational America*, 157.

39. Grewal, "'Women's Rights as Human Rights.'"

40. Bumiller, *In an Abusive State.*

41. The version of the PWDVA that was passed into law was drafted by the Lawyers' Collective, the same legal advocacy organization that served as the legal representatives for the Naz Foundation writ against Section 377. See Jaising, "Bringing Rights Home" for a detailed discussion on PWDVA.

42. Singh and Butalia, "Challenging Impunity on Sexual Violence in South Asia."

43. Abram et al., "Planning by Numbers," 249.

44. Brown and Boyle, "National Closets."

45. Kinnar and Aravani are forms of self-identity embraced by some in an effort to distance themselves from the pejorative connotations of hijra. Kinnar is more likely to be used in northern India while Aravani has resonance in the southern regions of the country.

46. Bhaskaran, "The Politics of Penetration."

47. This discussion is indebted to Foucault's speculations on the biopolitical in the last section of the *History of Sexuality*, and then more fully in his March 17, 1976 lecture at Collège de France, published in *Society Must Be Defended.*

48. On the first dimension, see Epstein, *Inclusion*; Ong, "Making the Biopolitical Subject"; Rose, *The Politics of Life Itself.* On the second, see Agamben, *Homo Sacer*; Giroux, *Stormy Weather*; Hardt and Negri, *Empire*; Mbembe, "Necropolitics"; Pease, "The Global Homeland State." For Hardt and Negri, the passage from disciplinary to biopolitical power means that whereas under disciplinary society power corresponds to the resistance of the individual body, under biopolitical power it comprises the whole social body (*Empire*, 24). Through Foucault and Deleuze and Guattari, they also stress that just as power unifies and envelops every aspect of social life, it reveals a new context, a singularity, an event (25).

49. Foucault, *Society Must Be Defended*, 254. For exceptions, see Giroux, *Stormy Weather*; Ong, "Making the Biopolitical Subject"; Puar, *Terrorist Assemblages.*

50. Foucault, *Society Must Be Defended*, 252. By invoking the metaphor of *homo sacer* and the rule of exception, Agamben seeks to reveal the paradox whereby citizens and others are increasingly stripped of their political and natural rights in the interests of the body politic. His contribution is to lay bare the grammar of the body politic through the idioms of refugee and the camp, the exceptions that illustrate the principle of widespread exclusion, whereby citizens gradually start to resemble refugees. Even though modern democracy justifies itself as a vindication and liberation of *zoē*, the bare life that is common to all living beings, by incorporating it into *bios*, or political life, it systematically denies this inalienable right.

51. Mbembe, "Necropolitics."

52. Gupta, *Red Tape*, especially chapter 5 and chapter 7, 251–52.

53. Gupta, "Section 377 and the Dignity of Indian Homosexuals," 4820.

54. On the deployment of vagrancy laws to regulate gender and sexual minorities, also see Gupta, "The Presumption of Sodomy."

55. Thangarajah and Arasu, "Queer Women and the Law in India."

56. A safari suit consists of a monochromatic pair of trousers and short-sleeved jacket-like shirt.

Chapter 3

1. The numbers were for the period 1996–2005, although the numbers for 2005 were incomplete. No cases were reported for the state of Jammu and Kashmir as the Indian Penal Code and constitutional protections have been troublingly suspended since 1990 under the Armed Forces Special Powers Act (AFSPA) of 1958. A few cases were reported for the states of Arunachal Pradesh, Assam, Meghalaya, Sikkim, and Tripura, but none for Manipur, Mizoram, and Nagaland, even though AFSPA was first deployed in these northeastern states. No cases were reported for the states of Jharkhand and Chattisgarh, which were carved out of the existing states of Bihar and Madhya Pradesh, respectively, in 2000. No cases were reported for the union territories of Andaman and Nicobar, Dadra and Nagar Haveli, Daman and Diu, or Lakshwadeep.

2. These numbers are from 2005; see NCRB, "Crime against Women."

3. For the years, 1999–2003, the number of records for Section 377 varies between 49 and 67, while they range between 381 and 490 for Section 375.

4. Khaitan, "*Koushal v. Naz.*"

5. For a useful critique of how consent is dismantled in cases of sexual violence against women due to its location in systems of exchange, property, and marriage, see Basu, "Sexual Property."

6. Seth, "To the Government of India, Members of the Judiciary, and All Citizens." For the endorsement, see Sen, "A Statement in Support of the Open Letter by Vikram Seth and Others." Both texts are available at http://orinam.net/377/wp-content/uploads/2013/12/377_OpenLetter_AmartyaSen.pdf.

7. See Guha, "Chandra's Death," in *Subaltern Studies V*; Weber, *Economy and Society*, vol. 2. Even though the ironies of the "rule of law" in colonial contexts have been repeatedly noted, the hallmark of the modern state is still seen as equality before the law. Critical race legal theorists have also discredited the neutrality and objectivity of law by pointing to the institutionalized biases of law in the United States.

8. Galanter, "The Uses of Law in Indian Studies"; Arondekar, *For the Record*.

9. Nair, *Women and Law in Colonial India*.

10. Indian Law Commissioners, *A Penal Code*, 47.

11. Narrain, *Queer*, 49.

12. See Macaulay, "Introductory Report upon the Indian Penal Code." Macaulay, who steered the drafting of the penal code, clarifies, "These illustrations will, we trust, greatly facilitate the understanding of the law, and will at the same time often serve as a defence of the law" (321).

13. In his discussion on the criminal justice system of nineteenth-century England in "Macaulay and the Indian Penal Code of 1862," Skuy describes the efforts of early Victorian reformers to reduce capital offenses in the statute book. Known as the Bloody Code, the two hundred statutes punished the majority of crimes with death but were unenforced due to the disproportionate punishment.

14. For Blackstone's language, see *Blackstone's Commentaries on the Laws of England*, book 4, chapter 15, p. 215. For a discussion of the Offences against Persons Act of 1828 and the Criminal Law Amendment Act of 1885, see Cohen, *Talk on the Wilde Side*, chapter 4.

15. In England by the nineteenth century the meaning of the term *sodomy* had come to cohere around transgressions of normative maleness, including homosexuality. In his discussion of the changing legislation and meanings of sodomy in England in *Talk on the Wilde Side*, Cohen traces a gradual shift from sodomy as a crime against God to a felony against the state, from a religious to a social transgression, from a sin to a crime against persons, and eventually to a normative transgression, especially associated with males. In *Homosexuality in Renaissance England*, Bray notes that sodomy was strongly associated with debauchery, and in *The Worst of Crimes* Goldsmith states that its meaning comes to rest on the effeminate homosexual, or the molly. Even as notions of sodomy and homosexuality extant in England may have shaped the syntax of Section 377, the specificities of the colonial context had a bearing as well. Extending the analytics of colonialism and criminality introduced by Anand Yang and Satadru Sen, Arondekar in *For the Record* underscores the unsubstantiated beliefs among British colonial administrators that sodomy was characteristic of and widely prevalent in the colony.

16. Haldar, *Law, Orientalism and Postcolonialism*, 2.

17. There is a divergence among legal historians about the particular set of factors that triggered the process of codification by the 1830s, even as subsequent colonial administrators contested it. Bernard S. Cohn explains that British interests in law in India were inextricable from the tax and revenue systems (*Colonialism and Its Forms of Knowledge*), while Nair emphasizes that a body of substantive law had not been established by the 1830s (*Women and Law in Colonial India*). In "Codification and the Rule of Colonial Difference," Kolsky suggests that there was some concern among legislators in England about the East India Company's administration of justice in making and executing laws, which prevailed in the early 1830s while the Company's royal charter was being renewed.

18. Macaulay, "Introductory Report upon the Indian Penal Code," 315.

19. Jain, *Outlines of Indian Legal History*, 603.

20. Cohn, *Colonialism and Its Forms of Knowledge.*

21. Presidency towns were the urban-centered colonial administrative units and the mofussils were the non-urban or rural areas. In *Colonialism and Its Forms of Knowledge* Cohn identifies established competing colonial ideologies between the colony as lawless and despotic and the colony as theocratic. If one aspect of the ideological scaffolding of British rule in the eighteenth century was that India had thus far been governed capriciously and autocratically, thereby requiring the rule of law, then another aspect was the reification of extant legal systems into Hindu and Muslim law.

22. Even though Macaulay only names the French Code and the Louisiana Code in the preparation of the draft on pages 320–21 of his "Introductory Report upon the Indian Penal Code," Skuy argues that Macaulay's code represents the transplanting of English law in India ("Macaulay and the Indian Penal Code of 1862").

23. Kolsky, "Codification and the Rule of Colonial Difference."

24. Singha, *A Despotism of Law.*

25. Macaulay, "Introductory Report upon the Indian Penal Code," 322, 432.

26. See Goldsmith's discussion of Bentham's writing, which appears to have been first published in 1978 (*The Worst of Crimes*, 19).

27. Narrain, *Queer*, 37.

28. Gupta, "Section 377 and the Dignity of Indian Homosexuals."

29. Dutta, "Retroactive Consolidation of 'Homophobia,'" 164.

30. Arondekar, *For the Record.*

31. Narrain, *Queer*, 48.

32. Bhaskaran, "The Politics of Penetration"; Bhaskaran, *Made in India*; Khanna, "Gay Rights"; Gupta, "Trends in the Application of Section 377."

33. Merry, *Colonizing Hawai'i.*

34. At least five cases in the archive are about women filing for divorce from their husbands partly on the grounds of being coerced into unnatural sex. While Indian law does not recognize marital rape, divorce was granted in all of these cases. For more detailed discussions, see Bhaskaran, "The Politics of Penetration"; Gupta, "Section 377 and the Dignity of Indian Homosexuals."

35. Gupta, "Trends in the Application of Section 377."

36. In 2012 the scope of Section 375 was expanded and the Protection of Children from Sexual Offences Act was passed.

37. Agnes, "Protecting Women against Violence?" 522. For the full text of the ruling on the *Jhaku* case, see Smt._Sudesh_Jhaku_vs_K.C.J._And_Others_on_23_May, 1996.pdf.

38. Gupta, "Trends in the Application of Section 377."

39. The details of the victims were unreported in ten cases; gender was unknown in one case; and the age of the man or boy was unclear in two cases.

40. *Government v. Bapoji Bhatt* 1884 Mysore LR 280; *Queen-Empress v. Khairati* 1884 ILR 6 ALL 204.

41. *Sardar Ahmad v. Emperor* 1914 AIR Lahore 565.

42. *Ganpat v. Emperor* 1918 AIR Lahore 322.

43. *State of Himachal Pradesh v. Yash Paul* 2010 Manupatra.

44. *Raju v. State of Haryana* 1998 Cri. L. J. 2587, 2591 (P&H).

45. *Mirro v. Emperor* 1935 AIR Sind. 78.

46. Arondekar, *For the Record*.

47. *Ghanashyam Misra v. The State of Orissa* 1958 AIR 78.

48. *Government v. Bapoji Bhatt* 1884 Mysore LR 280.

49. *Khanu v. Emperor* 1925 AIR Sind 286.

50. *Lohana Vasantlal Devchand and Others v. The State* 1968 AIR SC 252.

51. Narrain, *Queer*, 53.

52. *State of Kerala v. Kundumkara Govindam and Anr.*, 1959 Cri. L.J. 818 (Kerala HC).

53. *Fazal Rab Choudhary v. State of Bihar* 1982, 3 SCC 9.

54. *Naz Foundation v. Government of NCT of Delhi and Others*, accessed February 16, 2012, http://www.lawyerscollective.org/files/Naz%20Foundation%20Judgement.pdf 6.

55. *State of Maharashtra v. Rahul alias Raosaheb Dashrath Bhongale*, High Court of Bombay, 2002, Manupatra.

56. Ministry of Home Affairs, Criminal Procedure Code, accessed May 12, 2011, http://mha.nic.in/sites/upload_files/mha/files/pdf/ccp1973.pdf.

57. Tarlo, *Unsettling Memories*.

58. Gupta, "Section 377 and the Dignity of Indian Homosexuals." In his nuanced analysis, Gupta argues that when the Delhi High Court initially dismissed the Naz Foundation writ against Section 377 in 2004, it was correct that the law was not being used against consenting homosexual persons (see chapter 5) but without conceding that such biases may be present in trial court proceedings which are archived differently.

59. Gupta, "Section 377 and the Dignity of Indian Homosexuals."

60. *Nowshirwan Irani v. Emperor* 1934 AIR Sind 206.

61. *D. P. Minwalla v. Emperor* 1935 AIR Sind 78.

62. See Yang, *Crime and Criminality in British India*; Sen, *Disciplining Punishment*; Radhakrishna, *Dishonoured by History*.

63. Sen, *Disciplining Punishment*, 51, 204.

64. Notably, in the online edition of the *Oxford English Dictionary*, the meaning of *habitual* is associated with belonging to innate or inward dispositions.

Chapter 4

1. Chauncey, *Gay New York*; Goodman, "Beyond the Enforcement Principle"; Kulick, *Travesti*; Lowman, "Violence and the Outlaw Status of (Street) Prostitution in Canada"; Rhodes et al., "Police Violence and Sexual Risk among Female and Transvestite Sex Workers in Serbia"; Warner, *The Trouble with Normal*.

2. Fernandez and Gomathy, *The Nature of Violence Faced by Lesbian Women in India.*

3. See Gupta, "Section 377 and the Dignity of Indian Homosexuals."

4. People's Union for Civil Liberties, "Human Rights Violations against the Transgender Community."

5. Foucault, "*Omnes et Singulatim.*"

6. For examples of analyses of the impact of policing, see Bell, "The Police and Policing"; Bernstein and Kostelac, "Lavender and Blue"; Khalidi, *Khaki and Ethnic Violence in India*; Lowman, "Violence and the Outlaw Status of (Street) Prostitution in Canada"; Sanders, "The Risks of Street Prostitution"; Shah, *Contagious Divides*; Silliman and Bhatacharjee, *Policing the National Body*; Watts and Zimmerman, "Violence against Women." For exceptions that more thoroughly analyze the institution, see Bellur, "Why Do the Police Use Deadly Force?"; Hansen, "Governance and State Mythologies in Mumbai"; Amar, *New Racial Missions of Policing.*

7. In contrast with interviews that would likely make police more circumspect, the discussion groups had the advantage of allowing members of the Delhi Police to express their views relatively securely and even disagree from each other. My count of the number of those present for the second group discussion was between forty-six and forty-eight.

8. As noted previously, I gathered FIRs and statistics of the crimes registered under Section 377 in the Delhi area as well as nationally. This required repeated visits to a number of police stations spread across Delhi and also the Delhi Police Headquarters, which presented further opportunities for informal encounters with constables and police who occupy the middle ranks as inspectors and station heads. I also had discussions with police officials in Delhi, including meetings with two police commissioners and one former commissioner of Delhi, as well as police officials in Chennai and Kolkota.

9. Although accounts by members of the Delhi Police give insight into their perspectives on same-sex sexualities and the antisodomy law, the extent to which they shape policing practices cannot be deduced.

10. *Communalism* is a concept peculiar to India and other South Asian nations, used to describe sectarian difference, competition, and conflict between Hindus, Muslims, Sikhs, Christians, Jains, Buddhists, and Parsis, among others.

11. For example, Jains are not typically racialized, while the naturalized differences imposed on Muslims and Christians can be distinct.

12. Loomba, "Race and the Possibilities of Comparative Critique," 508.

13. Hansen and Stepputat, introduction to *Sovereign Bodies*, 1–2.

14. Quoted in Desai, "Red Herring in Police Reforms," 9.

15. The report is available at Human Rights Watch, "Broken System," 5.

16. Dhillon, *Police and Politics in India.*

17. Arnold, "Bureaucratic Recruitment and Subordination in Colonial India"; Verma, *The Indian Police.*

18. "Martial races" was a category invented by the British to create groups who

seemed well suited for warring and policing. These groups were described as physically strong, fearless, and loyal to British interests and were recruited for the military and police. The groups varied regionally. British administrators grouped together various ethnic and caste groups as "Brahmans" or "low castes" in a related strategy of reducing and enumerating the tremendous cultural, religious, class, and caste-based differences in the subcontinent.

19. Arnold, "Bureaucratic Recruitment and Subordination in Colonial India."

20. Dhillon, *Police and Politics in India*; Subramanian, *Political Violence and the Police in India*; Verma, *The Indian Police*.

21. In his discussion of political violence and the police, Subramanian suggests that the two-tier system of policing may be attributed to tensions between state control of civilian police and paramilitary forces under central control (*Political Violence and the Police in India*, 65).

22. Arnold, "Bureaucratic Recruitment and Subordination in Colonial India"; Dhillon, *Police and Politics in India*; Pathak, "The Beat(en)"; Subramanian, *Political Violence and the Police in India*.

23. Pathak, "The Beat(en)."

24. Human Rights Watch, "Broken System."

25. Ghosh, "Only 7% Women in Delhi Police."

26. Verma, *The Indian Police*.

27. Hansen and Stepputat, introduction to *Sovereign Bodies*, 4.

28. See the OED for a discussion on the adjacent terms *communal* and *communalism*.

29. Kaviraj, "The Imaginary Institution of India."

30. Given the innumerable differences in Hindu religious sects and practices, languages, geography, history, castes, and more, there is no single "Hindu" religious holiday that is observed across the country. Similarly the right-wing parties, the Shiv Sena in the state of Maharashtra, the Vishva Hindu Parishad with a stronger hold in the central and northern parts of the country, and the Tamil Protection Movement in the state of Tamil Nadu have numerous ideological differences and do not speak in a single voice.

31. Pandey, *The Construction of Communalism in Colonial North India*.

32. This is not to discount the formations of complex alliances in which Hindu Dalits are at the forefront of the violence against Muslims and Christians, for example, incited by upper-caste Hindu groups. See Chatterji. *Violent Gods*, for an insightful discussion.

33. The complete report is available online at Government of India, "Social Economic and Educational Status of the Muslim Community of India."

34. Bharucha, "Muslims and Others," 4246.

35. Chatterjee, *Gender, Slavery and Law in Colonial India*; Loomba, "Race and the Possibilities of Comparative Critique."

36. The relationships between minority communities and the abstract majoritarian Hindu community or the state are characterized by different histories and

imperatives. While Sikhs have felt the need to delineate physical and biological differences from Hindus (and Muslims), Muslims, often accused of being aliens, have not developed a political grammar of physical or biological differences.

37. Pandey, *The Construction of Communalism in Colonial North India*.

38. Arnold, "Bureaucratic Recruitment and Subordination in Colonial India."

39. Gilroy, *Against Race*; especially see the chapter, "The Crisis of 'Race' and Raciology."

40. Loomba, "Race and the Possibilities of Comparative Critique."

41. On the point about the multiple genealogies of race and racisms, see Goldberg, *Anatomy of Racism*; Macedo and Gounari, *Globalization of Racism*; Moore et al., *Race, Nature, and the Politics of Difference*.

42. For example, in his ethnography of the 2002 genocide of Muslims in Gujarat, "*Ahimsa*, Identification and Sacrifice in the Gujarat Pogrom," Ghassem-Fachandi notes that meat eating, excessive sexual appetites—especially for Hindu young women—and excessive violence is consistently ascribed to Muslims by majoritarian Hindus. See also Ghaseem-Pachandi, "The Hyperbolic Vegetarian."

43. See Jeffery and Jeffery, "Saffron Demography." Despite the fact that fertility rates among Muslims have decreased over time, the Hindu right has twisted data and reports to fan fears about an explosive fertility rate among Muslims, pejoratively called the Muslim growth rate, especially after the release of reports from the 2001 census. On this, see Bose, "Beyond Hindu-Muslim Growth Rates"; Gupta, "Censuses, Communalism, Gender, and Identity"; Gill, "Politics of Population Census Data in India."

44. Bharucha, "Muslims and Others," 4239.

45. Bacchetta, "When the (Hindu) Nation Exiles Its Queers," 143.

46. Khalidi, *Khaki and Ethnic Violence in India*.

47. V. N. Rai, quoted in Khalidi, *Khaki and Ethnic Violence in India*, 78.

48. Setalvad, "When Guardians Betray."

49. Brass, *The Production of Hindu-Muslim Violence in Contemporary India*; Das, *Life and Words*; Setalvad, "When Guardians Betray"; Pandey, "In Defence of the Fragment"; Pandey, "Hindus and Others"; Wilkinson, "Introduction." The violence unleashed in Gujarat in 2002 was preceded by instructions from none other than the director general of police, the highest-ranking police official in the state, to all police stations to gather detailed information on Muslims and Christians, whereas no such information was gathered on Hindu communities (Varadarajan, *Gujarat*).

50. Kapur, *Sikh Separatism*.

51. Axel, *The Nation's Tortured Body*.

52. Das, *Life and Words*.

53. Khalidi, *Khaki and Ethnic Violence in India*, 78.

54. For example, see Setalvad's "When Guardians Betray."

55. Gupta suggests that when police encounter those they perceive to be homosexual, they are likely to solicit money or sex, thereby committing the crimes

that they are supposed to be preventing ("Section 377 and the Dignity of Indian Homosexuals").

56. Radhakrishna, *Dishonored by History*, 2.

57. Narrain, *Queer*, 59.

58. Hereditary criminality is hard to account for a group that does not reproduce internally and must rely on socializing young and adult outsiders.

59. Radhakrishna, *Dishonored by History*, 55.

60. Puri, *Woman, Body, Desire in Post-Colonial India*.

61. *The Mahendra Caturvedi Practical Guide to Hindi-English Dictionary* associates *adhika'r* with right, entitlement, and even jurisdiction and occupation.

62. Richardson, "Constructing Sexual Citizenship."

63. I owe this point to a personal conversation with Maitrayee Chaudhuri.

64. Chatterjee, "Alienation, Intimacy, and Gender"; Cohen, "What Mrs. Besahara Saw."

65. Engaging Frantz Fanon's discussion of "epidermalization" in *Black Skins, White Masks*, Gilroy explains that it is about a historically specific system that makes bodies intelligible by endowing them with qualities of "color" (*Against Race*, 46).

66. Ghosh and Chakrabarty, "A Conversation on Provincializing Europe."

67. Balibar analyzes comparable forms of racisms, such as anti-Semitism, as "culturalist" racism, the kind that does not rely on the pseudo-biological concept of race as its driving force ("Is There a Neo-Racism?" 24). In "Race and the Possibilities of Comparative Critique" Loomba explains that Balibar's reference point is the racism directed largely at Muslim immigrants in Europe, but that this racialization of religion is hardly new and has deep historical roots. My purpose here is not to collapse the differences between unambiguously naturalized representations of race and the ones that naturalize qualities as innate to faith, but to connect their similarities.

68. Field notes, Chennai, July 2005. *Aravani* is the term preferred over *hijra* among some in the Chennai area. The arrests followed a report in the English-language daily *Indian Express*, itself based on complaints from middle-class residents in the area.

69. Section 8 B reads, "Solicits or molests any person, or loiters or acts in such manner as to cause obstruction or annoyance to persons residing nearby or passing by such public place or to offend against public decency for the purpose of prostitution."

Chapter 5

1. Civil Writ Petition 7455 of 2001.

2. In Mumbai a coalition including the Forum against the Oppression of Women (FAOW), the Human Rights Law Network, and Stree Sangam (now LABIA) led a signature campaign asking for Section 377 to be repealed. FAOW is the same

organization that conducted surveys among bar dancers in Mumbai and published reports to intervene in the state government's crackdown against the women performing in dance bars. As a nonfunded autonomous women's group, it brings together issues of labor, social class, and justice across sexual orientation and gender expressions. In Patna, a city in central India, an organization, AASRA, disseminated a pamphlet calling Section 377 an outdated colonial law and a health hazard (on file with the author).

3. http://nazindia.org, accessed May 17, 2011. Among its programs are outreach and a drop-in center for MSM; an outpatient clinic for people who are HIV-positive; home-based care for people living with AIDS; a care home for HIV-positive orphans; peer education–related training on gender-based violence and sexual health; and training programs, workshops, and resources related to HIV/AIDS and sexual health.

4. Shaleen Rakesh, Naz representative for the writ against Section 377, personal interview, July 2003. The Infinity Foundation in New Jersey, with Hindu nationalist leanings, initially provided a small amount of funding to Naz for the outpatient department. This is surprising given the group's leanings. However, this funding was inexplicably withdrawn, according to Anjali Gopalan, director of Naz (India) (personal communication, 2005).

5. Personal interview with Anjali Gopalan, June 2005. The point about police harassment was confirmed in a discussion group with Naz Foundation outreach workers, as one of them, Pammy, said at the outset in Hindi, "The police harass us, check our bags, hit and beat us, they threaten us that if we don't stop working, they will imprison us under Section 377" (group discussion, Naz, July 2005).

6. Lawyers' Collective HIV/AIDS Unit is based in Mumbai; see their website, http://www.lawyerscollective.org/.

7. Personal interview, July 2003.

8. Personal interview, July 2003.

9. Personal interview, June 2003.

10. ABVA published the groundbreaking book *Less Than Gay—A Citizens' Report on the Status of Homosexuality in India* (1991), in which it took a position against Section 377 by first seeking legislative recourse. It filed a writ in the Petitions Committee of Parliament in 1992 to repeal the law on the grounds that it violated fundamental rights, but when no member of Parliament was willing to introduce it as a bill for discussion, the writ was revised into a PIL and submitted to the Delhi High Court. The ABVA petition argued that Section 377 violated the following fundamental rights: right to protection against discrimination, right to freedom of speech and expression, and right to life and liberty, including the right to privacy—anticipating the Naz Foundation writ.

11. Baxi also notes the limitations of social action litigation in his essay "Taking Suffering Seriously." For a more thorough critique of PILs, see Aggrawal, *The Public Interest Litigation Hoax*.

12. Supreme Court of India, Compilation of Guidelines to be Followed for Entertaining Letters/Petitions Received in This Court as Public Interest Litigation, accessed May 18, 2011, http://supremecourtofindia.nic.in/circular/guidelines/pil guidelines.pdf. See the general principles of PIL in Upadhyay, *Public Interest Litigation in India*, 10–12.

13. For a useful overview of the cultural climate of the 1990s and thereafter from the perspective of same-sex desire, see Shahani, *Gay Bombay*.

14. See Kapur, *Erotic Justice*; Patel, "On Fire"; Dave, *Queer Activism*.

15. This was also the period that resulted in landmark legal judgments alternately upholding and undermining the rights of HIV-positive persons.

16. Cohen, "The Kothi Wars."

17. Despite the law criminalizing same-sex sexual practices, NACO recognizes the presence of MSM and their susceptibility to HIV/AIDS and directs prevention efforts toward them.

18. Personal interview, June 2003.

19. For descriptions of the articles of fundamental rights, see Bakshi, *The Constitution of India*.

20. The position that privacy is the right to be left alone is attributed to Thomas Cooley; see, Glancy, "The Invention of the right to Privacy."

21. Civil Writ Petition 7455, 23.

22. Civil Writ Petition 7455, 46.

23. Civil Writ Petition 7455, 18.

24. In 2001 in the city of Lucknow, nine members of two NGOs, Bharosa Trust and Naz Foundational International, focused on HIV/AIDS, were arrested by the police and held in prison for forty-five days and charged under Section 377, among other penal codes.

25. For a useful account of the early responses and concerns especially of lesbian feminist groups in Delhi and Mumbai to the Naz Foundation writ, see Dave, *Queer Activism*.

26. Personal interview, May 2005.

27. See Basu, *She Comes to Take Her Rights*; Menon, "Rights, Bodies and the Law."

28. Personal interview, June 2005.

29. Personal interview, June 2005. The memorandum shows the following organizations represented at the meeting: All India Women's Conference, Butterflies, CALERI, Human Right Law Network, Humnawaz, Humrahi, Naz, Nirantar, Partners for Law and Development, Positive Life, Sakshi, Sangini, TORCH, Women's Right Initiative, and Young Women's Christian Association (on file with the author). Letters of interest but regrets for being unable to attend were sent by Joint Women's Program, Jagori, UNIFEM, TARSHI, AAG, and Parivar Seva Sansthan.

30. While the meeting in Bangalore was held in December 2000 and the one in Mumbai in early 2001, I could not ascertain the precise dates.

31. The letter was dated January 8, 2002 (on file with the author).

32. On file with author.

33. Even though transcripts are not available, the list of orders given by the presiding justices can be obtained through the Delhi High Court and are on file with the author.

34. The JACK intervention was filed by the legal counsel Ravi Shankar Kumar on November 25, 2002.

35. In my joint interview with Mulloli and Singh, Mulloli took the position that there is little evidence to support claims of the prevalence of HIV and that the crisis is the effect of a conspiracy between the multinationals, the U.S. Central Intelligence Agency, politicians, police, NACO, government bureaucrats, and, not least, NGOs like Naz.

36. In the interview with Mulloli and Singh, Mulloli made no bones about the fact that he had an axe to grind with Anjali Gopalan and Naz Foundation as an organization. Not surprisingly the counteraffidavit questions the integrity of both Naz Foundation and the Lawyers' Collective.

37. Counter Affidavit on Behalf of Respondent Joint Action Council Kannur, Civil Writ Petition 7455 of 2001, 2.

38. The order was dated November 27, 2002.

39. For an earlier take on the government's reply, see Puri, "Sexualizing the State."

40. Rakesh Shukla, "Getting the State out of the Bedroom," *Indian Express*, October 30, 2003, accessed July 21, 2011, http://www.indianexpress.com/oldStory/34330/.

41. Counter Affidavit on Behalf of Respondent No. 5, Civil Writ Petition 7455/2001, 2003, 4–5.

42. In June 2003 I met with the director at the Judicial Division, G. Venkatesh, who supervised the drafting of the government's reply, and his successor, Kamala Bhasin, in May 2005. Perhaps because he was no longer at the Judicial Division, Venkatesh was forthcoming about the process through which the government's response was formulated, which was confirmed by subsequent interviews in the department, including with the joint secretary. Even though he was transferred to a completely different state institution by then, I met Venkatesh again in May 2005 since he was still following the Naz legal case with interest. I have also used pseudonyms here because of the first director's request for anonymity.

43. Throughout the interview he sought information related to homosexuality but quickly asserted distance at my offer to make resources accessible to him, perhaps because the interview occurred a few months before the government filed its reply in September 2003.

44. Counter Affidavit on Behalf of Respondent No. 5, Civil Writ Petition 7455/2001, 2003, 5.

45. Counter Affidavit on Behalf of Respondent No. 5, Civil Writ Petition 7455/2001, 2003, 11.

46. Interview, New Delhi, May 2005.

47. Interview, New Delhi, June 2005.

48. *Naz Foundation v. Govt. of NCT Delhi & Ors*, Delhi High Court, September 2, 2004.

49. Remarkably the Delhi meetings were held at the office of Saheli, indicating the sea change in positions among those who had been Naz Foundation's fiercest critics. Humsafar Trust hosted the meeting in Mumbai.

50. While the upper courts may rule on any laws, matters of fundamental rights are brought before the Supreme Court.

51. As many as 140 people attended the Bangalore meeting, representing some forty-six organizations, and thirty-seven organizations participated in the January 2005 meeting in Mumbai.

52. The minutes are on file with the author.

53. An SLP may be filed when an appeal to a high court or tribunal to review its decision is turned down and a petitioner wishes to challenge the order. For more details, see the Supreme Court of India website, http://supremecourtofindia.nic.in/.

54. At the final meeting in Mumbai, forty-nine participants supported and only five opposed filing an SLP in the Supreme Court.

55. This was later converted to Civil Appeal No. 952 of 2006.

56. *PUCL and Anr. v. Union of India* 9 SCC 580, Supreme Court of India, 2004.

57. SLP (Civil) No. 7217-7218 of 2005, 12.

58. The government's reply to the Naz Foundation SLP in the Supreme Court was filed promptly on September 26, 2005.

59. Government's reply to SLP (Civil) No. 7217-7218 of 2005, 7.

60. Government's reply to SLP (Civil) No. 7217-7218 of 2005, 8.

61. Supreme Court order, February 3, 2006.

62. Menon, "Rights, Bodies and the Law," 286; Menon, *Recovering Subversion*.

63. Basu, *She Comes to Take Her Rights*.

64. Personal interview, July 2003.

65. Derrida, "Force of Law."

66. Anand Grover, personal interview, July 2003.

67. Kaviraj, introduction to *Politics in India*, 11.

Chapter 6

1. Epigraph text is available at http://kafila.org/2013/12/11/justice-will-prevail/.

2. More than one critic has noted that the ruling seems hastily written. See Khaitan's discussion of the Supreme Court justices' considerable docket that likely accounts for the ruling's cavalier tone, "*Koushal v Naz*."

3. For further information on Voices against Section 377, see their facebook page: https://www.facebook.com/voicesagainst377.

4. Personal interview, May 2005.

5. "Campaigning for Sexuality Minority Rights," Sangama, February 3, 2007,

accessed July 26, 2011,http://sangama.org/campaigns/SexualityMinorityRights #attachments.

6. Among the most egregious examples of lurid reporting was on the murder of two men, Pushkin and Kuldeep, in what came to be called the Pushkin affair. For a useful analytical commentary, see Cohen, "Song for Pushkin."

7. First pioneered in Kolkata in 2003, the gay/queer pride or queer *azadi* (freedom) march became an annual event in the major metropoles by 2008, and also gradually began to be organized in the smaller cities.

8. Alternative Law Forum, accessed August 31, 2011, http://www.altlawforum .org/. That law is inherently political was the guiding orientation of the Alternative Law Forum when it was established in 2000 as a legal service provider focusing on issues of social and economic injustice. Arvind Narrain is a founding member.

9. The Voices coalition included Amnesty International India, Campaign for Human Rights; Anjuman, the JNU Students' Queer Collective; Breakthrough: Building Human Rights Culture; CREA (Creating Resources for Empowerment and Action); Haq, Centre for Child Rights; Jagori, Women's Training, Documentation and Resource Centre; Nigah Media Collective; Nirantar, Centre of Gender and Education; Partners for Law in Development, Legal Resource Group; PRISM (Persons for the Rights of Sexual Minorities), a forum for issues relating to sexual and gender identities; Saheli Women's Resource Centre, an autonomous women's group; SAMA, Resource Group for Women and Health; TARSHI (Talking about Reproductive and Sexual Health Issues). The coalition's leadership came in part from PRISM, whose members brought experience in responding to human rights violations as well as doing advocacy work with the state, and was supplemented by representatives of other groups, especially Nirantar and TARSHI. An autonomous forum, PRISM was created in 2001 to help free the four workers of Bharosa Trust, an HIV/AIDS-related organization based in the city of Lucknow, who were charged under Section 377, among other codes, for doing HIV/AIDS advocacy work.

10. Civil Miscellaneous writ of 2006 in the matter of CWP No. 7455 of 2001, 13, on file with the author.

11. Civil Miscellaneous Writ, 20.

12. Civil Miscellaneous Writ, 28.

13. In 2006 Lucknow police arrested four persons at a restaurant, falsely charging them under Section 377 for having sex in a public place.

14. The equivalence between sati and decriminalizing homosexuality was also noted by state agents in the Ministry of Home Affairs but excised from the government's reply filed in the Delhi High Court in 2003 (see chapter 5).

15. Gautam Bhan, "On Freedom's Avenue," *Indian Express*, July 3, 2009, accessed September 7, 2011, http://lassnet.blogspot.com/2009/07/on-freedoms-avenue.html. Also reprinted in Narrain and Eldridge, *The Right That Dares to Speak Its Name*. Complete information about this decision is available at International Gay and Lesbian Human Rights Commission, 2012, www.iglhrc.org.

16. Atul is a pseudonym.

17. However, the news made barely a dent in the U.S. media, which at the time was captivated by Michael Jackson's death.

18. For example, see Agnes, *Law and Gender Inequality*; Menon, *Recovering Subversion*. Menon problematizes the feminist argument that what is needed to protect women in India, and elsewhere, from sexual assault are better formulated laws. She points to the decreasing number of successful convictions and the assumption underlying even successful convictions.

19. The court interpreted the Naz Foundation writ as a plea with two options: declare Section 377 constitutionally invalid insofar as it affects private sexual acts among consenting adults or simply narrow Section 377 to exclude the same (*Naz Foundation v. Government of NCT of Delhi and Others*, WP(C) 7455/2001, High Court of Delhi at New Delhi, July 2, 2009, 23, on file with the author; the full text of the judgment can be accessed at http://lobis.nic.in/dhc/APS/judgement/02–07–2009/APS02072009CW74552001.pdf). On the issue of health as a fundamental right, the justices take their cue from the International Covenant on Economic, Social and Cultural Rights, "International Covenant on Economic, Social, and Cultural Rights," Office of the United Nations High Commissioner for Human Rights, accessed September 6, 2011, http://www.availablea.ohchr.org/EN/ProfessionalInterest/Pages/CESCR.aspx. Especially see Article 12 on matters of health.

20. Numerous citations in the judgment supporting the decision to decriminalize homosexuality were introduced during court hearings by the legal counsel for Voices. They included references to the Yogyakarta Principles, which oblige states to respect, protect, and fulfill the human rights of all persons regardless of their sexual orientation or gender identity; a study on the impact of sodomy laws on homosexuals in South Africa by the legal scholar Ryan Goodman; the Criminal Tribes Act; case law from Fiji and Nepal; and the *Lawrence v. Texas* decision in the United States.

21. *Naz v. Government*, 26.

22. *Naz v. Government*, 83.

23. Narrain and Eldridge, *The Right That Dares to Speak Its Name*.

24. *Naz v. Government*, 97, 100.

25. A particularly useful document is Narrain and Eldridge, *The Right That Dares to Speak Its Name*.

26. From all accounts, Siras was secretly videotaped having sex with another man and suspended from his position at the university as a result. Although a regional high court ordered his reinstatement, he was subsequently found dead, apparently from suicide. A highly publicized case, it stirred much discussion about the role of the university in framing Siras but also the ineffectiveness of the Delhi High Court's ruling to protect individuals like him from harm.

27. Vikram Raghavan, "Taking Sexuality Seriously: The Supreme Court and the

Koushal Case," *Law and Other Things*, December 14, 2013, accessed March 5, 2014, http://lawandotherthings.blogspot.in/2013/12/taking-sexuality-seriously-supreme.html. For the full text of the judgment, see Civil Appeal No. 10972 of 2013, Supreme Court of India, http://judis.nic.in/supremecourt/imgs1.aspx?filename=41070.

28. Vaibhav Vats, "A Conversation with Lawyer and Activist Gautam Bhan," *New York Times*, December 11, 2013, accessed March 5, 2014, http://india.blogs.nytimes.com/2013/12/11/a-conversation-with-lawyer-and-activist-gautam-bhan/?_php=true&_type=blogs&_r=0.

29. *Suresh Kumar Koushal and another v. Naz Foundation and others*, Civil Appeal No. 10972 of 2013, Supreme Court of India, New Delhi, December 11, 2013, 57.

30. For particularly useful analyses by legal scholars, see Raghavan, "Taking Sexuality Seriously"; Khaitan, "*Koushal v Naz*"; Gautam Bhatia, "The Unbearable Wrongness of *Koushal v. Naz*, *Outlook*, December 11, 2013, http://www.outlookindia.com/article/the-unbearable-wrongness-of-koushal-vs-naz/288823.

31. The unofficial transcripts for the Delhi High Court hearings were posted on the Yahoo group LGBT-India, then edited and reproduced in the primer on the 2009 judgment, Narrain and Eldridge, *The Right That Dares to Speak Its Name*. The transcripts for the Supreme Court hearings were compiled from various note takers present at the time and posted on the Yahoo group LGBT-India primarily by Vikram Doctor. A sanitized version of the transcripts is available at http://www.globalhealthrights.org/wp-content/uploads/2013/12/Koushal-v.-Naz-Foundation-record-of-proceedings.pdf.

32. Vikram Doctor, day three of the hearings, posted on the listserv LGBT-India, posted Februay 16, 2012, accessed March 7, 2014. An edited version of these hearings can also be found at http://orinam.net/supreme-court-hearings-on-naz-full-transcript-2012/.

33. *Naz v. Government* also includes a discussion of Sections 375 and 376 but in the context of the 172nd Law Commission's recommendation to amend these provisions and, at the same time, delete Section 377.

34. "Supreme Court Judgement on Section 377," Orinam, 2013, accessed March 7, 2014, http://orinam.net/377/supreme-court-verdict-2013/, 7.

35. Baxi, "*Suresh Koushal v. Naz Foundation.*"

36. I consider the sexual assault laws more fully in the conclusion to this book and make the point that they were hastily passed in the aftermath of the rape and death of a young woman in Delhi. Still, this incorrect point, that Section 377 had been come up repeatedly in Parliament, was introduced by a representative for the government, Additional Solicitor General P. P. Malhotra, who also initially misled the court into thinking that the government was indeed continuing to challenge the Delhi High Court's bid to decriminalize homosexuality. As it turned out, the government did not seek to challenge the outcome and was not an appellant in the Supreme Court.

37. Gupta and Sivaramakrishnan, "Introduction."

38. On the concept of law struggles, see Sundar, "The Rule of Law and the Rule of Property," 188. Also see Gupta and Sivaramakrishnan, "Introduction."

39. For particularly useful commentaries on the postliberalization context, see Gupta and Sivaramakrishnan, "Introduction"; Sharma and Gupta, "Introduction"; Sharma, "Crossbreeding Institutions, Breeding Struggle."

40. For useful critiques of the gay rights regime, see Duggan, *The Twilight of Equality?*; Richardson, *Desiring Sameness*; Brown, *States of Injury*; Collins and Talcott, "A New Language."

41. Consider here the predication of funding from the West on the promotion of gay rights in settings such as India.

42. *Naz v. Government*, 34.

43. The key cases include *Kharak Singh v. The State of U.P.* (1964), *Gobind v. State of M.P.* (1975), *Maneka Gandhi v. Union of India* (1978), R. *Rajagopal v. State of T.N.* (1994), and *District Registrar and Collector, Hyderabad and Another v. Canara Bank and Another* (2005).

44. *Naz v. Government*, 39–40.

45. For example, see Vikram Raghavan's argument that the Delhi High Court's persuasively nuanced reasoning presented a nonspatial and portable understanding of privacy, "Navigating the Noteworthy and Nebulous in Naz Foundation-1," *Law and Other Things*, July 7, 2009, accessed January 5, 2010, http://lawandotherthings.blogspot.com/2009/07/navigating-noteworthy-and-nebulous-in.html. In a subsequent post Raghavan qualifies his praise of this delocalized understanding of privacy that is presented mostly through selective citations of case law and not adequately supported by a substantive discussion by the justices: "Navigating the Noteworthy and Nebulous in Naz Foundation—Part II," *Law and Other Things*, July 8, 2009, accessed January 5, 2010, http://lawandotherthings.blogspot.com/2009/07/navigating-noteworthy-and-nebulous-in_08.html.

46. Franke, "The Domesticated Liberty of *Lawrence v. Texas*."

47. See Shah's discussion of the implications of the *Lawrence v. Texas* decision, "Policing Privacy, Migrants, and the Limits of Freedom."

48. The sexual health perspective in which the writ is framed means that though lesbians and bisexual women, hijras, and others are included, the focus remains on those who are seen as especially vulnerable to the spread of HIV and AIDS-related complications, namely MSM and gay men. The police have frequently used Section 377 to intimidate lesbians and bisexual women, often at the behest of family members. Even though lesbians are not immune to the threat of Section 377, they are sidelined in the writ as a group at low risk for HIV infections. Especially since the language of the law emphasizes penetration in its explanation of Section of 377, it leaves open the possibility of prosecuting lesbians.

49. If only private consenting sex were to be excluded from the purview of Section 377, same-sex sexual activity in public would still carry the harsh punishment

of up to ten years' imprisonment. On the other hand, without the proviso of privacy, same-sex sexual activity in public would be treated similarly to heterosexual activity in public, which means being charged under a different and less harsh section of the Indian Penal Code.

50. While not all males who have sex with males are economically marginal, the term MSM was coined to set apart typically lower-middle-class and poor males from middle- and upper-class English-speaking men who are likely to identify as gay. See Khan, "Kothi, Gays and (Other) MSM"; Khan, "A Rose by Any Other Name."

51. Sharma, *Logics of Empowerment.*

52. I am grateful to Chaitanya Lakkimsetti for sharing with me B. P. Singhal's intervention. For a fuller discussion of his intervention, see Lakkimsetti, "Governing Sexualities." B. P. Singhal is a former director general of police, erstwhile member of Parliament, a bureaucrat, and appointee to the Central Board of Film Certification. His intervention haphazardly spanned issues of homosexuality, criminality, health, and public well-being, among others.

53. For the text of Ambedkar's speech, see "Constituent Assembly of India."

54. On this point, see also Narrain and Eldridge, *The Right That Dares to Speak Its Name.*

55. *Naz v. Government*, 22.

56. "Constituent Assembly of India."

57. Narrain, "Persecuting Difference."

58. The *Naz v. Government* judgment quotes Ambedkar at length to argue that constitutional principles—especially a commitment to equality—and democratic values need to be cultivated in the Indian context. On the point about the values of a democratic nation, see Mehta, "Its about All of Us," On the issue of sexual citizenship, see Gitanjali Misra, "Decriminalising Homosexuality in India," Reproductive Health Matters, 2009, accessed February 2, 2012, http://www.countmeinconference.org/downloads/RHM.MISRA.pdf. In a commentary entitled "Good for All Minorities," Khaitan argues that if the *Naz v. Government* judgment were to be upheld by the Supreme Court, it would provide unprecedented constitutional protection from discrimination to all vulnerable minorities (120). In a longer version of the commentary, "Reading *Swaraj* into Article 15," *Khaitan* makes the thought-provoking case that the potential innovation of the judgment does not solely lie in the fact that it has extended the list of factors in the constitutional right to prohibition from discrimination to include sexual orientation, but also in linking protection from discrimination to matters of personal autonomy and the strict scrutiny test (limiting the state's infringement of constitutional protections).

59. Liang and Narrain, "Striving for Magic in the City of Words."

60. For example, see Kapur and Cossman, "On Women, Equality and the Constitution."

61. In his review of the discourse of minorities, "India's Minorities," Weiner ar-

gues that the category has come to mean non-Hindu in which Muslims and Sikhs loom especially large as minority groups.

62. Hasan, "Social Inequalities, Secularism and Minorities in India's Democracy."

63. Pandey, *The Construction of Communalism in Colonial North India*, 271; Pandey, "The Secular State and the Limits of Dialogue."

64. *Koushal v. Naz*, 96.

65. References to Coca-Cola and fashion parades occurred during the hearings.

66. Spivak, *A Critique of Postcolonial Reason*, 361.

67. Narrain, "Queering Democracy," 3–4.

68. Rancière, *Dis-Agreement*.

69. On this point, also see Narrain and Gupta, introduction to *Law Like Love*, xxii.

70. Legal scholars have noted that the senior Supreme Court justice has not shied away from judicial activism in previous cases and assuredly not in a ruling he delivered merely forty-eight hours before *Koushal v. Naz*, in which he issued sweeping orders to curb the abuse of red lights on government cars (thereby giving government and state officials special privileges); for example, see Vikram Raghavan, "Taking Sexuality Seriously: The Supreme Court and the Koushal Case, Part II," *Law and Other Things*, December 16, 2013, accessed April 2, 2014, http://www.lawandotherthings.blogspot.in/2013/12/taking-sexuality-seriously-supreme_16.html.

Afterlives

1. The full text of this judgment can be found at Writ Petition (Civil) No. 400 of 2012, Supreme Court of India, http://supremecourtofindia.nic.in/outtoday/wc40012.pdf.

2. The first seventy-four pages are attributed to Justice K. S. Radhakrishnan; Justice A. K. Sikri elaborates, clarifies, and sharpens the spirit of the ruling in the rest of the document.

3. Aniruddha Dutta, "Thoughts on the Supreme Court Judgment on Transgender Recognition and Rights," Orinam, April 19, 2014, accessed September 22, 2014, http://orinam.net/thoughts-supreme-court-judgment-transgender-recognition-rights/.

4. *Nirbhaya*, which translates as *fearless*, was the pseudonym popularly assigned to the young woman to shield her identity. The contexts of sexual violence vary considerably; while violence occurs at the hands of the military and paramilitary forces in Kashmir and the Northeastern States under military occupation, the troubling mix of caste and gender exposes Dalit women to higher caste men in the states of Haryana and Punjab. The systematic targeting of Sikh women in Delhi in 1984 and Muslim women in Gujarat in 2002 speaks to how women of minority religious communities are vulnerable during pogroms and genocide (see Tanika Sarkar, "Ethnic Cleansing in Gujarat; Sarkar, "Semiotics of Terror"; Citizen's Ini-

tiative, "How Has the Gujarat Massacre Affected Minorty Women?"). Numerous reports also document the fact that sexual violence is not limited to women and girls but also includes the shocking extent of sexual violence by police against hijras, kothis, and other queer subjects.

5. See the numerous critical interventions by a range of commentators and collectives published on the blog site Kafila.org.

6. The full text of the report is available at "Report of the Committee on Amendments to Criminal Law," January 23, 2013, accessed February 2, 2013. http://www.thehindu.com/multimedia/archive/01340/Justice_Verma_Comm_1340438a.pdf.

7. For a critical overview of sexual violence as it is believed to play out at the village level in India, see Grewal, "Outsourcing Patriarchy."

8. Contrary to the "Justice Verma Committee Report," marital rape is omitted from the modifications, unless the couple resides separately. For additional critiques of the Criminal Law (Amendment) Act of 2013, see Aarti Mundkur and Arvind Narrain, "Betraying the Third Way," *Hindu*, April 19, 2013, accessed June 5, 2013, http://www.thehindu.com/opinion/op-ed/betraying-the-third-way/article4630899.ece; Madhu Mehra, "Taking Stock of the New Anti-Rape Law," Kafila, May 5, 2013, accessed June 5, 2013, http://kafila.org/2013/05/05/taking-stock-of-the-new-anti-rape-law-madhu-mehra/.

9. Ratna Kapur, "The New Sexual Security Regime," *Hindu*, February 5, 2013, accessed June 5, 2013, http://www.thehindu.com/opinion/op-ed/the-new-sexual-security-regime/article4379317.ece.

10. For particularly useful analyses of sexuality, state, and immigration, see Lubhéid, *Entry Denied*; Lubhéid, "Queer/Migration"; Shah, *Stranger Intimacy*.

11. Civil Writ Petition No. 3170 of 2001, on file with the author.

12. Ramachandran, "'Operation Pushback.'

13. Ramachandran, "'Operation Pushback'; Citizen's Campaign for Preserving Democracy, "Democracy, Citizens, and Migrants: Nationalism in the Era of Globalization," Delhi, 2005.

14. Quoted in Dutt's writ to Delhi High court, CWP No. 3170 of 2001, 8, on file with the author.

15. Personal interview, November 2009.

16. The justices directed state agencies, especially the Delhi Police and the Union of India, to deport at least one hundred unauthorized Bangladeshi migrants from the city on a daily basis. To better understand the procedures I followed up with police in charge of the Bangladeshi cells in Delhi police stations that are aimed apprehending and deporting migrants. Among other things, these meetings confirmed what activists have long claimed, that it is typically difficult to decipher between Indian Muslim Bengalis and Muslim Bangladeshi migrants and that police often rely on information provided by informants in immigrant communities.

17. Personal interview, November 2009.

18. Canaday, *The Straight State*. Canaday describes the historical role of the Bureau of Immigration, the military, and federal agencies in the United States in disbursing welfare benefits and, in the process, producing homosexuality as a category of differential citizenship.

19. Mendras, *Russian Politics*. Also see Robinson, *Russia*.

20. Essig, *Queer in Russia*.

21. See Miriam Elder, "Russia Passes Law Banning Gay 'Propaganda,'" *Guardian*, June 11, 2013, accessed October 17, 2014, http://www.theguardian.com/world/2013/jun/11/russia-law-banning-gay-propaganda.

BIBLIOGRAPHY

Abram, Simone, Jonathan Murdoch, and Terry Marsden. "Planning by Numbers: Migration and Statistical Governance." In *Migration into Rural Areas: Theories and Issues*, edited by Paul Boyle and Keith Halfacree. Chichester, NY: Wiley, 1998.

Abrams, Philip. "Notes on the Difficulty of Studying the State (1977)." *Journal of Historical Sociology* 1.1 (1988): 58–89.

Agamben, Giorgio. *Homo Sacer: Sovereign Power and Bare Life*. Translated by Daniel Heller-Roazen. Stanford, CA: Stanford University Press, 1995.

Aggrawal, Shobha. *The Public Interest Litigation Hoax: Truth before the Nation. A Citizen's Report on How PIL Fails to Provide Justice to Those Who Need It Most*. New Delhi: Shobha PIL Watch Group, 2005.

Agnes, Flavia. "Hypocritical Morality: Mumbai's Ban on Bar Dancers." *Manushi* 149 (2005): 10–19.

———. *Law and Gender Inequality*. New Delhi: Oxford University Press, 1999.

———. "Protecting Women against Violence?" In *State and Politics in India*, edited by Partha Chatterjee. New Delhi: Oxford University Press, 1997.

———. State Control and Sexual Morality: The Case of the Bar Dancers of Mumbai." In *Enculturing Law: New Agendas for Legal Pedagog*, edited by Matthew John and Sitharamam Kakarala. New Delhi: Tulika Books, 2007.

———. "The Right to Dance: Mumbai High Court Judgment Strikes the Right Note." *Manushi* 154 (2005): 20–24.

Alexander, Jacqui M. "Not Just (Any) Body Can Be a Citizen: The Politics of Law, Sexuality, and Postcoloniality in Trinidad and Tobago and the Bahamas." *Feminist Review* 48 (1994): 5–23.

———. *Pedagogies of Crossing: Meditations on Feminism, Sexual Politics, Memory, and the Sacred*. Durham: Duke University Press, 2005.

———. "Redrafting Morality: The Postcolonial State and the Sexual Offences

Bill of Trinidad and Tobago." In *Third World Women and the Politics of Feminism*, edited by Chandra Talpade Mohanty, Ann Russo, and Lourdes Torres. Bloomington: Indiana University Press, 1991.

Amar, Paul E., ed. *New Racial Missions of Policing: International Perspectives on Evolving Law Enforcement Practices*. London: Routledge, 2011.

Anandhi, S. "Feminist Contributions from the Margins: Shifting Conceptions of Work and Performance of the Bar Dancers of Mumbai." *Economic and Political Weekly* 45.44–45 (2010).

Appadurai, Arjun. "Number in the Colonial Imagination." In *Orientalism and the Postcolonial Predicament*, edited by Carol A. Breckenridge and Peter van der Veer. Philadelphia: University of Pennsylvania Press, 1993.

Arendt, Hannah. *Origins of Totalitarianism*. San Diego: Harcourt, 1968.

Aretxaga, Begoña. "The Sexual Games of the Body Politic: Fantasy and State Violence in Northern Ireland." *Culture, Medicine and Psychiatry* 25.1 (2001): 1–27.

———. *States of Terror: Begoña Aretxaga's Essays*. Edited by Joseba Zulaika. Reno, NV: Center for Basque Studies, 2005.

Arnold, David. "Bureaucratic Recruitment and Subordination in Colonial India: The Madras Constabulary 1859–1947." In *Subaltern Studies IV: Writings on South Asian History and Society*, edited by Ranajit Guha. New York: Oxford University Press, 1990.

Arondekar, Anjali. *For the Record: On Sexuality and the Colonial Archive in India*. Durham: Duke University Press, 2009.

Axel, Brian Keith. *The Nation's Tortured Body: Violence, Representation, and the Formation of the Sikh "Diaspora."* Durham: Duke University Press, 2001.

Bacchetta, Paola. "When the (Hindu) Nation Exiles Its Queers." *Social Text* 17.4 (1999): 141–66.

Bakshi, P. M. *The Constitution of India*. 6th ed. Delhi: Universal Law Publishing, 2005.

Balibar, Etienne. "Is There a Neo-Racism?" In *Race, Nation, Class: Ambiguous Identities*, edited by Etienne Balibar and Immanuel Maurice Wallerstein. New York: Verso, 2011.

Banerjee-Guha, Swapna. "Neoliberalising the 'Urban': New Geographies of Power and Injustice in Indian Cities." *Economic and Political Weekly*, 44.22 (2009): 95–107.

Basu, Srimati. "Sexual Property: Staging Rape and Marriage in Indian Law and Feminist Theory." *Feminist Studies* 37.1 (2011): 185–211.

———. *She Comes to Take Her Rights: Indian Women, Property, and Propriety*. Albany: State University of New York Press, 1999.

Baxi, Pratiksha. "*Suresh Koushal v. Naz Foundation*: Pratiksha Baxi." Kafila. December 16, 2013. Accessed March 7, 2014. http://kafila.org/2013/12/16/suresh-koushal-v-naz-foundation-pratiksha-baxi/.

Baxi, Upendra. "Taking Suffering Seriously: Social Action Litigation in the Supreme Court of India." *Third World Legal Studies* 4 (1985): 107–32.

Bell, Jeannine. "The Police and Policing." In the *Blackwell Companion to Law and Society*, edited by Austin Sarat. Oxford: Blackwell, 2004.

Belur, Jyoti. "Why Do the Police Use Deadly Force? Explaining Police Encounters in Mumbai." *British Journal of Criminology* 50 (2010): 320–41.

Berlant, Lauren, ed. "Intimacy." Special issue of *Critical Inquiry* 24.2 (1998): 281–88.

———. *The Queen of America Goes to Washington City: Essays on Sex and Citizenship.* Durham: Duke University Press, 1997.

Bernstein, Mary. "Paths to Homophobia." *Sexuality and Research Policy* 1.2 (2004): 41–55.

Bernstein, Mary, and Constance Kostelac. "Lavender and Blue: Attitudes about Homosexuality and Behavior toward Lesbians and Gay Men among Police Officers." *Journal of Contemporary Criminal Justice* 18.3 (2002): 302–28.

Bharucha, Rustom. "Muslims and Others: Anecdotes, Fragments, and Uncertainties of Evidence." *Economic and Political Weekly* 38.40 (2003): 4238–50.

Bhaskaran, Suparna. *Made in India: Decolonizations, Queer Sexualities, Transnational Projects.* New York: Palgrave Macmillan, 2004.

———. "The Politics of Penetration: Section 377 of the Indian Penal Code." In *Queering India: Same-Sex Love and Eroticism in Indian Culture and Society*, edited by Ruth Vanita. New York: Routledge, 2001.

Blackstone's Commentaries on the Laws of England. Avalon Project. Accessed December 15, 2010. http://avalon.law.yale.edu/subject_menus/blackstone.asp.

Bose, Ashish. "Beyond Hindu-Muslim Growth Rates: Understanding Socio-Economic Reality." *Economic and Political Weekly* 40.5 (2005): 370–74.

Bose, Brinda. Introduction to *Translating Desire: The Politics of Gender and Culture in India*, edited by Brinda Bose. New Delhi: Katha, 2002.

Brass, Paul. *The Production of Hindu-Muslim Violence in Contemporary India.* Seattle: University of Washington Press, 2003.

Bray, Alan. *Homosexuality in Renaissance England.* New York: Columbia University Press, 1996.

Brown, Michael P., and Paul Boyle. "National Closets: Governmentality, Sexuality, and the Census." In *Closet Space: Geographies of Metaphor from the Body to the Globe*, edited by Michael P. Brown. London: Routledge, 2000.

Brown, Wendy. *States of Injury: Power and Freedom in Late Modernity.* Princeton: Princeton University Press, 1995.

Brown, Wendy, and Janet Halley, "Introduction." In *Left Legalism / Left Critique*, edited by Wendy Brown and Janet Halley. Durham: Duke University Press, 2002.

Bumiller, Kristin. *In an Abusive State: How Neoliberalism Appropriated the Feminist Movement against Sexual Violence.* Durham: Duke University Press, 2008.

Bunsha, Dionne. "Morality Check in Mumbai." *Frontline.* Online. http://www

.frontline.in/static/html/fl2209/stories/20050506001104700.htm. Accessed January 26, 2011.

Butalia, Urvashi. *The Other Side of Silence: Voices from the Partition of India*. Durham: Duke University Press, 2000.

Canaday, Margot. *The Straight State: Sexuality and Citizenship in Twentieth-Century America*. Princeton: Princeton University Press, 2009.

Charusheela, S. "Gender and the Stability of Consumption: A Feminist Contribution to Post-Keynesian Economics." *Cambridge Journal of Economics*, 34.6 (2008): 1145–56.

Chatterjee, Indrani. "Alienation, Intimacy, and Gender: Problems for a History of Love in South Asia." In *Queering India: Same-Sex Love and Eroticism in Indian Culture and Society*, edited by Ruth Vanita. New York: Routledge, 2001.

———. *Gender, Slavery, and Law in Colonial India*. New Delhi: Oxford University Press, 1999.

Chatterjee, Partha. "Introduction: A Political History of Independent India." In *State and Politics in India*, edited by Partha Chatterjee. New Delhi: Oxford University Press, 1997.

Chatterjee, Partha, and Gyanendra Pandey, eds. *Subaltern Studies*. Vol. 7: *Writings on South Asian History and Society*. New Delhi: Oxford University Press, 1993.

Chatterji, Angana. *Violent Gods: Hindu Nationalism in India's Present; Narratives from Orissa*. Gurgaon, Haryana: Three Essays Collective, 2009.

Chauncey, George. *Gay New York: Gender, Urban Culture and the Making of the Gay Male World, 1890–1940*. New York: Basic Books, 1994.

Citizen's Campaign for Preserving Democracy. "Democracy, Citizens, and Migrants: Nationalism in the Era of Globalization." A Report. Delhi: Hazard's Centre, 2005.

Citizen's Initiative. "How Has the Gujarat Massacre Affected Minority Women? The Survivors Speak." Coalition against Communalism, April 16, 2002. Accessed January 28, 2011. http://cac.ektaonline.org/resources/reports/womens report.htm.

Cohen, Ed. *Talk on the Wilde Side: Toward a Genealogy of a Discourse on Male Sexualities*. New York: Routledge, 1993.

Cohen, Lawrence. "The Kothi Wars: AIDS Cosmopolitanism and the Morality of Classification." In *Sex in Development: Science, Sexuality, and Morality in Global Perspective*, edited by Vicanne Adams and Stacy Leigh Pigg. Durham: Duke University Press, 2005.

———. "Song for Pushkin." In *Law Like Love: Queer Perspectives on Law*, edited by Arvind Narrain and Alok Gupta. New Delhi: Yoda Press, 2011.

———. "What Mrs. Besahara Saw: Reflections on the Gay Goonda" In *Queering Inida: Same-sex Love and Eroticism in Indian Culture and Society*, edited by Ruth Vanita. New York: Routledge, 2002.

Cohn, Bernard S. *Colonialism and Its Forms of Knowledge: The British in India*. Princeton: Princeton University Press, 1996.

Collins, Dana, and Molly Talcott. "A New Language that Speaks of Change Just as It Steps Toward It: Transnationalism, Erotic Justice and Queer Human Rights Praxis." *Sociology Compass* 5.7 (2011): 576–90.

"Constituent Assembly of India, Volume II," Parliament of India, November 4, 1948, accessed January 6, 2012, http://indiankanoon.org/doc/843976/.

Cooper, Davina. "An Engaged State: Sexuality, Governance, and the Potential for Change." *Journal of Law and Society* 20.3 (1993): 257–75.

Corrigan, Philip, and Derek Sayer. *The Great Arch: English State Formation as Cultural Revolution*. Oxford: Basil Blackwell, 1985.

Das, Veena. *Life and Words: Violence and the Descent into the Ordinary*. Los Angeles: University of California Press, 2007.

Dave, Naisargi N. *Queer Activism in India: A Story in the Anthropology of Ethics*. Durham: Duke University Press, 2012.

Derrida, Jacques. "The Force of Law: The 'Mystical Foundation of Authority'." In *Deconstruction and the Possibility of Justice*, edited by Drucilla Cornell, Michael Rosenfeld, and David G. Carlson. New York: Routledge, 1992.

Desai, Mihir. "Red Herring in Police Reforms." *Economic and Political Weekly* 44.10 (2009): 8–11.

Dhillon, K. S. *Police and Politics in India*. New Delhi: Manohar, 2005.

Duggan, Lisa. "Queering the State," *Social Text* 39 (1994): 1–14.

———. *The Twilight of Equality? Neoliberalism, Cultural Politics, and the Attack on Democracy*. Boston: Beacon Press, 2003.

Dutta, Aniruddha. "Retroactive Consolidation of 'Homophobia.'" In *Law Like Love: Queer Perspectives on Law*, edited by Arvind Narrain and Alok Gupta. New Delhi: Yoda Press, 2011.

Epstein, Steven. *Inclusion: The Politics of Difference in Medical Research*. Chicago: University of Chicago Press, 2007.

Essig, Laurie. *Queer in Russia: A Story of Sex, Self, and the Other*. Durham: Duke University Press, 1999.

Fanon, Frantz. *Black Skin, White Masks*. Translated by Richard Philcox. New York: Grove Press, 2008.

Ferguson, James, and Akhil Gupta. "Spatializing States: Toward an Ethnography of Neoliberal Governmentality." *American Ethnologist* 29.4 (2002): 981–1002.

Fernandes, Leela, and Patrick Heller. "Hegemonic Aspirations: New Middle Class Politics and India's Democracy in Comparative Perspective." *Critical Asian Studies* 38.4 (2006): 495–522.

Fernandez, Bina, and N. B. Gomathy. *The Nature of Violence Faced by Lesbian Women in India*. Mumbai: Research Centre on Violence against Women, Tata Institute of Social Sciences, 2003.

Foucault, Michel. *The Birth of Biopolitics: Lectures at Collège de France 1978–1979*. Edited by Michel Senellart. Translated by Graham Burchell. New York: Palgrave Macmillan, 2008.

———. "Governmentality." In *The Foucault Effect*, edited by Graham Burchell, Colin Gordon, and Peter Miller. Chicago: University of Chicago Press, 1991.

———. *History of Sexuality, Volume 1: An Introduction*. Translated by Robert Hurley. New York: Vintage Books, 1978.

———. "*Omnes et Singulatim*: Toward a Critique of Political Reason." In *The Essential Foucault*, edited by Paul Rabinow and Nikolas Rose. New York: New Press, 2003.

———. *Society Must Be Defended*. Translated by David Macey. New York: Picador, 1997.

———. "The Subject and Power." In *The Essential Foucault*, edited by Paul Rabinow and Nikolas Rose. New York: New Press, 2003.

Franke, Katherine M. "The Domesticated Liberty of *Lawrence v. Texas*." *Columbia Law Review* 104.5 (2004): 1399.

Fuller, C. J., and Véronique Bénéï, eds. *The Everyday State and Society in Modern India*. Delhi: Social Science Press, 2000.

Fuller, C. J., and John Harriss. "For an Anthropology of the Modern Indian State." In *The Everyday State and Society in Modern India*, edited by C. J. Fuller and Véronique Bénéï. New Delhi: Social Science Press, 2000.

Galanter, Marc. "The Uses of Law in Indian Studies." In *Languages and Areas Studies, Presented to George V. Bobrinskoy*. Chicago: University of Chicago Press, 1967.

Ghassem-Pachandi, Parvis. "*Ahimsa*, Identification, and Sacrifice in the Gujarat Pogrom." *Social Anthropology* 18.2 (2010): 1–21.

———. "The Hyperbolic Vegetarian: Notes on a Fragile Subject in Gujarat." In *Being There: The Fieldwork Encounter and the Making of Truth*, edited by John Borneman and Abdellah Hammoudi. Berkeley: University of California Press, 2009.

Ghosh, Amitav, and Dipesh Chakrabarty. "A Conversation on Provincializing Europe." *Radical History Review* 83 (2002): 146–73.

Ghosh, Dwaipayan. "Only 7% Women in Delhi Police and Few Officers." *Times of India*. March 9, 2010. Accessed May 12, 2015. http://timesofindia.indiatimes.com/city/delhi/Only-7-women-in-Delhi-Police-and-few-officers/articleshow/5660657.cms.

Gill, Mehar Singh. "Politics of Population Census Data in India." *Economic and Political Weekly* 42.3 (2007): 241–49.

Gilroy, Paul. *Against Race: Imagining Political Culture beyond the Color Line*. Cambridge, MA: Harvard University Press, 2000.

Giroux, Henry A. *Stormy Weather: Katrina and the Politics of Disposability*. Boulder, CO: Paradigm, 2006.

Glancy, Dorothy. "The Invention of the Right to Privacy." *Arizona Law Review* 21.1 (1979): 1–39.

Goldberg, David Theo. *Anatomy of Racism*. Minneapolis: University of Minnesota Press, 1990.

———. *The Racial State*. Malden, MA: Blackwell, 2002.

Goldsmith, Netta Murray. *The Worst of Crimes: Homosexuality and the Law in Eighteenth-Century London*. London: Ashgate, 1998.

Goodman, Ryan. "Beyond the Enforcement Principle: Sodomy Law, Social Norms, and Social Panoptics." *California Law Review* 89.3 (2001): 643–740.

Gopal, Meena. "Caste, Sexuality and Labour: The Troubled Connection." *Current Sociology* 60.2 (2012): 222–38.

Government of India, Prime Minister's High Level Committee, Cabinet Secretariat. "Social Economic and Educational Status of the Muslim Community of India." November 2006. Accessed September 16, 2011. http://zakatindia.org/Files/Sachar%20Report%20(Full).pdf.

Grewal, Inderpal. "Outsourcing Patriarchy: Feminist Encounters, Transnational Mediations, and the Crime of "Honour Killings" *International Feminist Journal of Politics* 15.1 (2013): 1–19.

———. *Transnational America: Feminism, Diasporas, Neoliberalisms*. Durham: Duke University Press, 2005.

———. "'Women's Rights as Human Rights': Feminist Practices, Global Feminism, and Human Rights Regimes in Transnationality." *Citizenship Studies* 3.3 (1999): 337–54.

Grosz, Elizabeth. "Bodies-Cities." In *Sexuality and Space*, edited by Beatriz Colomina. Princeton: Princeton Architectural Press, 1992.

Guha, Ranajit. "Chandra's Death. In *Subaltern Studies V: Writings on South Asian History and Society*, edited by Ranajit Guha. New York: Oxford University Press, 1990.

Gupta, Akhil. "Blurred Boundaries: The Discourses of Corruption, the Culture of Politics, and the Imagined State." *American Ethnologist* 22.2 (1995): 375–402.

———. *Red Tape: Bureaucracy, Structural Violence, and Poverty in India*. Durham: Duke University Press, 2012.

Gupta, Akhil, and K. Sivaramakrishnan. "Introduction: The State in India after Liberalization." In *The State in India after Liberalization: Interdisciplinary Perspectives*, edited by Akhil Gupta and K. Sivaramakrishnan. London: Routledge, 2011.

Gupta, Alok. "The Presumption of Sodomy." In *Law Like Love: Queer Perspectives on Law*, edited by Arvind Narrain and Alok Gupta. New Delhi: Yoda Press, 2011.

———. "Section 377 and the Dignity of Indian Homosexuals." *Economic and Political Weekly* 41.46 (2006): 4815–23.

———. "Trends in the Application of Section 377." In *Humjinsi: A Resource Book on Lesbian, Gay and Bisexual Rights in India*, complied and edited by Bina Fernandez. Mumbai: India Centre for Human Rights and Law, 2002.

Gupta, Charu. "Censuses, Communalism, Gender, and Identity." *Economic and Political Weekly* 39.39 (2004): 4302–4.

Hacking, Ian. "Biopower and the Avalanche of Printed Numbers." *Humanities in Society* 5 (1982): 279–95.

———. "How Should We Do the History of Statistics?" In *The Foucault Effect*, edited by Graham Burchell, Colin Gordon, and Peter Miller. Chicago: University of Chicago Press, 1991.

Haldar, Piyel. *Law, Orientalism and Postcolonialism: The Jurisdiction of the Louts-Eaters*. New York: Routledge-Cavendish, 2007.

Hansen, Thomas Blom. "Governance and State Mythologies in Mumbai." In *States of Imagination: Ethnographic Explorations of the Postcolonial State*, edited by Thomas Blom Hansen and Finn Stepputat. Durham: Duke University Press, 2001.

Hansen, Thomas Blom, and Finn Stepputat. Introduction to *States of Imagination: Ethnographic Explorations of the Postcolonial State*, edited by Thomas Blom Hansen and Finn Stepputat. Durham: Duke University Press, 2001.

Hansen, Thomas Blom, and Finn Stepputat, eds. *Sovereign Bodies: Citizens, Migrants, and States in the Postcolonial World*. Princeton: Princeton University Press, 2005.

Hardt, Michael, and Antonio Negri. *Empire*. Cambridge, MA: Harvard University Press, 2000.

———. *Multitude: War and Democracy in the Age of Empire*. New York: Penguin Press, 2004.

Hasan, Zoya. "Social Inequalities, Secularism and Minorities in India's Democracy." In *Will Secular India Survive?* edited by Mushirul Hassan. New Delhi: Imprint One, 2004.

Hennessy, Rosemary. "Queer Theory, Left Politics." *Rethinking Marxism* 7.3 (1994): 85–111.

———. "Queer Visibility in Commodity Culture." *Cultural Critique* 29 (Winter 1994–95): 31–76.

Holstein, James A., and Gale Miller. *Reconsidering Social Constructionism: Debates in Social Problems Theory*. New Brunswick, NJ: Aldine Transaction, 2006.

Human Rights Watch. "Broken System: Dysfunction, Abuse, and Impunity in the Indian Police." August 4, 2009. Accessed September 16, 2011. http://www.hrw.org/reports/2009/08/04/broken-system.

Hunter, Nan D. "Sexual Orientation and the Paradox of Heightened Scrutiny." *Michigan Law Review* 102.7 (2004): 1528–54.

Indian Law Commissioners. *A Penal Code*. Union, NJ: Lawbook Exchange, 2002. Accessed December 21, 2010. http://books.google.com/books?id=I-j1ESLqCj4C&printsec=frontcover#v=onepage&q&f=false.

Jain, M. P. *Outlines of Indian Legal History*. Bombay: N. M. Tripathi, 1966.

Jaising, Indira. "Bringing Rights Home: Review of the Campaign for a Law on Domestic Violence." *Review of Women's Studies* 44.44 (2009): 50–57.

Jeffrey, Roger, and Patricia Jeffrey. *Economic and Political Weekly* 40.5 (2005): 447–53.

Jessop, Bob. *State Power*. Cambridge: Polity, 2008.

John, Mary, and Janaki Nair, eds. *A Question of Silence? The Sexual Economies of Modern India*. New Delhi: Kali for Women, 1998.

Joseph, G. M., and D. Nugent, eds. *Everyday Forms of State Formation: Revolution and Negotiation of Rule in Modern Mexico*. Durham: Duke University Press, 1994.

Joseph, Miranda. "Family Affairs: The Discourse of Global/Localization." In *Queer Globalizations: Citizenship and the Afterlife of Colonialism*, edited by Arnaldo Cruz-Malavé and Martin F. Manalansan IV. New York: New York University Press, 2002.

———. "The Performance of Production and Consumption." *Social Text* 16.1 (1998): 26–61.

Joseph, Sarah. "Neoliberal Reforms and Democracy in India." *Economic and Political Weekly*, 42.31 (2007): 3213–18.

Kalpagam, U. "The Colonial State and Statistical Knowledge." *History of the Human Sciences* 13.2 (2000): 37–55.

Kapur, Rajiv A. *Sikh Separatism: The Politics of Faith*. London: Allen & Unwin, 1986

Kapur, Ratna. *Erotic Justice: Law and the New Politics of Postcolonialism*. Portland, OR: Glasshouse Press, 2005.

Kapur, Ratna, and Brenda Cossman. "On Women, Equality and the Constitution." In *Gender and Politics in India*, edited by Nivedita Menon. New York: Oxford University Press, 2011.

Kaviraj, Sudipta. Introduction to *Politics in India*, edited by Sudipta Kaviraj. New Delhi: Oxford University Press, 2001.

———. "The Imaginary Institution of India." In *Subaltern Studies* 7.

Keating, Christine. "Framing the Postcolonial Sexual Contract: Democracy, Fraternalism, and State Authority in India." *Hypatia* 22.4 (2007): 130–45.

Khaitan, Tarunabh. "Good for All Minorities." In *The Right That Dares to Speak Its Name: Naz Foundation v. Union of India and Others*, edited by Arvind Narrain and Marcus Eldridge. Bangalore: Alternative Law Forum, 2009.

———. "Reading *Swaraj* into Article 15—A New Deal for All Minorities." NUJS *Law Review* 419 (2009): 419–32.

———. "*Koushal v. Naz*: The Legislative Court." U.K. Constitutional Law Association. Accessed March 13, 2014. http://ukconstitutionallaw.org/2013/12/22/tarunabh-khaitan-koushal-v-naz-the-legislative-court/.

Khalidi, Omar. *Khaki and Ethnic Violence in India*. New Delhi: Three Essays Collective, 2003.

Khan, Owais. "A Rose by Any Other Name." *Trikone* 15.3 (2000): 15

Khan, Shivananda. "Kothis, Gays, and (Other) MSM." Naz Foundation International, 2000. Online.

Khanna, Shamona. "Gay Rights." In *Humjinsi: A Resource Book on Lesbian, Gay and Bisexual Rights in India*, compiled and edited by Bina Fernandez. Mumbai: India Centre for Human Rights and Law, 2002.

Kolsky, Elizabeth. "Codification and the Rule of Colonial Difference: Criminal Procedure in British India." *Law and History Review* 23.3 (2005): 631–83.

Kotiswaran, Prabha. "Labours in Vice or Virtue? Neo-liberalism, Sexual Commerce and the Case of Indian Bar Dancing." *Journal of Law and Society* 37.1 (2010): 105–24.

Kulick, Don. *Travesti: Sex, Gender, and Culture among Brazilian Transgendered Prostitutes.* Chicago: University of Chicago Press, 1998.

Lakkimsetti, Chaitanya. "Governing Sexualities: Biopower, Governmentality and Citizenship in Postcolonial India." PhD diss., University of Wisconsin, Madison, 2010.

Lefebvre, Henri. "Space and the State." In *State/Space: A Reader*, edited by Neil Brenner, Bob Jessop, Martin Jones, and Gordon Macleod. Malden, MA: Blackwell, 2003.

Less Than Gay: A Citizens' Report on the Status of Homosexuality in India. New Delhi: AIDS Bhedbhav Virodhi Andolan, 1991.

Liang, Lawrence, and Siddharth Narrain, "Striving for Magic in the City of Words" In *The Right That Dares to Speak Its Name: Naz Foundation vs. Union of India and Others*, edited by Arvind Narrain and Marcus Eldridge. Bangalore: Alternative Law Forum, 2009.

Loomba, Ania. "Race and the Possibility of Comparative Critique." *New Literary History* 40 (2009): 501–22.

Lowman, John. "Violence and the Outlaw Status of (Street) Prostitution in Canada." *Violence against Women* 6.9 (2000): 987–1011.

Lubhéid, Eithne. *Entry Denied: Controlling Sexuality at the Border.* Minneapolis: University of Minnesota Press, 2002.

———. "Queer/Migration: An Unruly Body of Scholarship." *GLQ: A Journal of Lesbian and Gay Studies* 14.2–3 (2008): 169–90.

Macaulay, T. B. "Introductory Report upon the Indian Penal Code." Internet Archive. http://www.archive.org/stream/speechesandpoemoomacagoog#page/n316/mode/2up/search/Indian+Penal+Code.

Macedo, Donaldo, and Panayota Gounari, eds. *Globalization of Racism.* Boulder, CO: Paradigm, 2006.

Makhija, Sonal. "Bar Dancers, Morality and the Indian Law." *Economic and Political Weekly*, 45.39 (2010): 19–23.

Mazzarella, William. "'A Different Kind of Flesh': Public Obscenity, Globalization, and the Mumbai Dance Bar Ban." Department of Anthropology, University of Chicago, 2014. https://www.academia.edu/3679511/_A_Different_Kind_of_Flesh_Public_Obscenity_Globalization_and_the_Mumbai_Dance_Bar_Ban.

Mbembe, Achille. "Necropolitics." Translated by Libby Meintjes. *Public Culture* 15.1 (2003): 11–40.

Mehta, Pratap Bhanu. "It's about All of Us." In *The Right That Dares to Speak Its Name: Naz Foundation v. Union of India and Others*, edited by Arvind Narrain and Marcus Eldridge. Bangalore: Alternative Law Forum, 2009.

Mehta, Suketu. *Maximum City: Bombay Lost and Found.* New York: Random House, 2004.

Mendras, Marie. *Russian Politics: The Paradox of a Weak State*. New York, Columbia University Press, 2012.

Menon, Nivedita. *Recovering Subversion: Feminist Politics beyond the Law*. Champaign: University of Illinois Press, 2004.

———. "Rights, Bodies and the Law." In *Gender and Politics in India*, edited by Nivedita Menon. New York: Oxford University Press, 2011.

Menon, Ritu, and Kamala Bhasin. *Borders and Boundaries: Women in India's Partition*. New Delhi: Kali for Women, 1998.

Merry, Sally Engle. *Colonizing Hawai'i: The Cultural Power of Law*. Princeton: Princeton University Press, 2000.

Miller, Gale, and James A. Holstein. "Reconsidering Social Constructionism." In *Reconsidering Social Constructionism: Debates in Social Problems Theory*, edited by James A. Holstein and Gale Miller. New Brunswick, NJ: Aldine Transaction, 2006.

Mitchell, Timothy. "Limits of the State." *American Political Science Review* 85.1 (1991): 77–96.

———. "Society, Economy and State Effect." In *State/Culture: State Formation after the Cultural Turn*, edited by George Steinmetz. Ithaca: Cornell University Press, 1999.

Moore, Donald S., Anand Pandian, and Jake Kosek. *Race, Nature, and the Politics of Difference*. Durham: Duke University Press, 2003.

Mosse, George. *Nationalism and Sexuality: Respectability and Abnormal Sexuality in Modern Europe*. New York: Howard Fertig, 1997.

Nair, Janaki. *Women and Law in Colonial India: A Social History*. New Delhi: Kali for Women, 1996.

Nandy, Ashis. *The Romance of the State and the Fate of Dissent in the Tropics*. New Delhi: Oxford University Press, 2003.

Narrain, Arvind. *Queer: Despised Sexuality, Law, and Social Change*. Bangalore: Books for Change, 2004.

———. "Queering Democracy." In *Law Like Love: Queer Perspectives on Law*, edited by Arvind Narrain and Alok Gupta. New Delhi: Yoda Press, 2011.

———. "Persecuting Difference." In *Law Like Love: Queer Perspectives on Law*, edited by Arvind Narrain and Alok Gupta. New Delhi: Yoda Press, 2011.

Narrain, Arvind, and Marcus Eldridge. *The Right That Dares to Speak Its Name: Naz Foundation v. Union of India and Others*. Bangalore: Alternative Law Forum, 2009.

Narrain, Arvind, and Alok Gupta. "Introduction." In *Law Like Love: Queer Perspectives on Law*, edited by Arvind Narrain and Alok Gupta. New Delhi: Yoda Press, 2011.

National Crime Records Bureau, *Crime in India: 2011 Statistics*. National Crime Records Bureau, Ministry of Home Affairs. http://ncrb.nic.in/CD-CII2011/Home.asp. Accessed October 24, 2012.

Navaro-Yashin, Yael. *Faces of the State: Secularism and Public Life in Turkey*. Princeton: Princeton University Press, 2002.
NCRB. "Crime against Women." Ministry of Home Affairs. Accessed October 30, 2010. http://ncrb.nic.in/cii2007/cii-2007/CHAP5.pdf.
———. "Empowering Indian Police with IT—Origin." Ministry of Home Affairs. Accessed July 23, 2007. http://ncrb.nic.in/origin.htm.
———. "Empowering Indian Police with IT—Quality Policy." Ministry of Home Affairs. Accessed July 23, 2007. http://ncrb.nic.in/objectives.htm.
Nigam, Sanjay. "Disciplining and Policing the 'Criminals by Birth,' Part 2: The Development of a Disciplinary System, 1871–1900." *Indian Economic and Social History Review* 21.3 (1990): 257–87.
Oldenburg, Philip. "Face to Face with the Indian State: A Grass Roots View." In *Experiencing the State*, edited by Lloyd I. Rudolph and John Kurt Jacobsen. New Delhi: Oxford University Press, 2006.
Ong, Aihwa. *Flexible Citizenship: The Cultural Logics of Transnationality*. Durham: Duke University Press, 1999.
———. "Making the Biopolitical Subject: Cambodian Immigrants, Refugees Medicine, and Cultural Citizenship in California." *Social Science Medicine* 40.9 (1995): 1243–57.
Pandey, Gyanendra. *The Construction of Communalism in Colonial North India*. New York: Oxford University Press, 2006.
———. "Hindus and Others: The Militant Hindu Construction." *Economic and Political Weekly* 26.52 (1991): 2997–3009.
———. "In Defense of the Fragment: Writing about Hindu-Muslim Riots in India Today." *Economic and Political Weekly* 26.11–12 (1991): 559–72.
———. "The Secular State and the Limits of Dialogue." In *The Crisis of Secularism in India*, edited by Anuradha Dingwaney Needham and Rajeswari Sunder Rajan. Durham: Duke University Press, 2007.
Pandit, Maya. "Gendered Subaltern Sexuality and the State." *Economic and Political Weekly*, 48.32 (2013): 33–38.
Parker, Kunal M. "Observations on the Historical Destruction of Separate Legal Regimes." In *Religion and Personal Law in Secular India: A Call to Judgment*, edited by Gerald James Larson. Bloomington: Indiana University Press, 2001.
Patel, Geeta. "Advertisements, Proprietary Heterosexuality, and Hundis: Postcolonial Finance, Nation-State Formations, and the New Idealized Family." *Rethinking Marxism* 24.4 (2012): 516–35.
———. "On Fire: Sexuality and Its Incitements." In *Queering India: Same-Sex Love and Eroticism in Indian Culture and Society*, edited by Ruth Vanita. New York: Routledge, 2001.
Pathak, Neeraj. "The Beat(en)." *Sahara Time*, October 11 (2008): 18–21.
People's Union for Civil Liberties. "Human Rights Violations against the Trans-

gender Community: A PUCL Report." September 2003. Accessed September 16, 2011. http://www.pucl.org/Topics/Gender/2004/transgender.htm.
Pease, Donald E. "The Global Homeland State: Bush's Biopolitical Settlement." *boundary 2* 30.3 (2003): 1–18.
Peterson, V. Spike. "Political Identities / Nationalism as Heterosexism." *International Feminist Journal of Politics* 1.1 (1999): 34–65.
Povinelli, Elizabeth A. "Disturbing Sexuality." *South Atlantic Quarterly* 106.3 (2007): 566–76.
———. *The Empire of Love: Toward a Theory of Intimacy, Genealogy, and Carnality*. Durham: Duke University Press, 2006.
———. "Notes on Gridlock: Genealogy, Intimacy, Sexuality." *Public Culture* 14.1 (2002): 215–38.
———. "Sex Acts and Sovereignty: Race and Sexuality in the Construction of the Australian Nation." In *The Gender/Sexuality Reader: Culture, History, Political Economy*, edited by Roger N. Lancaster and Michaela di Leonardo. London: Routledge, 1997.
Prakash, Gyan. *Another Reason: Science and the Imagination of Modern India*. Princeton: Princeton University Press, 1999.
———. *Mumbai Fables: A History of an Enchanted City*. Princeton: Princeton University Press, 2010.
Puar, Jasbir. *Terrorist Assemblages: Homonationalism in Queer Times*. Durham: Duke University Press, 2007.
Puri, Jyoti. *Encountering Nationalism*. Malden, MA: Blackwell, 2004.
———. "Forging Hetero-Collectives: Obscenity Law in India." In *Obscenity and the Limits of Liberalism*, edited by L. Glass and C. Williams. Columbus: Ohio State University Press, 2011.
———. "Sexualizing the State: Sodomy, Civil Liberties, and the Indian Penal Code." In *Contesting the Nation: Gendered Violence in South Asia. Notes on the Postcolonial Present*, edited by Angana P. Chatterji and Lubna Nazir Chaudhry. New Delhi: Zubaan, 2012.
———. "States' Sexualities: Theorizing Sexuality, Gender and Governance." In *The Sage Handbook of Feminist Theory*, edited by Mary Evans et al. Los Angeles: Sage.
———. *Woman, Body, Desire in Post-Colonial India: Narratives of Gender and Sexuality*. New York: Routledge, 1999.
Radhakrishna, Meena. *Dishonored by History: Criminal Tribes and British Colonial Policy*. New Delhi: Orient Longman, 2001.
Rajan, Rajeswari Sunder. *The Scandal of the State: Women, Law, and Citizenship in Postcolonial India*. Durham: Duke University Press, 2003.
Ramachandran, Sujata. "'Operation Pushback': Sangh Parivar, State, Slums, and Surreptitious Bangladeshis in New Delhi." *Economic and Political Weekly* 38.7 (2003): 637–47.

Rancière, Jacques. *Dis-Agreement: Politics and Philosophy*. Minneapolis: University of Minnesota Press, 2004.

Rhodes, Tim, Milena Simic, Stadjana Baros, Lucy Platt, and Bojan Zikic. "Police Violence and Sexual Risk among Female and Transvestite Sex Workers in Serbia: Qualitative Study." *British Medical Journal* 337 (2008). Online.

Richardson, Diane. "Constructing Sexual Citizenship: Theorizing Sexual Rights." *Critical Social Policy* 20.1 (2000): 105–35.

———. "Desiring Sameness? The Rise of a Neoliberal Politics of Normalisation." *Antipode* 37.3 (2005): 515–35.

Robinson, Neil. *Russia: A State of Uncertainty*. London: Routledge, 2002.

Rose, Jacqueline. *States of Fantasy*. Oxford: Clarendon Press, 1996.

Rose, Nikolas. "Governing by Numbers: Figuring Out Democracy." *Accounting, Organizations and Society* 16.7 (1991): 673–92.

———. *The Politics of Life Itself: Biomedicine, Power, and Subjectivity in the Twenty-first Century*. Princeton: Princeton University Press, 2006.

———. *Powers of Freedom: Reframing Political Thought*. Cambridge: Cambridge University Press, 1999.

Rudolph, Lloyd I., and John Kurt Jacobson, eds. *Experiencing the State*. Oxford: Oxford University Press, 2006.

SAHRDC. "Armed Forces Special Powers Act: A Study in National Security Tyranny." South Asia Human Rights Documentation Centre. Accessed February 16, 2011. http://www.hrdc.net/sahrdc/resources/armed_forces.htm.

Sanders, Teela. "The Risks of Street Prostitution: Punters, Police, and Protestors." *Urban Studies* 41.9 (2004): 1703–17.

Sarkar, Tanika. "Ethnic Cleansing in Gujarat: An Analysis of a Few Aspects." *Akhbar*, July 2002. Accessed January 28, 2011. http://www.indowindow.com/akhbar/article.php?article=99&category=2&issue=17.

———. "Semiotics of Terror: Muslim Children and Women in Hindu Rashtra." Mukto-mona, July 13, 2002. Accessed January 28, 2011. http://groups.yahoo.com/group/mukto-mona/message/12585.

Scott, James C. *Seeing Like a State: How Certain Schemes to Improve the Human Condition Have Failed*. New Haven: Yale University Press, 1998.

Sedgwick, Eve Kosofsky. *Between Men: English Literature and Male Homosocial Desire*. New York: Columbia University Press, 1985.

Sen, Satadru. *Disciplining Punishment: Colonialism and Convict Society in the Andaman Islands*. New Delhi: Oxford University Press, 2000.

Seshu, Geeta. "Bar Girls Seek Rights." *Boloji*, September 6, 2004. Accessed September 15, 2011. http://www.boloji.com/index.cfm?md=Content&sd=Articles&ArticleID=6103.

Setalvad, Teesta. "When Guardians Betray: The Role of Police in Gujarat." In *Gujarat: The Making of a Tragedy*, edited by Siddharth Varadarajan. New Delhi: Penguin Books India, 2002.

Seth, Vikram. "To the Government of India, Members of the Judiciary, and all citizens." Online. http://p2.voicesagainst377.org/.

Shah, Nayan. *Contagious Divides: Epidemics and Race in San Francisco's Chinatown.* Berkeley: University of California Press, 2001.

———. "Policing Privacy, Migrants, and the Limits of Freedom." *Social Text* 23.3–4 (2005): 275.

———. *Stranger Intimacy: Contesting Race, Sexuality, and the Law in the North American West.* Berkeley: University of California Press, 2011.

Shahani, Parmesh. *Gay Bombay: Globalization, Love and (Be)longing in Contemporary India.* New Delhi: Sage, 2008.

Sharma, Aradhana. "Crossbreeding Institutions, Breeding Struggle: Women's Employment, Neoliberal Governmentality, and State (Re)Formation in India." *Cultural Anthropology* 21.1 (2006): 60–95.

———. *Logics of Empowerment: Development, Gender, Governance in Neoliberal India.* Minneapolis: University of Minnesota Press, 2008.

Sharma, Aradhana, and Akhil Gupta. "Introduction: Rethinking Theories of the State in an Age of Globalization." In *The Anthropology of the State: A Reader*, edited by Aradhana Sharma and Akhil Gupta. Malden, MA: Blackwell Publishing, 2006.

Silliman Jael, and Anaya Bhatacharjee, eds. *Policing the National Body: Race, Gender, and Criminalization.* Boston: South End Press, 2002.

Singh, Navsharan, and Urvashi Butalia. "Challenging Impunity on Sexual Violence in South Asia: Beginning a Discussion." *Economic and Political Weekly* 47.28 (2012): 58–63.

Singha, Radhika. *A Despotism of Law: Crime and Criminal Justice in Colonial India.* New Delhi: Oxford University Press, 2001.

Skuy, David. "Macaulay and the Indian Penal Code of 1862: The Myth of the Inherent Superiority and Modernity of the English Legal System Compared to India's Legal System in the Nineteenth Century." *Modern Asian Studies* 32.3 (1998): 513–57.

Smith, Richard Saumarez. "Rule-by-Records and Rule-by-Reports: Complementary Aspects of the British Imperial Rule of Law." *Contributions to Indian Sociology* 19.1 (1985): 153–76.

SNDT-FAOW. "After the Ban: Women Working in Dance Bars." Study conducted by Research Centre for Women's Studies, SNDT Women's University, Mumbai, and Forum against Oppression of Women, Mumbai, December 2006.

———. "Backgrounds and Working Conditions of Women Working as Dancers in Dance Bars." Study conducted by Research Centre for Women's Studies, SNDT Women's University, Mumbai, and Forum against Oppression of Women, Mumbai, 2005.

Spector, Malcolm, and John I. Kitsuse. *Constructing Social Problems.* Piscataway, NJ: Transaction, 2000.

Spivak, Gayatri Chakravorty. *A Critique of Postcolonial Reason: Toward a History of the Vanishing Present*. Cambridge, MA: Harvard University Press, 1999.

Steinmetz, George, ed. *State/Culture: State Formation after the Cultural Turn*. Ithaca: Cornell University Press, 1999.

Stevens, Jacqueline. *Reproducing the State*. Princeton: Princeton University Press, 1999.

Stoler, Ann Laura. "Affective States." In *A Companion to Anthropology of Politics*, edited by David Nugent and Joan Vincent. Malden, MA: Blackwell, 2004.

———. *Carnal Knowledge and Imperial Power: Race and the Intimate in Colonial Rule*. Berkeley: University of California Press, 2002.

———, ed. *Haunted by Empire: Geographies of Intimacy in North American History*. Durham: Duke University Press, 2006.

———. *Race and the Education of Desire*. Durham: Duke University Press, 1995.

Subramanian, K. S. "Police and Politics in India." *Economic and Political Weekly* 40.27 (2005): 2915–16.

———. *Political Violence and the Police in India*. New Delhi: Sage, 2007.

Sundar, Nandini. "The Rule of Law and the Rule of Property: Law-Struggles and the Neo-liberal State in India." In *The State in India after Liberalization*, edited by Akhil Gupta and K. Sivaramakrishnan. London: Routledge, 2011.

Sunder Rajan, Rajeswari. *Scandal of the State: Women, Law, and Citizenship in Postcolonial India*. New Delhi: Permanent Black, 2003.

Tarlo, Emma. *Unsettling Memories: Narratives of the Emergency in Delhi*. Berkeley: University of California Press, 2003.

Taussig, Michael. *The Nervous System*. New York: Routledge, 1992.

Thangarajah, Priyadarshini, and Ponni Arasu. "Queer Women and the Law in India." In *Law Like Love: Queer Perspectives on Law*, edited by Arvind Narrain and Alok Gupta. New Delhi: Yoda Press, 2011.

Uberoi, Patricia. "Introduction: Problematising Social Reform, Engaging Sexuality, Interrogating the State." In *Social Reform, Sexuality and the State*, edited by Patricia Uberoi. New Delhi: Sage, 1996.

Upadhyay, Videh. *Public Interest Litigation in India: Concepts, Cases, and Concerns*. London: LexisNexis, 2007.

Varadarajan, Siddarth. *Gujarat: The Making of a Tragedy*. New Delhi: Penguin Books India, 2002.

Verma, Arvind. *The Indian Police: A Critical Evaluation*. New Delhi: Regency, 2011.

Voices against 377. "Rights for All: Ending Discrimination against Queer Desire under Section 377." Online. http://files.creaworld.org/files/Voices_Report_English.pdf.

Watts, Charlotte, and Cathy Zimmerman. "Violence against Women: Global Scope and Magnitude." *Lancet* 359 (2002): 1232–37.

Weber, Max. *Economy and Society: An Outline of Interpretive Sociology*. Vols. 1 and 2. Berkeley: University of California Press, 1978.

Weiner, Myron. "India's Minorities: Who Are They? What Do They Want?" In *State and Politics in India*, edited by Partha Chatterjee. New Delhi: Oxford University Press, 1997.

Weston, Kath. "A Political Ecology of 'Unnatural Offences.'" *GLQ: A Journal of Lesbian and Gay Studies* 14.2–3 (2008): 217–37.

Wilkinson, Steven I. "Introduction." In *Religious Politics and Communal Violence*, edited by Steven I. Wilkinson. New Delhi: Oxford University Press, 2005.

Wittig, Monique. *The Straight Mind and Other Essays*. Boston: Beacon Press, 1992.

Yang, Anand, ed. *Crime and Criminality in British India*. Tucson: University of Arizona Press, 1985.

INDEX